The American Latino

The American Latino

Psychodynamic Perspectives on Culture and Mental Health

Edited by
Salman Akhtar and
Solange Margery Bertoglia

ROWMAN & LITTLEFIELD
Lanham • Boulder • New York • London

Published by Rowman & Littlefield
A wholly owned subsidiary of The Rowman & Littlefield Publishing Group, Inc.
4501 Forbes Boulevard, Suite 200, Lanham, Maryland 20706
www.rowman.com

Unit A, Whitacre Mews, 26-34 Stannary Street, London SE11 4AB

British Library Cataloguing in Publication Information Available

Library of Congress Cataloging-in-Publication Data

The American Latino : psychodynamic perspectives on culture and mental health issues / edited by Salman Akhtar and Solange Margery Bertoglia.
pages cm
Includes bibliographical references and index.
ISBN 978-1-4422-4856-4 (cloth : alk. paper) -- ISBN 978-1-4422-4857-1 (electronic)
1. Hispanic Americans--Social conditions. 2. Hispanic Americans--Mental health. 3. Hispanic Americans--Psychology. I. Akhtar, Salman, 1946 July 31- II. Bertoglia, Solange Margery.
E184.S75A823 2015
305.868'073--dc23

2015002928

™ The paper used in this publication meets the minimum requirements of American National Standard for Information Sciences Permanence of Paper for Printed Library Materials, ANSI/NISO Z39.48-1992.

Printed in the United States of America

To

ANGEL GARMA (1904-1993)

whose book on dreams had a profound effect on me

—SA

ADRIAN & NATALIA

my friends since childhood

—SMB

Contents

Acknowledgments

Thirteen distinguished colleagues devoted their time and effort to writing original papers, upon our request, for inclusion in this book. They abided by the deadlines we set and responded to our editorial suggestions with utmost grace. Drs. Andrew Logamasino and Carmela Perez helped us in subtle and not-so-subtle ways. The Hispanic-American psychiatric residents whose clinical work the senior co-editor supervised over the last three decades, especially Drs. Aurora Casta, Vivian Charneco, Elena Del-Busto, Carmen Irrizary, Elaine Martin, Lisa Moldanado, Neftali Ortiz, Norah Kramer, and Sarah Ramos, have been important sources of information about the matters contained in this book. Ms. Jan Wright prepared the manuscript of this book with her usual diligence, extraordinary skill, and good humor. To all these individuals, our sincere thanks indeed.

Introduction

Sonia Sotomayor's appointment as a Justice of the United States Supreme Court in 2009 drew everyone's attention to the nation's Hispanic community. Her poignant autobiography, *My Beloved World* (Vintage, 2013), depicted a valorous saga of ambition, perseverance, and the transformation of dreams into reality. She became a poster child for the country's educated Hispanic population and an ego-ideal for the rags-to-riches aspirations of its disenfranchised youth. But not all members of this subpopulation have obtained such astounding recognition. Nor are they so impoverished as Sotomayor was during her formative years in the Bronx, New York. Most Hispanic or Latino Americans live ordinary lives, with desires and concerns no different from those of other ethnic and linguistic groups in the United States. Since they are not homogenously distributed over the map of this country and since social disadvantage often casts them away from the glare of popular media, few facts about them are known to their fellow citizens. To be sure, this is not true of the particular regions of the country where the Hispanic population is thick but in other areas, stereotypes comfortably masquerade as familiarity. Hence, it might be best to begin by underscoring some realities in this realm.

- The United States of America has the second largest population of Hispanics world wide; only Mexico exceeds this number.
- Hispanic or Latino Americans constitute 17 percent of the population of the United States. Their projected population for 2060—just 45 years from now—will constitute 31 percent of the nation's population by that date.
- The states with a population of one million or more Hispanic residents are Arizona, California, Colorado, Florida, Illinois, New Jersey, New York, and Texas.
- Spanish is the most prevalent non-English language in the United States, with 37.6 million persons of ages five years and older speaking it at home.

- While almost all countries of Central and South America, as well as the Caribbean, are represented in the North American Hispanic population, Mexico, Puerto Rico, and Cuba are the three regions with the highest number of immigrants to the United States.
- While often not noticed as such, Latino Americans have acquired prominence in diverse aspects of our civic life, including *community organization* (e.g., César Chavez), *government* (e.g., Bill Richardson as Governor of New Mexico, Alberto Gonzales as US Attorney General, and Henry Cisneros, as Secretary of Housing and Urban Development), *sports* (e.g., Oscar de la Hoya, Roberto Duran, and Bobby Chacon in boxing, Jose Cortez and Martin Grammatica in football, Roberto Clemente in baseball), *medicine* (e.g., Antonio Coello Novello as the Surgeon General of the United States), *news media* (e.g., Geraldo Riviera, Ruben Salazar, and Rudolfo Anaye), *fashion* (e.g., Oscar de la Renta), *entertainment* (e.g., Christina Aguilera, Desi Arnez, Cameron Diaz, Jose Ferrar, Jennifer Lopez, Ricardo Montalban, Freddy Prince, and Anthony Quinn), and *literature* (e.g., Julia Alvarez, and Richard Blanco).

Such splashes and sparks constitute only window-dressing for a market of talents and ideas that is as varied as it is rich. The tapestry of American Latino life is historically complex, demographically diverse, economically layered, and culturally variable. It is for bringing a colorful "super-size" portrait of this population to the attention of its fellow North American citizens that we have devised this book. Though our target audience is mental health professionals, educated laity and college students will find much of use contained in these pages as well.

The book opens with a thorough survey of the history or migration from various Central and South American nations to the United States and it closes with a personal account of how it feels to be working in this country as a psychotherapist of Hispanic origin. Sandwiched between the opening and closing chapters are eight nuanced essays on the cultural and clinical aspects of Hispanic American life. Written specifically for this book and published here for the first time, these essays by distinguished psychiatrists and psychologists delineate the patterns of child-rearing, gender roles, the importance of religion and spirituality, vulnerability of youth to drugs and gang-related violence, and the stresses related to geo-cultural dislocation. Together, they create a panoramic gestalt of Hispanic American life in the United States. Familiarity with the faces, voices, idioms, traditions, concerns, fears, ambitions, and talents that reside at the heart of this population is intended to enrich empathy, create respect, and enhance socio-clinical skills in dealing with the members of this group. The book therefore has both mental-health related and humanitarian aims. To what degree it has succeeded in achieving this goal is up to you—the reader—to decide.

ONE

A Brief History of Latino Immigration to the United States

Kelly Lopez

Variously designated as "Hispanics," "Latinos," and "South Americans," immigrants from the nations of South America, Central America, and the Caribbean hardly constitute a homogenous cultural group in the United States. A common language, Spanish, is deemed to act as a glue for this ethnic collage but this too, is not sacrosanct since English, Creole, French, and Portuguese are the mother tongues of many people in this group. Subgroups in the "Latino" population also differ in the degree of their adaptation of a North American identity and vary in their continuing emphasis upon their national origins. Moreover, the psychosocial concerns faced by each subgroup also vary.

> Mexicans and Mexican Americans experience the pressures of legalities and legalism; Puerto Ricans confront the challenges of dual identities; Cubans face the joys and pains of economic assimilation; Dominicans are subjected to blatant racism because of their predominantly African phenotype; and countless South Americans contend with the ambiguities of detachment and belonging. (Comas-Diaz, 2006, p. 436)

Such heterogeneity is highlighted and better understood if one takes into account the varying immigration patterns among the subgroups of the American Latino population. This forms the topic of my contribution. Dividing my survey into the broad regions of South America, Central America, and the Caribbean, I will offer the details of how people from various countries in these regions arrived in the United States. While my discourse will be largely historical and sociopolitical, it is my hope that a nuanced familiarity with what underlies matters of demography will enhance the readers' empathy in both social and clinical settings.

IMMIGRATION FROM SOUTH AMERICA

Argentina

The majority of Argentines who settled in the United States in the 1960s were professionals who came in search of greater educational and economic possibilities. Many of them held academic degrees and many were physicians or scientists. New York was a focus of Argentine immigration, with 20 percent of Argentine immigrants living there in the 1970s, illustrating the tendency for Argentines to immigrate to metropolitan areas. In the 1980s, that percentage increased to just over 23 percent, and the 1990 US Census recorded that New York City had 17,363 Argentine Americans, followed by Los Angeles, which had 15,115.

The existing Argentine and Italian communities in New York helped to fuel this immigration, as many Argentines are of Italian origin. With the goal of helping its Argentine population, the government of the city created several organizations such as the Argentine-American Chamber of Commerce, which promotes business ventures between Argentina and the United States. The 1990 US Census recorded 92,563 Argentines, showing that nearly half of the Argentine immigrants arrived in the last two decades alone.

Bolivia

Bolivian immigration into the United States occurred in two significant phases. The first phase occurred subsequent to and during the 1952 National Revolution in Bolivia. Most of these immigrants consisted of middle- to upper-middle income occupational professionals or political dissidents who identify with Bolivia's White or Criollo society. The next phase of Bolivian immigration was a result of Bolivia's fiscal policies in the 1970s, which gave way to the hyperinflation throughout most of the 1980s. Most of these immigrants consisted of lower-income Mestizo and Indigenous Bolivians obtaining work posts as service and manual laborers. Many Bolivians who immigrated to the United States came as tourists but remained indefinitely in the country, settling with family and friends. This made it difficult to know the number of Bolivians living in the United States. Between 1984 and 1993, only 4,574 Bolivians received United States citizenship (Eigo, 2014).

Brazil

In the 1960s, the first recorded Brazilians began to immigrate to the United States. From the 1960s until the mid-1980s, between 1500 and 2300 Brazilian immigrants arrived in the United States. Since the mid-1980s, economic hardship in Brazil increased, and as a result, between 1986 and 1990 1.4 million Brazilians immigrated to the United States, Japan, and Europe. It was not until the 1980s that Brazilian immigration reached significant levels. The 1990 US Census recorded that there are about 60,000 Brazilians living in the United States (United States Census Bureau).

Chile

Most Chilean immigration to the United States has occurred within the last twenty-five years. For the most part, Chileans left as either political asylees or refugees during the dictatorship of Augusto Pinochet, or for economic hardship. Also, there have been others that have immigrated to seek scholastic or employment opportunities. Many Pinochet-era immigrants (i.e., 1973–1990) were of middle- or upper-class origin. A significant proportion of them arrived with advanced educations and well-developed skills. They had close networks with other Chilean exiles and formed tight-knit communities forged around a shared sense of identity.

Colombia

The first Colombian community formed after World War I, when several hundred professionals migrated to New York City. The growth of Colombian neighborhoods was slow until 1940, when Colombian immigration to New York increased. Most Colombians who arrived after the mid-1960s were visiting the United States temporarily. Despite a succession of immigration laws, the Colombian population in the United States continued to grow, with New York remaining the most popular destination. Smaller communities formed in Los Angeles, San Francisco, Houston, Philadelphia, and Washington, DC (US Census Bureau). Initially, many Colombians settled in Little Havana, Florida, a large Cuban neighborhood. Many of them engaged in business and trade between Miami and Latin America. The area also attracted the Colombian wealthy, who settled there to get medical care, send their children to school, and escape from social, economic, and political turmoil in Colombia. By 1987, Colombian Americans were one of the fastest growing Hispanic groups in Miami. By the early 1990s, many Colombian Americans left the metropolitan centers for the suburbs due to crime and the high cost of living. This trend was probably started for the first time in the coastal towns of Connecticut and New York. In 1990 and 1991, 43,891 Colombians were admitted to the United States, more than from any other South American country. Both 1992 and 1997 were years in which the guerrillas in Colombia increased, so nearly 75,000 Colombians immigrated to the United States in this period, many of them fleeing to and remaining in California (US Census Bureau).

Ecuador

Most Ecuadorian immigration to the United States began in the early 1970s, fueled by several different factors. First, the United States's immigration law changed, making it easier for Latin Americans and other foreign groups to immigrate here. In addition, the price of air travel lowered, making immigration more accessible to Latin Americans. They were drawn to the United States for economic opportunities and political freedoms (Hanratty, 1991). During the 1970s, most of the Ecuadorians came from the northern and central highlands, including the area around Quito. In the 1980s, many Ecuadorians came from the coast. And in the 1990s, most of them came from the southern highlands, near the border with Peru. The majority of Ecuadorian immigrants immigrated to New York City. In fact, the 1990 census recorded that 60 percent of Ecuadorians living in the United States lived in the New York area; the second-largest group, 10 percent, lived in Los Angeles. Those areas, along with Connecticut and Florida, have the largest populations of Ecuadorians in the United States (US Census Bureau).

Guyana

Following the independence of Guyana from Great Britain in 1966, Guyanese immigration to the United States increased exponentially. Political and economic uncertainty prompted many Guyanese who could to make the move to seek opportunities abroad. Many of the first Guyanese immigrants to the United States were of African descent. They were women who were recruited as domestic workers or nursing assistants. Prior to the Immigration and Nationality Act of 1965, Guyanese of Asian descent faced immigration restrictions because of US Immigration policy that was more pro-European. Since the 1960s, the majority of Guyanese immigrants to the United States have been women. In 1980, the US Census Bureau registered a total of 48,608 people of Guyanese descent living in the United States, half of whom were women, 26,046 people. In 1990, approximately 81,665 people Guyanese were already living in this country (US Dept. of Homeland Security).

Nicaragua

Nicaraguans began to immigrate to the United States in the early 1900s, with a precipitous increase in the late 20th century. The Nicaraguan community is mainly concentrated in three major urban areas: Metropolitan Miami, Greater Los Angeles, and the San Francisco Bay Area. According to Immigration and Naturalization Service figures, more than 20,000 Nicaraguans were admitted as permanent residents between 1976 and 1985; more than 75,000 were admitted between 1986 and 1993; and almost 100,000 between 1994 and 2002, with a total of approximately 200,000 Nicaraguan immigrants being granted legal status since 1976 (Orlov). The earliest documentation of immigration from Nicaragua to the United States was combined in total with those of other Central American countries. However, according to the US Census Bureau, some 7,500 Nicaraguans legally immigrated from 1967 to 1976. An estimated 28,620 Nicaraguans were living in the United States in 1970, 90 percent of whom self-reported as "white" on the 1970 census. Most Nicaraguan immigrants during the late 1960s were women: there were only sixty male Nicaraguan immigrants for every one hundred female immigrants during this period. Over 62 percent of the total documented immigration from 1979 to 1988 occurred after 1984. In 1998, more than two million Nicaraguans were left homeless due to Hurricane Mitch; as a result many

Nicaraguans received permanent residence or temporary protected status (TPS) in the late 1990s. According to the 1990 US Census, 168,659 of the total 202,658 documented Nicaraguans in the United States were born in Nicaragua. In 1992, approximately 10 to 12 percent of the Nicaraguan population had emigrated. These emigrants tended to be disproportionately of working age, better educated, and more often white-collar workers than nonimmigrants. In addition, emigrants were more likely to come from larger pre-immigration households and higher income households (Konczal, 2011). Another major wave of Nicaraguans to the United States, consisting primarily of blue-collar workers, peaked in a large exodus in early 1989; most of them sought escape from both political and economic torment in their homeland.

Paraguay

It is estimated that the first Paraguayans arrived in the United States between the years of 1841 and 1850. At that time, Paraguayans were not coming directly to the United States from Paraguay, but through other countries such as Brazil, Argentina, and Peru. Paraguayan residents in the United States were included in the early records in the group of other South Americans. During those years, 3,579 other immigrants arrived. In the 1960s, one-fourth of all Paraguayans were registered as living in countries outside Paraguay, with a majority in Argentina, Brazil, and Uruguay. In 1979, close to 11,000 Paraguayans immigrated to the United States, but the numbers declined rapidly. In 1982, 4,000 Paraguayans immigrated to the United States. The reasons of migration were varied, but many immigrants were young people who wanted educational opportunities to get professional knowledge, gain skills and have better jobs (National Geographic). Additionally, some of the immigrants arrived for political reasons or to escape civil riots. The women exceeded the male immigrants slightly in number, and more than half of the immigrants lacked occupations. Many Paraguayan immigrants were also infants adopted by American families. More than a thousand Paraguayan infants were adopted in this country—254 in 1989, 405 in 1993, and 351 in 1995 (United Nations).

Peru

The majority of Peruvians who immigrated to the United States have arrived since the 1990s. Peruvians typically immigrated for economic reasons, to escape poverty and pursue a better quality of life. Significant numbers of Peruvians can be found in New Jersey, New York, Miami and Los Angeles (yumimmigrantcity.com).

Suriname

Surinamese began migrating to the United States beginning in 1975, through a permanent visa which enabled them to acquire American citizenship. Some of these people were political refugees who fled the Bouterse regime. Even though many Surinamase migrated to United States in search of better lives and opportunities, many still have migrated for work and tourism (Human Development Report).

Uruguay

The history of Uruguayan immigration to the United States is very recent. Before 1960, the Uruguayan living conditions were favorable, as many Uruguayans had steady employment, education, and healthcare. The few Uruguayans who left their mother country migrated to other Hispanic countries. However, after 1960, the standard of living in Uruguay fell due to the emergence of serious economic and political problems after World War II, particularly financial crises and employment shortages during the 1960s and 1970s in addition to an oppressive military regime. These factors contributed to a major exodus of Uruguayan immigrants. The continued employment problems of the late 1980s developed yet another impetus for the youth of Uruguay to seek employment and new lives in other countries. Some of them went to the United States, but most of the Uruguayan immigrants continued migrating to Argentina (American Community Survey). According to the 2010 census, there are about 56,884 people of Uruguayan descent in the United States. The majority of Uruguayans that migrated to the United States arrived in the 1960s and 1970s. Between 1963 and 1975 (when the country's economy suffered a huge drop), 180,000 Uruguayans left their country. Later on, between 1975 and 1985, during the period of oppressive military control, 150,000 Uruguayans fled. Finally, by 1989, only 16,000 of these citizens had returned to their native country (Ancestry Map).

Venezuela

Until the twentieth century, there was no clear record of the number of Venezuelans who immigrated to the United States. From 1910 to 1930, it is estimated that over 4,000 South Americans each year immigrated to the United States. Since the early 1980s, the reasons for Venezuelan immigration have changed to include hopes of earning a higher salary and due to the economic hardship (US Census Bureau). The largest concentration of Venezuelans in the United States lives in South Florida, especially the suburbs of Doral and Weston. Other main states with Venezuelan American populations are, according the 1990 census, New York, California, Texas, New Jersey, Massachusetts, and Maryland. Some of the urban areas with a highly populated Venezuelan community include Miami, New York City, Los Angeles, and Washington, DC (epodunk).

IMMIGRATION FROM CENTRAL AMERICA

Belize

About one out of every three Belizeans now live overseas and outside of Belize; the majority have migrated to English-speaking countries, especially the United States, where there are some 300,000 Belizeans, and the United Kingdom, with around 3,000 Belizeans. Smaller numbers now live in Canada. Kriols and other ethnic groups emigrated mostly to the United States, but also to the United Kingdom and other developed nations in search of better lives. Based on the latest US Census, Belizeans in the United States are primarily of the Kriol and Garinagu ethnic groups and comprise approximately 70,000 legal residents and naturalized citizens (Belize Central Statistical Office).

Costa Rica

There have not been large waves of migration from Costa Rica to the United States. The Immigration and Naturalization Service records indicate that very few Costa Ricans have actually tried to enter the country illegally. This is because they have not been forced to immigrate to the United States for political oppression or extreme economic circumstances. Since 1931, only 57,661 Costa Ricans have immigrated to the United States. The number of Costa Rican immigrants has been increasing very slowly, which is very different from the pattern of immigration from most other Central American countries. In fact, the other two countries in this region that have had a continuously slow rate of immigration are Belize and Panama (Colonial Times). Most Costa Ricans who live in the United States reside in California, Florida, Texas, and the New York City/New Jersey area. The areas with the largest Costa Rican populations are Los Angeles and its surrounding areas, the New York City area, Miami and surrounding area, and in the Houston-Galveston area of Texas. There is also a significant Costa Rican American population in the Chicago, Illinois, and Gary, Indiana, areas. The geographical preferences of Costa Ricans become evident in the statistics from the Immigration and Naturalization Service, as consistent with the findings of the 1990 census (state.gov).

El Salvador

Salvadoran immigration to the United States is a fairly recent phenomenon. The movement is small in comparison with some of the great immigration waves of the past, but it has a profound significance for both El Salvador and the United States. The exodus of Salvadorans was a result of both economic and political problems. The largest immigration wave occurred as a result of the Salvadoran Civil War in the 1980s, in which 20 to 30 percent of El Salvador's population immigrated. About 50 percent, or up to 500,000 of those who escaped, migrated to the United States, which was already home to over 10,000 Salvadorans, making Salvadoran Americans the third-largest Hispanic or Latino American group, after the Mexican American majority and Cubans (and when not including Stateside Puerto Ricans). As civil wars engulfed several Central American countries in the 1980s, hundreds of thousands of Salvadorans fled their country and came to the United States (US Census Bureau). Between 1980 and 1990, the Salvadoran immigrant population in the United States increased nearly fivefold from 94,000 to 465,000. The number of Salvadoran immigrants in the United States continued to grow in the 1990s and 2000s as a result of family reunification and new arrivals fleeing a series of natural disasters that hit El Salvador, including earthquakes and hurricanes. By 2008, there were about 1.1 million Salvadoran immigrants in the United States. Salvadorans are the country's sixth-largest immigrant group after Mexican, Filipino, Indian, Chinese, and Vietnamese foreign-born. The immigrant population from this tiny Central American country is now nearly as large as the immigrant population from much larger China (US Census Bureau).

Guatemala

Guatemalans have emigrated to the United States since the 1930s and 1940s. Similar to other Central American countries like Costa Rica, they first arrived by way of Mexico and settled in urban areas like Chicago, Houston, Los Angeles, New Orleans, New York City, and San Francisco. The heightening of the Guatemalan Civil War during the 1970s and 1980s led to the arrival of tens of thousands of Guatemalan refugees into the United States via Mexico, by both legal and illegal means. Guatemalan refugees became an important political and economic influence on seeking an end to the civil war, which finally came about in 1996. They also organized to change policies of the Mexican government in dealing with Guatemalan immigrants' legal status, their experiences in Mexico, and difficulties of Guatemalans in Mexico immigrating to the US (US Census Bureau). During the Guatemalan civil war, there was massive destruction of rural villages and farmlands. In the 1996 peace accords, there was a free exchange of civilian land to favor the rise of corporate agribusinesses with the drop of prices of local agricultural products. This heavily affected farm workers and inhabitants of the countryside and they had to immigrate into the US through Mexican territory. After September 11, 2001, Mexican officials made new laws through an initiative limiting immigration visas and other repressive measures on the southern Mexican border through Plan Sur, a binational treaty with the Guatemalan government. Half of the Guatemalan population is situated in two parts of the US—the Northeast and Southern California. A combined population of 267,335 resides in Los Angeles, Orange, Riverside, San Bernardino, and San Diego counties. The Northeast megalopolis, extending from Northern Virginia to north of Boston is home to a population of 257,729 Guatemalans. Cities such as Langley Park, Maryland; Trenton, New Jersey; Stamford, Connecticut; Providence, Rhode Island; and Lynn, Massachusetts have significant concentrations of Guatemalans along the corridor (US Census Bureau).

Honduras

The late eighteenth and early nineteenth centuries marked the beginning of Honduran immigration to the United States, when the continental portion of Central America declared its independence from Spain and became the republic of Honduras. Since the first large influx, periods of conflict have precipitated Honduran immigration to the United States. Most of the individuals who arrived were migrant farm workers and fled to large cities where they had extensive support networks established by previous immigrants. In the 1990s most Honduran Americans lived in New York City, Los Angeles, and Miami (Honduran Americans).

Mexico

The immigration history of Mexico and the United States can be traced as early as the 1820s, when immigrants from Europe and the Americas began to settle in "Tejas", now Texas, which at that time was part of Mexico. The newly arrived American transplants ended up declaring war on the Mexicans in 1836, ultimately defeating the Mexican army and sealing the independence of Texas. These tensions culminated in the Mexican/American war, spanning almost two years from 1846 to 1848. This war was fought over the southwestern part of the current United States, most of which was previously controlled by Spain and then Mexico. The United States fought with the motive that it was the nation's destiny to pursue the war and expand westward. The Annexation of Texas occurred in 1845, followed by the signing of the Treaty of Hidalgo in 1848 (Gonzalez, 1969).

The result of the Mexican/American war was the relinquishing of a large area of Mexican territory, which now represents Arizona, California, parts of Colorado, Nevada, New Mexico, Texas, Utah, and parts of Wyoming. A later treaty, completed by James Gadsden in 1853, would grant the United States an additional portion of previous Mexican territory. The majority of Hispanic citizens living on the gained territories stayed where they were and became full United States citizens; very few returned to Mexican territories. Citizenship in the United States offered a promise of prosperity that many were unable to achieve under the previous Mexican presidency. Unfortunately, legislation passed after the Gadsden treaty led to the surrender of formerly Mexican-owned land via lawsuits before state and federal courts, even though the treaty promised protection of landowners' territories and full protection as citizens of the United States. One example is the stripping of land from landowners in New Mexico, creating a largely property-less population, by the "Santa Fe Ring," a group of relentless and powerful land speculators and attorneys during the late 19th and early 20th centuries (De la Garza et al., 1992).

Upward of 25,000 Mexican miners arrived in California at the time of the California gold rush and were met with great success and wealth. Most Hispanic Americans arriving during that time period were industry men, working in railroads and mining and meanwhile contributing to the growth of Spanish-speaking communities in the surrounding locales. The precipitously growing labor needs of the railroad industry in the late 19th century brought Mexican immigrants from deep in Mexico, not simply border areas. The advent of railroads also helped to bring agricultural jobs to Mexican immigrants, perhaps a foreshadowing of the goals of future immigration to the United States. With the aid of railroad travel, Mexicans began to develop colonies further within the United States, such as Kansas, Utah, and Illinois. During World War I, many Mexicans migrated to Detroit, Minneapolis, and Pennsylvania to work in the steel and automobile manufacturing industry (US Census Bureau).

The stage for the largest influx of Mexican immigrants was set in the early 1900s, with the cessation of Japanese worker migration to the United States. The curtailment of Japanese immigration occurred in 1907, initiated by the "Gentleman's Agreement," an informal agreement between the United States and the Empire of Japan stating that Japan would no longer grant passports for Japanese citizens wishing to work in the continental United States, with assurance from the United States to accept the presence of Japanese immigrants already residing in America. This agreement created a subsequent deficit in an economically advantageous labor force in the United States, and thus, the first large wave of Mexican immigrants began to migrate in the early years of the twentieth century.

The Mexicans entering the States arrived as agricultural laborers farming the valleys in the southern ends of the border states of California, Arizona, New Mexico, and Texas. These laborers were hired by Americans to work in the region's agricultural areas, most notably farming tomatoes, carrots, lettuce, grapes, strawberries, and citrus fruit. Large-scale emigration from central Mexico to the United States began in the 1920s. Mexico was exempted from the system of quotas created by the

Immigration Act of 1924, with Untied States politicians hoping to dissuade the revolutionary government from carrying out the close guarding of the nation's oil reserves decreed in the 1917 Constitution of Mexico. The establishment of a major Mexican presence in California dates back to these years. During this period, Mexicans began to migrate to areas outside the Southwest; they were imported to work in the steel mills of Chicago during a strike in 1919, and again in 1923. Many would find work on the assembly lines of automobile factories in Detroit, and in the meat-packing plants of Chicago and Kansas City. Still more of the arriving immigrants entered the agricultural sector, participating in cotton production in Texas, integrating themselves in the preexisting colonies which had existed since the Spanish colonial era. They followed the cotton crop westward; beginning in settlements in the Rio Grande valley and venturing to new colonies (Gonzalez, 1969).

In the years of the Great Depression, the United States Immigration and Naturalization Service adopted a repatriation policy, and approximately 400,000 Mexican immigrants and their children left the country. The infamous Texas Rangers forcibly evicted Mexicans who refused to accept voluntary repatriation, while Illinois, Indiana, and Michigan paid for special trains to take Mexicans to the border.

When the United States entered World War II, wartime labor shortages were filled by Mexican immigrants. In August 1942, the Bracero Program was born, allowing for the importation of temporary contract laborers from Mexico. Over the following two decades, more than 4 million Mexican farm workers arrived in the United States under this guest worker program, most of them destined for the cotton fields and orchards of California's Central Valley and the Pacific Northwest, and the ranches and sugar beet farms of the Midwest. Texas chose to opt out of the Bracero program and hire farm workers directly from Mexico (US Census Bureau).

Mexican Americans, mestizos especially, also faced heightened racism during World War II, most famously during the Zoot Suit Riots, when sailors in Los Angeles attacked Mexican American youths in 1943, and in the Sleepy Lagoon Case, in which a number of young men were wrongly convicted in a case marked by sensationalized press coverage and overt racism from the prosecution and judge. That trial and verdict, overturned on appeal after a broad-based committee was created to support the defendants, is depicted in Luis Valdez's play and film *Zoot Suit* (Universal

Pictures, 1991). At the same time, the United States was importing thousands of Mexican farm workers under the Bracero program that used them as temporary labor, without employment rights.

According to the National World War II Museum, between 250,000 and 500,000 Hispanic Americans served in the Armed Forces during WWII. Thus, Hispanic Americans comprised 2.3 percent to 4.7 percent of the Army. The exact number, however, is unknown, as Hispanics at the time were classified as whites. Generally Mexican American World War II servicemen were integrated into regular military units. However, many Mexican American war veterans were discriminated against and even denied medical services by the United States Department of Veterans Affairs when they arrived home. In 1948, war veteran Dr. Hector P. Garcia founded the American GI Forum to address the concerns of Mexican American veterans who were being discriminated against (De la Garza et al., 1992).

At the height of the Bracero Program, over 437,000 guest workers entered the United States annually under it, which was discontinued in 1964, as the invention of a mechanical cotton harvester reduced labor needs, and scandals over the exploitation of guest workers led the Department of Labor official overseeing the program to denounce it as "legalized slavery." More recently, beginning in significant numbers in the 1970s, Mexican immigrants have moved in large numbers to the Midwest, attracted by jobs in the packinghouse industry, and to the southeastern United States, where they have displaced many African Americans and contract workers from the Caribbean in agriculture and related industries. The Mexican immigrants of this large wave were attracted to low-paid labor jobs, and an equally high number moved to low-income communities, such as industrial suburbs of Los Angeles in ethnic neighborhoods known as barrios and the agricultural sector of Imperial Valley, California (De la Garza).

The Immigration and Nationality Act of 1965 set strict quotas on the number of persons who could legally enter the United States from Latin American nations, and most new Mexican migration to the United States in the 1960s and 1970s was temporary and short-term. Since the 1980s, Mexican migration has increased dramatically. The Immigration Reform and Control Act of 1986 granted amnesty to illegal immigrants who had resided in the United States before 1982, while imposing penalties on employers who hired illegal immigrants. Several factors led to an increase in Mexican immigration to the United States.

The Latin American debt crisis of the 1980s led to high rates of unemployment in Mexico and destroyed the savings of a large portion of the middle class, as did the 1994 Mexican Peso Crisis. In 1991, Mexican president Carlos Salinas dismantled the communally owned *ejidos*, one of the most important legacies of the Mexican Revolution, and the enactment of NAFTA brought a flood of subsidized United States goods into the Mexican market, driving down grain prices and forcing hundreds of thousands of people from rural areas to migrate in search of better economic opportunities. The 2000 Census showed that the foreign-born population of the United States increased by 11.3 million people in the 1990s, and Mexican immigrants accounted for 43 percent of that growth. The region which had the fastest growing immigrant population was the Southeast, where many Mexicans found work in construction, as migrant agricultural laborers, and in textile mills and chicken processing plants. The Latino populations of Georgia, North and South Carolina, and Arkansas increased between 300 and 400 per cent from 1990 to 2000 (Gonzalez).

Panama

Since 1820, more than one million immigrants from Central and South America migrated to the United States. Until 1960, the US Census Bureau did not produce statistics that separated the Panamanians, South Americans, and Central Americans. After World War II the flow of immigrants from Panama remained small even though there were no immigration restrictions on the people from the Western Hemisphere. Panamanian immigration increased dramatically after the 1965 Immigration Act, which imposed a ceiling of 120,000 admissions from the hemisphere. This remarkably increased Panamanian immigration and by 1970, Panamanians were one of the largest Central American groups in the United States (Panamanian American).

Most Panamanian immigrants were non-white women, with many of the female immigrants working in service, domestic, or low-paid, white-collar positions in order to earn money to send back home. Since 1962, the percentage of employed newcomers who are domestic servants has remained high, ranging from 15 to 28 percent. The entry of homemakers and children after 1968 was eased by the immigration preference system favoring family reunions. They had already amassed 86,000 people of Panamanian ancestry living in the United States.

During the nineteenth and twentieth centuries, Panamanian immigrants gathered in urban centers, especially in very large metropolitan cities, with New York City containing the largest urban population of Panamanians. Unlike most other Hispanic groups, the vast majority of Panamanian Americans are black, with the remaining being mainly Mestizo. Although most Panamanian Americans speak Spanish, the group tends to identify itself more with West Indian groups rather than with other Hispanic groups. Most Panamanians, along with Dominicans, Puerto Ricans, Cubans, Colombians, and Venezuelans have higher percentages of African descent than other Hispanic groups (Panamanian American).

IMMIGRATION FROM THE CARIBBEAN

Cuba

The history of Cuban immigration to the United States traces back to the Spanish colonial period in 1565 when St. Augustine, Florida, was established by Pedro Menéndez de Avilés, and hundreds of Spanish-Cuban soldiers and their families moved from Cuba to St. Augustine to begin new lives. Thousands of Cuban settlers also immigrated to Louisiana between 1778 and 1802 and Texas during the period of Spanish rule. In 1870, the number of Cuban immigrants increased to almost 12,000, of which about 4,500 resided in New York, about 3,000 in New Orleans, and 2,000 in Key West. The causes of these movements were both economic and political (US Census Bureau).

The year 1869 marked the beginning of one of the most significant periods of emigration from Cuba to the United States, the epicenter of which was Key West. Hundreds of workers arrived, motivated by the search of prosperity in tobacco manufacturing. This influx was catalyzed by many breakthroughs in the manufacturing of tobacco products and snuff, as well as a clearer access to the United States market. Furthermore, the future of Cuba was uncertain, as the country had suffered years of economic, social, and political hardship. Other cities in Florida also greeted a large arrival of immigrants, most notably, Tampa. In 1880, the city had less than 1,000 Cuban inhabitants, and that number grew to greater than 5,000 in just a decade. Many immigrants returned to Cuba in the late 1800s to fight for independence on Cuban soil, however (Cuban Ancestry Map).

In 1885, Vicente Martinez Ybor moved his cigar operations from Key West to the town of Tampa, Florida, to escape labor shortages. Ybor City quickly attracted thousands of Cuban workers from Key West and Cuba proper. West Tampa, another new cigar manufacturing community, was founded nearby in 1892 and also grew quickly. Between these communities, the Tampa Bay area's Cuban population grew from almost nothing to the largest in Florida in just over a decade, and the city as a whole grew from a village of approximately 1,000 residents in 1885 to over 16,000 by 1900. Both Ybor City and Tampa were instrumental in Cuba's eventual independence. Inspired by revolutionaries such as Jose Martí, who visited Florida several times, Tampa-area Cubans and their sympathetic neighbors donated money and equipment toward the goal of a free Cuba. After the Spanish-American War, some Cubans returned to their native land, but many chose to stay in the United States due to the physical and economic devastation caused by years of fighting on the island.

In the early twentieth century (1900–1959), many small waves of Cuban emigration to the United States occurred, with most Cubans settling in Florida and the Northeast. The majority of an estimated 100,000 Cubans arriving in that time period usually came for economic reasons (the Great Depression of 1929, high sugar prices and labor contracts), but also included refugees fleeing the military dictatorship, who had favorable views towards the United States (US Census Bureau). Cuban migration during these years also included a small portion of the population who could afford to leave the country and live abroad. The United States territory was considered a favorite locale of the Cuban upper and middle classes of society, to which they sent their children for school, took vacations, and even established small and medium-sized businesses.

After the Cuban Revolution in 1959, led by Fidel Castro, a large Cuban exodus began as the new government allied itself with the Soviet Union and began to introduce communism. From 1960 to 1979, hundreds of thousands of Cubans left Cuba and began a new life in the United States, most of which were members of Cuba's upper and middle classes. Between December 1960 and October 1962, more than 14,000 Cuban children arrived alone in the United States. The motivation of this large influx of children was their parents' fear that their children would be sent to Soviet Bloc countries to be educated.

The United States Congress passed the Cuban Adjustment Act in 1966 in order to provide aid to recently arrived Cuban immigrants, with the Cuban Refugee Program providing more than $1.3 billion of direct financial assistance. Recent immigrants were also eligible for public assistance, Medicare, free English courses, scholarships, and low-interest college loans. Some banks even pioneered loans for exiles that did not have collateral or credit but received help in getting a business loan. These loans enabled many Cuban Americans to secure funds and start up their own businesses. With these financial incentives and low cost of living, Cuban-owned businesses began to appear in Miami, Florida, and Union City, New Jersey (dubbed Havana on the Hudson).

It was not until the mass exodus of the Cuban exiles in 1959 that Miami started to become a preferred destination. Westchester, Florida, was the area most densely populated by Cubans and Cuban Americans in the United States, followed by Hialeah, Florida. In 2010, Hialeah, Florida was the area most densely populated by Cubans and Cuban Americans in the United States, followed by Westchester, Florida. Another large wave (an estimated 12,000 people) of Cuban immigration occurred in the early 1980s with the Mariel boatlifts. Most of the "Marielitos" were people wanting to escape from communism, and had succeeded in establishing their roots in the US. Fidel Castro sent some twenty thousand criminals directly from Cuban prisons, as well as mentally ill persons from Cuban mental institutions, with the alleged double purpose of cleaning up Cuban society and poisoning the USA. Those people were labeled "inadmissible" by the US government, and with time, through many negotiations, have been returned to Cuba.

Since the mid-1990s, after the implementation of the "Wet Foot, Dry Foot" policy, immigration patterns changed. Many Cuban immigrants departed from the southern and western coasts of Cuba and arrived at the Yucatán Peninsula in Mexico; many landed on Isla Mujeres. From there, Cuban immigrants traveled to the Texas-Mexico border and found asylum. Many of the Cubans who did not have family in Miami settled in Houston; this has caused Houston's Cuban American community to increase in size. The term "dusty foot" refers to Cubans immigrating to the United States through Mexico. In 2005, the Department of Homeland Security had abandoned the approach of detaining every dry-foot Cuban who crossed through Texas and began a policy allowing most Cubans to obtain immediate parole.

Before the 1980s, all refugees from Cuba were welcomed into the United States as political refugees. This changed in the 1990s so that only Cubans who reach United States soil are granted refuge under the "wet foot, dry foot policy." While representing a tightening of United States immigration policy, the "wet foot, dry foot policy" still affords Cubans a privileged position relative to other immigrants to the United States. This privileged position is the source of a certain friction between Cuban Americans and other Latin citizens and residents in the United States, adding to the tension caused by the divergent foreign policy interests pursued by conservative Cuban Americans. Cuban immigration also continues with an allotted number of Cubans (20,000 per year) provided legal US visas.

Cuban Americans live in all fifty states, Washington, DC, and Puerto Rico, which received thousands of anti-Castro refugees as well in the 1960s, and Cuban American population growth is found in California, Georgia, Illinois, Indiana, Texas, Massachusetts, New York, New Jersey, Rhode Island, North Carolina, South Carolina, and Virginia.

Dominican Republic

Immigration records of Dominicans in the United States date from as far back as the late 16th century, and New York City has had a Dominican community since the 1930s. Sailor-turned-merchant Juan Rodriguez arrived in downtown Manhattan in 1613 from his home on the island now known as the Dominican Republic, making him the first visitor to spend a night in Manhattan.

From the 1960s onward, following the fall of General Rafael Trujillo's dictatorship, large waves of immigrants have arrived from the Dominican Republic. With increased immigration, Dominican diaspora communities have sprouted in New York, New Jersey, Miami, Philadelphia, Providence, and Boston. Smaller waves of immigrants have since settled in the metropolitan areas of Chicago; Washington, DC; Houston; Los Angeles; Portland, Oregon; Kansas City; Orlando; Buffalo; and New Orleans. Dominican immigrant communities have similar settlement patterns to that of the Puerto Rican population (US Census Bureau).

Almost half of all the Dominican Americans today have arrived since the 1990s, especially in the early part of the decade. There has been another surge of immigration in recent years as immigration from Mexico has declined, allowing more backlogged Dominican applicants to obtain legal residence. Dominican Americans are the fifth-largest Hispanic or Latino American group, after Mexican Americans, Stateside Puerto Ricans, Cuban Americans, and Salvadoran Americans.

As of 2010, the five largest concentrations of Dominican Americans are in New York, New Jersey, Florida, Massachusetts, and Pennsylvania. Rhode Island is the only state where Dominicans are the largest Hispanic group. In New York City, the borough of Manhattan (New York County) is the only county in the country where Dominicans are the largest ancestral group and its Washington Heights neighborhood has long been considered the center of the Dominican American community. The 2010 Census estimated the nationwide Dominican American population at 1,414,703 (US Census Bureau).

Puerto Rico

Since 1898, the end of the Spanish American War, Puerto Rico has been under the control of the United States, allowing free migration between the mainland and the island. Surprisingly, Puerto Ricans settled freely in the United States even when under Spanish rule. With its victory in 1898, the United States acquired Puerto Rico from Spain and has retained sovereignty since. The 1917 Jones–Shafroth Act made all Puerto Ricans US citizens, freeing them from immigration barriers. The massive migration of Puerto Ricans to the United States was the largest in the early and late twentieth century.

The manufacturing boom in Puerto Rico, with the creation of American factories, slowly transformed Puerto Rico's economy from one that was agrarian to an industrial one. These political and economic interventions in Puerto Rico created optimum conditions for emigration, "by concentrating wealth in the hands of US corporations and displacing workers." Policymakers promoted colonization plans and contract labor programs to reduce the population. The government supported United States companies in recruiting Puerto Ricans as a source of low-wage labor to the United States. The plight of the migrating Puerto Rican was similar to that of others, searching for higher-wage jobs, first to New York City, and later to other cities such as Chicago, Philadelphia, Boston, Cleveland, Miami, Tampa, and Orlando. Recently, many Puerto Ricans have chosen to migrate to states such as New Jersey and New York, for cultural and economic reasons (Lapp).

In the late 1900s, Puerto Ricans migrated to New York en masse, especially to the Bronx, and Spanish Harlem and the Lower East Side neighborhoods. In 1960, the number of stateside Puerto Ricans living in New York City was 88 percent, 69 percent of which were living in East Harlem. The strong community networks already in existence helped new immigrants to settle, find work, and build communities. In later years, Puerto Rican neighborhoods started to materialize in the Bronx because of its proximity to East Harlem and in Brooklyn because of its proximity to the Lower East Side. In 1980, the city's Puerto Rican population peaked. At that time there were about 930,000 Puerto Rican residents in the city and about 80 percent of the Hispanic population was Puerto Rican, representing about 15 percent of the city's total population then. The number and percentage are significantly lower now than they were in 1980 (Perez y Gonzalez).

Between 1990 and 2000, the stateside Puerto Rican population grew by 12.5 percent, from 3.2 to 3.4 million. This growth rate was significantly higher than the 8.4 percent growth of Puerto Rico during this same period.

In 1950, about a quarter of a million Puerto Rican natives lived stateside. In March 2012 that figure had risen to about 1.5 million. That is, only a third of the 4.6 million Puerto Ricans living stateside were born on the island. Puerto Ricans are also the second-largest Hispanic group in the USA after those of Mexican descent. In the most recent census in 2010, there were 4,623,716 Puerto Rican Americans, native and foreign born, representing 9.2 percent of all Hispanics in the United States.

CONCLUSION

In this contribution, I have offered a detailed survey of immigration to the United States from the various countries of South America, Central America, and the Caribbean. Addressing the historical and sociopolitical trajectory of each subgroup, I have prepared the ground for a culture-specific attunement with the psychosocial vulnerabilities and assets of them. Awareness of these variables will go a long way, I hope, in evolving a fundamentally humane and respectful attitude towards Latino Americans (and their offspring) in both social and clinical environments.

TWO

Child-Rearing by Latino Immigrants

April Fallon and Carol Quintana

Throughout most of the world, the family takes the primary responsibility for ensuring that the next generation will be physically and psychologically healthy and socially well-functioning. Specific child-rearing practices have both biological and cultural determinants within the context of the physical ecosystem. Super and Hark (1997) describe the child's environment as composed of (i) the child's physical setting, (ii) socially and culturally regulated customs of child care, and (iii) the psychology (with regard to child-rearing) of the caregivers. Stability in these three elements ensures consistent child-rearing practices coherent with the culture in which the child resides. Major change in one component may aggravate the equilibrium of the system and stress the fit of the other elements. The immigration process, which ruptures the child's previous physical backdrop and surrounding social expectations, may quash the success of previously well-established child-rearing practices.

In this chapter, we first explore Latino family values that are rooted in a common historical socioeconomic foundation. The overarching values of family closeness and respect/obedience underpin the psychology of homeland child-rearing practices. We then examine two processes involved in child-rearing. The first is the use of *refranes* and *dichos*. *Refranes* and *dichos,* popular sayings of Spanish origin handed down from generation to generation, are a common way in Latino culture to impart wisdom or advice on a wide range of human activities. We incorporate a number of *refranes* into the values section for illustration of their importance. The second is the use of firm discipline. We include findings from our empirical study that compared American and Mexican methods of discipline. We then present how these child-rearing values and practices become disrupted due to factors that are inherent to Latino families' experience of immigration/acculturation and to living as an ethnic minority within the United States. The impact of disruptions to child-rearing will be discussed and illustrated with clinical examples. We draw upon our experiences as clinicians, the professional literature and our empirical research.

LATINO CHILD-REARING VALUES

Latino American immigrant families come from a variety of countries of origin; they reside in the United States under very diverse circumstances. Sixty-two percent of those who identify as Latinos in the United States today are native-born. Of the remaining, most were born in Mexico. Mexico, Puerto Rico and Cuba (in that order) are the principle countries of origin (US Census Bureau, 2009). Our rationale for grouping these families together is that they share similar historical roots that lay the foundation for child-rearing practices with many values in common. These particular values emerge from a common world view and ways of being that have at their foundation a focus on shared, family-focused existence where the needs of the larger family collective take precedence over those of the individual. We recognize that variability in country of origin, circumstances and status of immigration and participation in the acculturation process is likely to influence these values, processes and practices (Buriel, 1993; Hill et al, 2003).[1] Latinos are far from homogenous and we are apologetic that there are likely to be exceptions to much of our discussion. We nonetheless present this framework as a starting point from which various groups and individuals may diverge.

Family Closeness

Family closeness and cohesiveness is promoted through the traditional Latino cultural values of *familismo, simpatía, personalismo,* and *respeto* (Guilamo-Ramos et al., 2007). *Familismo* refers to family closeness or interdependence. The term *familismo* is not common verbiage among Latino families themselves; the term *convivencia familiar* (shared family life) would be more apt. Nevertheless, it has come to denote Latino family closeness in the literature (Falicov, 1996, Garcia-Preto, 1996). *Familismo* expresses itself through the sharing of financial responsibilities, of raising and disciplining the children, of helping with problem solving, and the providing of support for lonely members (Falicov, 1996). It also involves the carrying out of family obligations, as well as the recognition of accomplishments by members of the family both nuclear and extended. Parents and children maintain a strong connection throughout the adult lives of the offspring. An additional component of this extended family support system is that of *Compadrazgo,* which refers to the participation and support of godparents in the lives of godchildren under their care (Chang and Liou, 2009).

Simpatía refers to the cultural practice of maintaining harmony and avoiding controversy and conflict. "*Al hogar, como a la nave, le conviene la mar suave*" (For a home, as for a ship, calm seas are preferred), a common saying, expresses the essence of this value. It refers to being polite, agreeable, and respectful toward others. Indirect, implicit, or covert communications are used as a means of circumventing angry feelings, avoiding making others uncomfortable, and keeping the peace (Falicov, 1996). Harkness and Super (in press) utilizing parents' diaries of their young children found that "being easy" or not "being difficult" was a more highly valued characteristic in Spain than the five other Western cultures studied.[2] *Simpatía* is shown in the warmth displayed by parents in their interactions with their children, which is one of the bases of child-rearing. For example, in parental interactions with adolescents, warmth and responsiveness are emphasized in an effort to maintain low-conflict relationships (Guilamo-Ramos et al, 2007).

Personalismo is a Latino value that represents the importance of displaying warmth in interpersonal relationships as well as the overriding centrality of interpersonal relationships in life. It refers to the value placed on personal character and inner qualities as well as the preference for relating to others belonging to one's own ethnic group. "*Si quieres tu estima ver crecer, trata a la gente bien*" (If you want your esteem to grow, treat people well) is a well-known Spanish dicho that captures this value. Warmth, trust, and respect shape the base of social relationships that function in "interpersonal connectedness, cooperation, and mutual reciprocity" (Guilamo-Ramos et al, 2007, p. 19). Latinos recognize that *person-*

alismo forms the central foundation for maintaining these relationships (Chang and Liou, 2009).

Respect and Obedience

Respeto (respect) is a central tenet of Latino interpersonal relations that helps maintain and support *familismo, simpatia,* and *personalismo. "Quien respeta a sus padres será respetado por sus hijos"* (Whoever respects their parents will be respected by their children) captures this belief. *Respeto* signifies an emotional dependence and dutifulness not implicit in the English version of the word. It represents the values of loyalty, respect, and obedience and is promoted through the hierarchical structure of the family unit (Falicov, 1996; Guilamo-Ramos et al, 2007). Children are expected to adhere to parental authority and follow rules of conduct without question. Respect must be shown to parents, elders, other authority figures, and to God, and is part of being a well-educated person. Well-educated, *bien educado,* refers not only to people's level of education, but to their social skills and ability to show respect (Chang and Liou, 2009). To achieve *respeto,* parents monitor their children's behavior, they do not ignore misbehavior, and they remain consistently strict (Guilamo-Ramos et al, 2007). *Respeto* forms part of the parenting dimension of demandingness.

Obediencia, or obedience, acts as the under girder to the support of parental authority through which the other family values are instilled in children. Parental authority is not only perceived as a means of enforcing the hierarchical family structure, but it is viewed as an expression of parental love as well (Chang and Liou, 2009). *"Hijo sin rienda, madeja sin cuerda,"* (A child without reins is like a tangled ball of yarn). Studies in Mexico, studies by the renowned psychologist Rogelio Diaz-Guerrero (2007) demonstrate the continuing importance of obedience in Mexican society. Diaz-Guerrero developed specific sociocultural historical premises from factor analysis of studies with middle school children conducted in 1959, 1970, and 1994 that indicated that the most important premise was that children should always obey their parents. Obedience is achieved in various ways, through this mixing of authority and love that expects compliance without question as well as through specific child-rearing practices. Children are taught forms of courtesy and good manners from an early age. In Mexico, for example, young children are taught to respond to elders with the phrases "a sus ordenes" (at your orders) or "para servirle" (in order to serve you), submissive phrases that are commonly employed in social interactions from childhood and throughout adulthood (Diaz-Guerrero, 2007). It is also achieved through the consistent and strict monitoring of behaviors (Guilamo-Ramos et al, 2007) which is discussed further in the next section.

Latinos share this respect for other social institutions such as the church and school. Latino parents' expectations of teachers and schools are often higher than Anglo-Americans. Petelo (2005), in an interesting comparison study of Latino and Anglo parents, found that Latino families believed more than Anglo families that parents should not question teachers' methods and that the most important thing that the school can teach is absolute obedience to adults. Children were viewed as naturally bad and in need of early training and that this would be a passive process where teachers fill children's minds with information. Although most Latino parents believe in the importance of education, their Latino children's lag behind other ethnic groups has often been attributed to the passive part of the student role. In a study of Latino students from impoverished backgrounds who were attending Yale, parents' encouragement and facilitation of their child's autonomy was one of the important elements in their success (Ceballo, 2004).

CHILD-REARING PRACTICES

The common child-rearing practices of Latinos reflect an emphasis on the values of obedience and firm discipline as well as warmth and interpersonal closeness. Baumrind's (1996) parenting dimensions and accompanying prototypes is a useful framework for connecting Latino family psychology and child-rearing. Baumrind's factor analytic research on child-rearing produced two principal dimensions of child-rearing: *responsiveness* and *demandingness*. Baumrind (1996) distinguished three parenting models based on these dimensions: the *permissive* model is high on responsiveness and low on demandingness; the *authoritarian* model is low on responsiveness and high on demandingness; and the *authoritative* model is high on both responsiveness and demandingness. Baumrind concluded that the optimal model was the authoritative one in that control is balanced with warmth and sensible demands with responsiveness (Baumrind, 1996). Additionally, Baumrind's research led her to conclude that extrinsic motivation in the form of aversive consequences, such as spanking, does not interfere with intrinsic motivation as long as parents are both responsive as well as intellectually stimulating (Baumrind, 1996).

Specifically, responsiveness consists of such basic components as warmth, reciprocity, clear communication and person-centered discourse, and attachment. We discuss two ways that these are conveyed. The first is the use of *dichos* or *refranes*. The storytelling and use of sayings is used to teach moral behavior and are always in the context of personal connection. The second is through modeling. Although neither of these (particularly the latter) is unique to Latinos, both occur with a goal of connection and warmth.

Demandingness constitutes direct confrontation, monitoring, intrusive-directiveness, as well as firm, consistent discipline that include demands for high maturity (Baumrind, 1989). Demandingness includes both restrictiveness and firm control. Restrictiveness constitutes forms of psychological control and the firm control represents forms of behavioral control (Darling and Steinberg, 1993). For Latinos, the use of firm and consistent discipline is significant. This can constitute the use of physical punishment; however, behavioral compliance can also be obtained through the instilling of shame or from the operation of overriding constructs that act in conjunction to maintain family structure and parental authority.

Refranes *and* Dichos

Refranes (historical proverbs), and *dichos* (popular sayings) are used to teach social expectations and proper moral behavior (Quinones-Mayo and Dempsey, 2005). These proverbs and sayings have their origins in Spanish literature. The discourse of Cervantes' character Sancho Panza in *Don Quijote de la Mancha* (1605) is characterized by frequent use of *refranes.* At one point, Don Quijote begs Sancho to refrain from using them (Perez, 1993). They serve to impart wisdom as well as transmit aspects of culture and social protocol. They are generally short and concise and often rhyme, making them easier to remember (Perez, 1993). Thus, *refranes* form part of an oral as well as literary tradition that is passed from one generation to the next in conjunction with the learning of Spanish language itself.

According to Perez (1993), *refranes* possess the virtue of springing up spontaneously when a situation encapsulated by a particular refrán presents itself. The following *refrán* speaks to this function: "*La gracia de cada refrán, es decirlo en el momento y el lugar en donde van*" (The grace of each *refrán* is to say it in the moment and place where it belongs).[3] More specifically, they serve as a tool to educate children on how to behave; "In a hierarchical society, such proverbs teach deference and proper social protocol, as well as critical thinking" (Quinones-Mayo and Dempsey, 2005, p. 661). The following examples illustrate this: "*A Dios, al padre y maestro, tenga el niño gran respeto*": (Children should have great respect for God, parents, and teachers); "*Lo que con tus padres hagas con tus hijos lo pagas*" (What you do to your parents, you will pay for with your own children) and "*Con buenas palabras y mejores hechos conquistaras el mundo entero*" (With good words and better actions you will conquer the whole world). Each of these examples speaks to teaching children how to relate to others. The first refers to the importance of treating God and other important adults with respect and clearly would be used when a child has spoken or acted in a thoughtless or disrespectful manner. The second speaks to the idea that what you sow, you will reap; in this case, if you treat your parents poorly, your own children will treat you the same way. The third *refrán* imparts the wisdom that if you interact in a positive manner with others you will accomplish much in life; it emphasizes the importance of reflecting on the effect actions in the present can have on the future. This last one is sometimes used with an adolescent when discussing how to resolve some interpersonal problem with a peer or teacher.

It is important to note that *refranes* and *dichos* may be employed directly with children as in the above examples, or indirectly through grandparents, godparents, or others in the extended family. Extended family often uses them with parents as a way of giving counsel on child-rearing. For example, the following *dicho* might be said to parents who are relying too heavily on corporal punishment: "*Al niño malo más amor y menos palo*" (Treat a bad child with more love and less stick). For parents who are gossiping or using bad language in the home, the following might apply: "*Lo que el niño oyo en el hogar, eso dice en el portal*" (What the child hears at home, he will say in the doorway). Thus, the use of *refranes* and *dichos* represents another way in which the importance of the extended family network is reflected in the raising of children in Latino culture.

Modeling of Adult Activities

Another important dimension of child-rearing involves the modeling of adult activities. This dimension encompasses gender role socialization as well as a wide range of aspects. Children participate in all types of family social activities from an early age. They are taken to weddings, funerals, and other events where they witness how adults behave with one another. This means that children may attend events that extend well into the night; however, they are collectively cared for by both parents and other extended family members. As children move into adolescence they are often chaperoned by adults until marriage. This child-rearing practice provides continuity and consistency to role acquisition (Quinones-Mayo and Dempsey, 2005). According to Fuller and Coll (2010), attending family dinners or completing household chores "advances intersubjective understanding between parent and child of how obligation to the household's interests trumps one's own preferences" (p. 562).

Firm Discipline

Firm discipline that often takes the form of physical punishment is a product of the fact that Latin American nations developed within the context of colonization. While colonization established a common language, religion,[4] and customs, this was accomplished through force and harshness (Garcia-Preto, 1996). As a result, the parenting practices that grew out of this context reflected the harshness of this experience (Fontes, 2005). These countries also have common agrarian economic roots. Children hold economic value in helping to provide materially, both while they are young, as well as when they grow to adulthood. Under these circumstances, child-rearing tends to focus on control and obedience to meet the demands of farming and tending animals. While family members depend on each other economically, they also need each other on an emotional level. A high level of emotional interdependence is normal under these circumstances. Family patterns and interactions reflect a priority of the group over the individual (Kagitcibasi, 1996). More specifically, family closeness, parental authority, and interpersonal relatedness have influenced and evolved common child-rearing practices (Zayas and Solari, 1994).

In addition, parental control often is exacted through the use of corporal punishment. Latin American families have been characterized as likely to take an authoritarian approach to discipline that relies on the use of physical punishment (Fontes, 2005). Use of physical punishment in Latin American families has been seen to be a by-product of colonization that mirrors the harshness of that experience (Fontes, 2005). However, the degree to which physical discipline is employed is also a function of the ecological context in which families reside. Families coming from an agrarian background are more likely to rely on physical discipline where children are likely to serve an economic function. In families from an urban industrial setting, children are less likely to serve this function and thus obedience in the form of physical punishment is not as necessary (Kagitcibasi, 1996). It may persist given the lasting impact of its historical roots on the one hand, and on the other, its prevalence will depend on the harshness of families' external environment. More controlling parenting practices may be required to survive in dangerous and impoverished urban neighborhoods (Harrison et al, 1990).

In general, harsh parenting practices have been linked to problematic behavior at school and in the context of peer relationships (Dumka, Gonzalez, Bonds and Milsap, 2009). Behavioral problems are associated with both verbal and corporal punishment, but also with inadequate nurturance (Perez and Fox, 2008). Fathers' harshness is more likely to result in aggressive and behavioral problems in boys. Mothers' strictness with girls is actually associated with higher grades for girls (Dumka et al, 2009). As this empirical work demonstrates, the harshness of punishment cannot be viewed in isolation and is often mitigated by warmth and monitoring. For Latinos, corporal punishment should not be confused with physical abuse. This lack of differentiation and inability to appreciate the broader cultural parenting context has been a source of Latino distrust and disappointment in mental health services available. Minority immigrant families also face poverty, segregation, and racial discrimination, which can increase parents' frustration and expression of aggression (Gracia Coll et al, 1996).

The common stereotype that assumes Latino families generally employ harsh physical punishment does not take socioeconomic status into consideration. Results of a recent study by Quintana (2014) run counter to this stereotype. In this comparative study of the experience and perception of physical punishment in childhood among Americans and Mexicans, Mexican participants did not report harsher physical punishment than Americans. In fact, the Mexicans in this predominantly urban upper-class sample experienced significantly less physical abuse than the Americans from a mostly working-class sample in the South. These findings support the role of socioeconomic context over culture in determining the degree to which physical discipline is utilized to exercise parental control. Likewise, the Mexicans in this sample had a lower threshold for abuse than the American sample. Another study with an even broader comparison group, comparing non-Hispanic Caucasians, Mexicans, Mexican immigrants and Mexican Americans (born in the United States), found that there was greater use of authoritarian parenting styles in parents of Mexican descent—first and second generation immigrants (Varela et al, 2004). This suggests that either immigration selects for this or the experience of immigration, with its inherent stresses and disappointments, creates this.

IMPORTANCE OF GENDER ROLES IN CHILD-REARING

The hierarchical structure of the Hispanic family unit has traditionally been based on the gender role constructs of male dominance and female submissiveness. The terms *machismo* and *marionismo* have been used in this regard. *Marionismo*, emerging from Hispanic women's devotion to the Virgin Mary, manifests as humility and virtue expressed in caregiving and stoicism. Motherhood traditionally has been perceived as more important than female sexuality. *Machismo* involves the attitudes and beliefs that come with the leadership role of men in the family as well as the community. Machismo can be perceived in both a positive and negative light: on the one hand it signifies being responsible, confident, and personable; on the other, it means being aloof, risk-taking, and aggressive. Although both parents and extended family contribute to responsiveness and demandingness, females are expected more than males to prioritize home and family above all other individual concerns. These distinct gender constructs affect how male and female children are socialized; parenting practices toward boys and girls may differ accordingly. The research on this has been somewhat mixed. Utilizing Puerto Rican and Dominican families, Guilamo-Ramos and associates (2007) found that parents tended to be more authoritative and egalitarian with their adolescent sons, while with their adolescent daughters they were stricter and more authoritarian. In contrast, Varela (et al, 1996) reported in a sample of Latinos of Mexican descent, both parents were more authoritarian with their boys than their girls. Interestingly, these differences were not related to education, socioeconomic status, immigrant status or degree of assimilation.

Problems related to gender roles often emerge during adolescence when the gender role difference between the parents, distribution of power in the family, and differential treatment of male and female teenagers diverge between the host culture and culture of origin. Conflicts around differences in the couple between gender role ideologies[5] are often masked with the children who become the identified patients.[6]

DISRUPTIVE FACTORS TO CHILD-REARING

The majority of Latino immigrants are motivated by economic circumstances and the desire to provide a safe and prosperous life for their children. "*Dos legados duraderos a los hijos—uno raíces, el otro alas.*" (Two lasting legacies to give to children: one, roots; the other, wings.) This Spanish proverb highlights the desire that Latino parents have for their children to have both roots and wings in their lives. Here, "roots" refers both to children having their feet planted firmly on the ground physically and psychologically, in order to provide for and support their families, and roots planted in the community and family. At the same time they wish for them to fly, to realize their dreams. Yet poverty and oppression may eclipse their efforts to do so in their native countries; "roots" in the native community conflicts with the well-being and success of the next generation. Within each family, the value of pursuing a better life for their progeny helps to ensure survival and success. Yet this desire and value embedded in the caretaker's psychology chafes against the other two components of the child's cultural environment—social setting and cultural childcare customs. To accomplish this requires uprooting the family from its social and physical environment and from the cultural supports, customs and norms with which they are familiar. Immigration often involves a process of family separation, later reunification, and a subsequent lifetime of ambivalence of whether to stay or return. Each stage of the immigration process has the potential to create traumatic experiences of loss and disequilibrium in the family system, resulting in psychological stress and deterioration in mental health. The experience of immigration and acculturation disrupts the ability of Latin American immigrant parents to impart their core values and employ many of their common child-rearing practices.

Separation of Families

Family closeness in terms of maintaining connections and receiving support from extended family members is often compromised when part of the family immigrates to the United States, leaving important loved ones behind. Grandparents, aunts, and uncles may remain in the country of origin, and contact may only be possible by phone or social media. A very frequent occurrence is that of one parent, often the father, immigrating alone to seek out employment, gathering savings and, a few years down the road, sending for his family to join him. Children often emigrate last. In the interim, attachment is disrupted in both the marital and parent-child relationship. Sometimes the effect of this disruption does not appear until years later, as seen in the following example.

A fourth-year college student came to treatment, reporting symptoms of depression and anxiety. In her history, she revealed that when she was four, her mother had left her in the care of her extended family while pursuing work in the United States. After four years she, her grandparents and two other unmarried children moved to the United States and had all lived together since that time, even though it was not a financial necessity.[7] She reported that it was not upsetting when her mother left because her grandparents and other extended family had lived together. She felt that her grandmother had been more of a caregiver than her mother. She alluded to some differences that she had with her mother but assured the therapist that she had a very close relationship with all of the family members. She reported that she had friends at school and liked her roommates. However, since her freshman year she returned home every other weekend, even though the college was about a five-hour bus ride from her home.

Her symptoms attenuated after ten sessions, but she asked to continue treatment, expressing fear that her symptoms would return. In the following three additional months of once-weekly therapy, the patient spoke about friends, school work, her impending graduation, and occasionally about squabbles between her mother and other family members. She was most comfortable with a practical problem-solving approach, and a rhythm of initial anxiety, examination of the problem, and decrease in anxiety was established for each session. The therapist provided a containing environment where, little by little, the patient felt freer to openly express negative affect to an outsider. The therapist described it as a deconditioning experience where the patient could feel reduction in anxiety without disruption of their relationship or fragmentation of the self. With six sessions left, the therapist brought up termination directly.

The next session, the patient appeared tearful and anxious. She revealed that she and her mother had been fighting, which was apparently not an unusual occurrence, even though she had not spoken before about it. Over the next several sessions, this patient revealed the cycle of her mother's frequent texting. There would be increasing urgency in these messages when the patient did not answer. This would eventuate in the patient answering her mother in monosyllables. With her mother's continued badgering and accusing phone messages of ungratefulness, the patient would become very angry and yell at her mother. She would then feel very guilty and bad about herself. This would happen often more than once between home visits. What emerged was a long-standing resentment toward her mother because she felt that her mother now wanted to be close, but it was "too late." She came to recognize that she had not forgiven her mother for leaving her when she was young. Here-and-now termination issues and connecting it to the earlier separation from the mother helped her to resolve intense negative emotionality that she was experiencing instead of becoming angry and irritated for her mother's culturally based intrusiveness.

The late revelation of her conflictual relationship with her mother was likely twofold. First, values of *simpatia* dictated the patient's reluctance to express the conscious negative feelings about her mother, particularly to someone both outside the family and ethnic group. Secondly, the discussion of termination and the ending of the supportive therapeutic relationship sparked the awareness of dormant unconscious unresolved issues of early separation from the mother. No discussion of this ever seemed appropriate to the patient since she realized that her mother had been brave and had endured poverty and discrimination alone for a number of years. The decision to emigrate had resulted in a very prosperous life for the family and many opportunities for her that would not have otherwise been available. Now on the cusp of a developmental transition in American life, the patient struggled with American age-appropriate issues of autonomy and individuation within a family that demanded togetherness and that embraced cultural norms of closeness. These occurred in the context of the early traumatic separation and an unconscious resolution of subtle withholding and withdrawal from the relationship with her mother after reunification. Contextually, the patient's depression and anxiety (and entrance into therapy) in her last year of college should be seen as more than a normative developmental crisis. It is both a struggle for personal and cultural identity.

UNITING PARENTS AND CHILDREN IN A NEW ENVIRONMENT

With a new environment, new social norms and internalized cultural norms from the old country, the instilling of respect in the Latino tradition may be compromised in several ways. If a split immigration has occurred in which children and parents have been separated for a number of years, it is frequently difficult for parents to receive the respect from their children that they may feel they automatically deserve. Parents of adolescents may struggle to gain respect from their children who have acculturated to the American lifestyle, one that accepts less hierarchical parent-child relations. If these same adolescents are angry and resentful from not having their emotional needs fully met during a period of separation from their parents, difficulties in achieving respect will be compounded. The traditional view that parental authority represents a form of parental love as well as a means of maintaining the family hierarchy is not likely to be accepted easily by these adolescents.

The case of a sixteen-year-old Latin female illustrates this situation. Her parents immigrated to the United States when she was seven or eight. She stayed in the care of her grandparents in Mexico. Once her parents had earned enough money to have a place of their own in which to live, she was reunited with them, eight years later. She was unwilling to comply with her parents' rules with respect to such things as a nightly curfew or with whom she could socialize. Tensions between them became so great that the daughter refused to live at home, preferring instead to stay with a nearby aunt. The parents did not understand how she could act this way, given the sacrifices they had endured to provide for her. They made frequent declarations to her in this regard but to no avail. Parents' visits to the aunt's home were riddled with a number of intense emotional outbursts. A report of abuse was filed with Child Protective Services, most likely called in by neighbors who heard the verbal fighting. The parents felt confused and humiliated by this government intrusion. Required family therapy was instituted.

Inclan (in press) suggests conceptualizing the problem of adolescent independence and transition to adulthood on a macro-level. This involves sharing with the family the cultural differences in norms and values of their Latino heritage as well as its clash with "American" values of independence and autonomy. The second step is to reframe the conflict between parents and their children as a problem that has its inception in the process of immigration.

Brought up in a traditional family, but functioning outside in a complex, less restrictive environment is difficult for an adolescent to negotiate. Hormones, lack of full executive functioning and culture clash conspire to overwhelm even the closest and most functional of families. Promoting *familismo* and *respeto* has been shown to improve adolescents' psychological functioning and reduce depression (Lorenzo-Blanco, Unger, Baezconde-Garbanati, Ritt-Olson and Soto, 2012). This, in conjunction with helping parents recognize the difficult but critical bridging role that their adolescent must negotiate, may be helpful in promoting a more positive parent-child interaction (Quinones-Mayo and Dempsey, 2005).

Differential Rates of Acculturation and Children as Language Brokers

There are a number of obstacles in maintenance of parental authority and obedience from children in Latin American immigrant families. The issue of language acquisition is a critical one; the reality is that immigrant children generally learn English quickly while their parents often lag behind, particularly in lower socioeconomic groups, where there was no exposure to English in school. While most first generation immigrant children understand both languages, it is common for them to prefer to speak in English and even refuse to speak in Spanish. This language differential subtly undermines the ability of parents to use verbal directives effectively. For example, a mother brought her four-year-old boy to treatment because teachers at the pre-school encouraged her to seek medicine for her son's severe symptoms of ADHD. While there were many issues related to the mother's ineffectual parenting, what was also very noticeable was the language barrier between her and her son. The mother spoke little English and spoke to her child in Spanish. The child, who spent much of his time watching cartoons on TV, appeared to speak only in English. The mother was basically unable to discipline her child due to this language barrier; it had severely debilitated her power to wield parental authority.

When Latino parents bring a child into treatment, as was the case with this mother, there is often the belief that the *doctor* will fix the child and ensuing frustration occurs if the therapist attempts to focus on the *parents'* actions. Thus, joining the parent in their frustrations of child-rearing and the travails of immigration is an important first set step. The use of psychoeducation and bolstering of parental skills that are consistent with their traditional values will help support their effectiveness as parents. Promoting a joint fluency, whether Spanish or English, will also improve parent-child relationships (Schoefield, Beaumont, Jochem, and Widaman, 2012).

Parental authority is often compromised by the fact that children acculturate so much quicker than their parents. This occurs through the children's ongoing emersion in school and peer activities while parents often remain insulated in the barrio. Thus, the child develops some degree of competence, negotiating layers of context and transitions from home to school (Fuller and Coll, 2010). This sense of agency may come in conflict with the parent's goal of achieving obedience and conformity to the larger family system and attendant acceptable pursuits and activities.

The practice of educating children in social mores and values through the use of *refranes* and *dichos* is another child-rearing practice that can get disrupted as the family attempts to assimilate and acculturate following immigration. Language differences between the older caregiving generation and the children interfere with the transmission of these educational proverbs. Children who only speak English may have difficulty understanding their meaning and will be unable to pass these pearls of wisdom on to their own offspring.

Another all too common obstacle to obtaining obedience occurs in relation to the use of physical punishment. Children become savvy to the rules for reporting physical abuse of children in the United States. Older children often threaten their parents with reporting them to the police if they use physical punishment as discipline. The parents, who lag behind in English usage and thus in their ability to inform themselves adequately of the specifics regarding physical abuse, are left wondering how to obtain obedience without using corporal punishment and are likely to experience feelings of impotence. Parents in this situation may vacillate between a permissive style of parenting in which children are given little structure and boundaries, and an authoritarian one when parents become extremely frustrated with their children's lack of compliance. They may strike out physically in an excessive manner when frustrated. Unfortunately, the latter approach may result in a report of abuse being filed when school personnel note marks or bruises, so the very outcome the parents were attempting to avoid in the first place results.

Staying and Going

One big difference between Puerto Rican immigrants and those of other Latino groups is that the former can come to and leave the United States with no VISA issues. With all other Latino groups, obtaining a legitimate VISA is paramount to an uninterrupted stay in the country. Thus, many families in this latter group have both documented and undocumented immigrant members. Despite many decades of life in the US, many families fear that children, parents and their extended families could be separated and some deported without warning. In 2005, it was estimated that 30 percent of the foreign-born population was undocumented (Passel, 2006). Four in ten second-generation immigrant children have at least one undocumented immigrant parent (Fry and Passel, 2009). The level of legal vulnerability to deportation has a tremendous effect on the family environment and child mental health (Brabeck and Xu, 2010). Unfortunately, this group tends not to seek medical or other mental health care for fear of being discovered. Many of them are not aware that despite their undocumented existence, their children (very often American citizens by birth) are entitled to health care.

For Puerto Rican families, the narrative is often different, with parts of families coming to the mainland for periods of time, but periodically returning to Puerto Rico, leaving some or all children with a "relative" in the United States. These separations, which are usually economically motivated, hamper consistent child-rearing and can leave children vulnerable to being physically, sexually, or emotionally abused by the informally designated caregivers. One example, not atypical of those we see, was a mother who was pushed into treatment by child welfare. She had left her three grade-school-aged children for a year with a stepfather who sexually abused the oldest daughter as she approached twelve. The patient had returned to Puerto Rico because her mother had become ill. She was well-intentioned in that she wished for her children to continue their school year. Although she had planned to bring them back to Puerto Rico at the end of the school year, without work, she decided that she did not have the financial base to return them to the US for the next school year.

Initially, it appeared that she struggled with whether her own mother or her children should have priority and was unable to find a guilt-free solution. It was later uncovered in therapy that her own unresolved anxieties about being physically apart from her mother (they had always lived together) were a motivating factor in her decision to leave her children. Although the therapy focused primarily on child development and its interface with social expectation in the United States, the mother did come to recognize that her own longings for physical proximity to her mother overpowered a rational review of purchasing three round trip tickets for her children after she left her job in the United States.

CONCLUDING COMMENTS

In this chapter, we outlined some of the important traditional Latino family values and a few of the child-rearing practices that are culturally tethered to produce a healthy and functioning next generation. The stresses of the immigration process, the concomitant and necessary separations in this close extended family unit, and the clash in cultural values and practices create the possibility of a toxic crucible for effective child-rearing in their new home. Therapists' sensitivities to these elements may support parents' dream of providing both roots and wings for their children.

NOTES

1. Phinney and Devich-Navarro (1997) provide a useful framework for acculturation which can be applied to Latinos. *Assimilated* Latinos have incorporated most of the "American" values. *Separated* Latinos are those who have rejected majority culture, often having little contact with mainstream American values, including not learning English. *Acculturated* Latinos balance traditional and majority culture and often enjoy the best mental health of all groups. *Marginalized* Latinos are those that struggle to identify with either their homeland or mainstream America.
2. Harkness and Super's (in press) parental ethno-theories study include parents from Spain, US, Australia, Italy, Sweden, and Netherlands.
3. *Refranes* were obtained from Refranero Castellano (n.d.)
4. Religion has been and remains often an important aspect of Latino culture (Garzon and Tan, 1992). The majority of Latinos are Roman Catholic (Pew Hispanic Center, 2007).
5. Latino women who embrace more traditionally oriented gender roles report more satisfaction in the marital relationship compared to those who are more egalitarian oriented (Falconier, 2013).

6. How this conflict plays out with children is complicated. There is some evidence that contrary to American egalitarian philosophy, promoting traditional gender roles in Latino girls may actually protect against depression (Lorenzo-Blanco et al, 2012).

7. Statistics from the census bureau (US Census Bureau, 2009) suggest that of all ethnic groups residing in the United States, Latinos are more likely than others to be living in a family setting.

THREE

Latino Ethnic Identity

Antonio Bullón and César A. Alfonso

The term Latino has displaced what we used to refer to as Hispanic, as we have come to realize that language affinity is not synonymous with cultural affinity. Latino seems to be a more encompassing term that broadens boundaries and context to consider other aspects of cultural affinity. These additional cultural elements include but are not limited to common heritage, religion, mythology, folklore, socioeconomic factors, artistic traditions, education, and political history. Latinos are the largest ethnic minority in the United States, with over 50 million or approximately 16 percent of the total USA population. The term "minority" is becoming paradoxical, since in four states in the United States, minorities outnumber majorities—Hawaii, New Mexico, California, Texas; nine other states have a sixty/forty percent majority to minority ratio: Maryland, Georgia, Nevada, Florida, Arizona, New Jersey, New York Louisiana, and Mississippi (Humes, 2011). The Pew Research Center projections estimate that in 2050, Latinos will constitute 29 percent of the US population (Passel, 2008).

The cultural complexity of Latin America is extraordinary, encompassing twenty countries, twelve thousand years of history, extensive ethnic inter-mixing and religious syncretism. Spanish and Portuguese are predominant languages in Latin America—close to half a billion people in America are Spanish speaking and a quarter of a billion Portuguese speaking. French Creole is spoken in Haiti by close to ten million people.

Quechua and Qichua have close to six million speakers, mostly in Peru, but also in all of its neighboring countries. One and a half million people in Mesoamerican regions speak Nahuatl. Guaraní is the official language of Paraguay. Aymara has 2.2 million speakers, mostly in Bolivia, some in Peru and other regions of the Andes. Miskito is spoken in Nicaragua, Honduras and El Salvador by close to 200,000 people. Sumu, related to Miskito, is spoken further south in Costa Rica, Panama and Colombia. The above cross-sectional view of the multiplicity of languages in the American Continent is part of the cultural complexity of Latin America.

In this chapter, we begin to address the resonance and juxtaposition of Latino ethnic identities within an overarching Latino culture, in turn finding its place within a broader American identity. First, however, in order to understand the construct of Latino ethnicity, it is helpful to examine contributions from anthropology and related social sciences to the study of ethnogenesis in addition to psychodynamic perspectives.

THE STUDY OF ETHNIC IDENTITY: CONTRIBUTIONS OF THE SOCIAL SCIENCES

Ethnicity can be defined in several ways. Etymologically, *ethnos*, from the Greek, can non-specifically signify a societal group, class, and culture, even a nation. In the eighteenth and nineteenth centuries, in the English language, ethnicity as a construct acquired connotations of the exotic, foreign, alien, distant, undiscovered, colorful and yet to be explored, referring to qualities of individuals belonging to immigrant or minority groups. In the social sciences, ethnicity is deconstructed into multiple elements, including kinship, language, customs, folklore, religion, rituals, mythology, artistic traditions, shared sociopolitical history, economic parameters, and citizenship. Cultural anthropology (Ember, 2006), ethnography (Brewer, 2000) and ethnology (Ortner, 2006) are social sciences fields of study of ethnicity and of the formation of ethnic identity.

Ethnography encompasses the study of groups that share a common heritage, while ethnology is the comparative study of groups of one culture within a nation or a conglomerate of other cultures. Ethnology and cultural anthropology share commonalities as fields of study and are often referred to interchangeably. While emphasis in anthropology is often placed in the other and on cultural differences, a more recent research focus highlights cross-cultural commonalities. The French School of Ethnologists, from the 1960s, spearheaded by Claude Levi-Strauss (1958, 1969), proposed that there were universal invariants across cultures and continents, a concept once controversial but now widely accepted as the world moves toward globalization, when similarities among groups overshadow differences.

Ethnogenesis refers to a process resulting in formation of an ethnic identity. Social changes, nationalism, acculturation, assimilation, and group or nation building sociopolitical forces contribute to the evolution of ethnic identity. Ethnogenesis can result from both subtle transgenerational determinants and sudden transformative experiences. An example of subtle transgenerational ethnogenesis would be the evolution of the Cult of the Virgin Mary in Latin America as a unifying ethnic force across geographical boundaries (Cunneen, 1996, Alfonso and Schwartz, 1999). Transformative ethnic-identity-building experiences of a more acute nature include changes in the American and Latino-American cultural landscape occurring, for example, as a result of the exodus of Puerto Ricans to El Barrio in East Harlem in the 1950s and Dominicans to Washington Heights in Upper Manhattan in the 1990s.

While social sciences research explores and addresses group dynamics and behavior, the biopsychosocial medical paradigm (Engel, 1977) and psychodynamic theory and practice (Cabaniss, 2011) can help clinicians understand the multifaceted individual determinants of identity formation. Clinical challenges in psychotherapy with Latino patients can be bridged when approached psychodynamically, resulting in diagnostic accuracy and effective treatment.

ETHNIC IDENTITY: PSYCHODYNAMIC PERSPECTIVES

The definition of ethnic identity eludes easy categorization. One aspect that we would like to stress in this chapter is the importance of individuals developing a sense of integration of the self. Affective experiences need explanation and expression. Culture provides expression through multiple avenues: the mirroring of emotions by the immediate family and surrounding community through gestures and body language, verbal manifestations expressed through culturally-sanctioned lexicon and prosody for each particular emotion, which in turn reflect the values of those emotions in the particular historical moment that the group of individuals live in. Other modes of expression such as art, music, food and smells also convey deep meanings and connections that are shared by individuals of the same group. Common kinship fears, wishes, and frustrations are communicated with cultural consonance. Consider Joan Manuel Serrat's (1981) lyricism in a popular Iberian musical verse from the song "*Esos locos bajitos*": "Our frustrations and wishes are communicated through the warm mother's milk and in each song." Wishes, frustrations and unfulfilled hopes are expressed through culture in multifaceted ways.

Ethnic cohesion is more consistent in small groups; if a particular group occupies a small geographical area, it is more difficult to maintain in a hyper-diverse community, such as in contemporary American society. As Latinos acculturate and assimilate, the group identity of both the host and the immigrant cultures evolve simultaneously. We propose that group dynamics, just as individual dynamics, exist in a continuum as amalgamated processes that are fluid and ever changing. Regardless of the culture in which an individual grows and develops, the culture of origin is not the sole determinant of the identity matrix. Other factors provide additional elements for identity formation, such as an individual's temperament, religious beliefs, and exposure to other ethnocultural groups through education, frequent international trips or migration. In addition, intense or frequent personal trauma (physical, emotional, sexual) and social conflict (war, poverty, discrimination) may affect attitudes toward other groups or the group of origin, in turn affecting one's potential to change the environment.

Jean-Paul Sartre's (1905–1980) aphorism, "The way others see you defines who you are," has particular relevance in the formation of ethnocultural categories in society. Dominant groups have the tendency to lump minority groups together according to some external characteristics (such as skin color, physical features, language, accent, dress, etc.) which, from the mainstream observer's perspective are considered strong and indisputable definers of distinct categories of individuals (Tajfel, 1981), when in fact, to the individuals being labeled, such commonalities may not be of great relevance. Stereotypes or overgeneralizations often become engrained in society, and immigrants who belong to marginalized or minority groups may identify with the stereotypes with counterphobic defense, and internalize parts of the stereotypes as a way to seek the solace and comfort of belonging and maintaining some frame of reference as a substrate for the formation of a new identity. Alternatively, some individuals from minority groups may reluctantly accept these labels in order to vaguely affirm their position in the demographic map of society. Others plainly reject external designations because of the concern that in accepting or using them there would be a threat of losing differentiation and identity (Akhtar, 1999).

Erik Erikson's concept of contextual development stresses the importance of the social milieu in a person's life trajectory, and the importance of adaptation as one is faced with changes in society. Acculturation and assimilation are thus understood as efforts in adaptation. Just as individuals have the right to autonomy and self-determination, acculturation and assimilation are choices that individuals and or groups will make, at different points in time, depending on the alignment of a multiplicity of variables. There is no right or wrong when it comes to acculturation and assimilation and as clinicians, our position should be neutral and nondirective. The exposure to a new environment can either be a threat to the integrity of the self or provide new opportunities for growth, or both (Akhtar, 1999).

The sense of self and ethnic identity of individuals and the characteristics of the community that harbors them are never static (Guarnaccia, 1996). Ethnogenesis is a fluid process that results from interaction, adaptation, evolution, and mutual change (Kirmayer, 2012; Modood, 2007; Burke, 2009). Consider how in New York City, the Puerto Rican El Barrio is no longer Puerto Rican; now renamed East Harlem, El Barrio is predominantly gentrified and intermixed with new groups of immigrants from Mexico and Central America. Puerto Ricans assimilated over the second half of the twentieth century and dispersed throughout major USA cities. Although they constitute the second largest Latino ethnic group in the United States, they are no longer bound by geographical boundaries in segregated communities.

Intergenerational conflicts surge as families relocate, regardless of the lesser or greater extent of the geographical transposition. These interpersonal conflicts permeate the treatment discourse of psychodynamic psychotherapy with Latino patients. The realities of each treatment dyad, however, often will not reflect cultural differences. Globalization may have changed the way we practice, bringing us back to emphasizing the fundamental processes common to all psychotherapies, enhancing supportive interventions with psychodynamic exploration, with cultural similarities often outweighing differences in the therapeutic dyad.

It is not easy then to define the identity of any ethnic group unless the group has been isolated geographically and historically from other groups in the world. We find that assumptions about ethnic identity in diverse and mixed societies can, at times, be useful but at others detrimental, because of reductionism. The official demographic categories developed by the US Census Bureau have historical and political antecedents and do not necessarily reflect the way individuals define themselves. The designation of the American demographic pentad world (Asian, White, Black, Native American and Pacific Islander, and Hispanic) is not based on uniform variables but in a conflation of dimensions that are as complex as they are different, such as language, race, geographical origin, and ethnicity (Hollinger, 1995). For the demographer and the researcher in any professional arena, the reification of artificial social constructs may be essential for the process of quantification and the study of certain variables that need to be analyzed in a static population. For the social advocate, on the other hand, it is crucial to define a population at risk. In the Civil Rights era, it was very helpful to categorize certain populations that were either vulnerable or lacked the same access to services in society. Regardless of its usefulness to decrease inequalities, this categorization now is anachronistically viewed as too simplistic. Good and colleagues (2011)[1] state:

> "The politically important cultural categories of race and ethnicity have been fundamental to promoting civil rights, to assessing inequalities and disparities in health, education, housing, and civil rights protection, and to identifying underrepresented minorities and yet, they now seem, at least in popular culture, to be social labels and analytic categories of another era with diminished political potency and meaning." (3)

As immigration adds layers of cultural complexity highlighting intergenerational differences even within a kin group, our social and ethnic labels fail to capture the dynamic and evolving cultural identities. Hyperdiversity—a term used by Hannah (Good et al., 2011)—refers to the nation's dynamic population transition to a complex mosaic-like mix of national origin, ethnicity, race, and immigration status. The Latino ethnic group is part of the hyperdiversity of American society and is also by itself a hyperdiverse group.

HISPANIC AND LATINO ETHNIC IDENTITY

The terms "Hispanic" or "Latino" carry the same difficulties of labeling as that of other groups. "Hispanic" was a term created to try to categorize the group of individuals living in the United States of America who had Spanish as the predominant language in their lives, or who could trace their ancestry to individuals who had Spanish as their mother tongue. The term "Hispanic" eventually felt offensive and limiting to some because it used Spanish as a language and Spain as the ultimate ancestral land. Focusing on Spain as the mainstay of identity dismissed other diverse cultural, historical, geographical and linguistic realities.

"Latino" gradually became the preferred label, because it was felt to be more inclusive of individuals that came from or could trace their ancestry to Latin America. In most of the world, America is a word that designates mainly the continent that comprises North, Central and South America (what in the United States is usually called the Americas) and not only to the United States of America. Latin America is a term that was first used at the end of the eighteenth century to designate the part of America that was occupied by Latin European countries (Mediterranean countries that were mainly Roman-Catholic and where romance languages were spoken, such as Portugal, Spain, France and Italy), which were differentiated from the Anglo-Saxon, Germanic and Teutonic countries of Northern Europe (England, Netherlands, Germany) where the population was mainly Protestant. Therefore, regions where languages other than Spanish are spoken such as Brazil (Portuguese), Haiti (French Creole), or many parts of South and Central America and Mexico where native ancestral languages are spoken are also considered part of Latin America.

But even now controversy surrounds the question—is the term "Latino" accurate, pertinent and useful? Many immigrants from Latin America are surprised to learn, when arriving in the United States, that they belong to a well-delineated group called Latinos. As fish do not know they are wet until out of the water, Latinos many times do not realize what is to be a Latino until the parameters of the host culture are imposed. Although the term "Latino" is not unknown in Latin America, it is almost always accompanied by the word American. In this sense, the term "Latino" is more inclusive linguistically than "Hispanic." However, the word "Latino" still stresses the European component instead of the mixed ancestry that would be implied in the more inclusive term Latin American.

The Pew Hispanic Center Survey, "When Labels Don't Fit: Hispanics and their Views of Identity" (published on 4/4/12), explores 1,220 Latinos' attitudes about their identity, language usage patterns, core values, and views about the United States and their families' country of origin. The survey concluded that the majority of respondents prefer to be identified according to their national origin (such as Cuban, Puerto Rican, Mexican, Dominican, etc.) rather than using a Latino pan-identity. The majority of those surveyed considered language as the main (and sometimes sole) shared connection. This survey crystallizes the experience of many Latinos, especially recent immigrants, who resist an immediate homogenization and blurring of national details and differences. The survey, however, fails to differentiate attitudes of second and third generation Latinos, individuals of mixed ancestry, and those who speak very little or do not speak Spanish, from that of recent immigrants. Clinical practice reflects other aspects of ethnic affiliation that are not evident in the Pew survey.

We have observed that Latinos in treatment, who are recent immigrants or belong to marginalized socioeconomic sectors, develop some sense of connection and identity with other Latinos as a reaction to feelings of alienation and otherness from mainstream USA society. When faced with distressing affects, Latinos from different backgrounds may realize that, in fact, there is some common ground, besides language, with people from other regions of Latin America. The complexities and conflicts of USA society may elicit commonalities that exist among Latinos that were previously below conscious awareness. Malleability in identity formation has been described among other marginalized populations around the globe (Tajfel, 1986).

CULTURAL COMPETENCE AND THE CARE OF LATINOS

In response to increased diversity, American society has made some efforts to advance understanding of its different groups. In response to either a societal mandate to improve delivery of care to minorities or to requirements from credentialing agencies, institutions have implemented cultural competency courses in the training curriculum and the continuing education of mental health and medical professionals (Qureshi, 2008). These courses have commonly included a list of traditional values shared by many Latinos in comparison with the wider American culture. Some of these cultural values and interpersonal attitudes include:

- *Familismo*: attachment to family as the main source of support and fulfillment.
- *Marianismo*: the sense of greater moral authority for women who also had to sacrifice themselves in the name of the family, sexual passivity and subordination after marriage, resignation in the face of adversity, abuse and neglect.
- *Machismo*: the sense of ultimate responsibility for the family in the hands of men, presenting men as condescending, histrionically fierce, and exemplary.
- *Respeto*: a sense of respectful attitude and compliance to people in authority, among them clinicians.
- *Simpatía*: outwardly expressed warmth in interactions with friends and respected people, including clinicians.
- *Personalismo*: the development of a relationship with an individual clinician and not with the institution for which the clinician works.
- *Fatalism*: a sense that one does not have control over one's fate, of fate being in the hands of God, with few things one can do to prevent suffering or improve life.
- *Somatization*: amplification of bodily sensations and greater expression of physical symptoms as manifestations of psychological distress.
- Greater physical expression of emotion (warmth, grief) in comparison to other groups in American society.
- Different perception of, and level of comfort with, interpersonal space and touch.

Although these concepts may be helpful to inform a clinician of Latino value systems as a whole, they also can be used blindly as simplistic reductionisms, and in some way may stump the exploration of the real life and experience of the individual patient. Obsessive cultural competence discourse may lead to overgeneralizations and stereotyping.

Some of the above-mentioned cultural characteristics of Latinos might misguide clinicians to have inaccurate impressions of the way Latinos experience and interpret emotions. For example, the prevalence of somatization in Latinos may relate to socioeconomic status, language proficiency, educational level, immigration status, and level of acculturation and assimilation, rather than to other ethnographic variables, and may not differ from that of other ethnic groups.

What the authors find most helpful is taking the stance of having a modicum of cultural curiosity, to approach cultural explorations with serenity, neutrality, and not so enthusiastically, as enthusiasm can deflect from affect-laden situations in therapy that may not be transcultural in origin. Willen, Bullon, and associates (2010) emphasize "cultural humility" (Tervalon, 1998) as a helpful notion that may prevent clinicians from countertransferential overinvestment. Psychotherapists should be inquisitive about cultural differences—but it is important to modulate enthusiasm, since too much cultural enthusiasm may dilute patients' negative affects and distress.

Kirmayer's (2012) thorough review on the concept of cultural competence recognizes the complex task of addressing and educating clinicians about culture and ethnicity. Kirmayer explains that in vulnerable populations, it is important to become acquainted with the cultural characteristics of the patients, and to be blind to the cultural dimension (language, health and treatment beliefs, interpersonal costumes and values) can produce great damage. However, cultural sensitivity is not enough, and probably may not the most crucial factor with marginalized populations. In these circumstances, the clinician should not only be a skilled practitioner of cultural humility, but also an active promoter of cultural safety—a purposeful reflection of the implications of the actions of the clinician and the medical establishment (Papps, 1996) as powerful agents of the dominant culture, which can unintentionally produce greater alienation of these patients and contribute to healthcare disparities. It follows that clinicians should expect that patients' cultural and ethnic values would present in the context of the nature of structural sources of inequality of a particular locality or country. Lastly, we may add that although it is impractical and detrimental to consider Latinos as a monolithic group, it is still important to review the cultural characteristics and socioeconomic contexts that put certain subpopulations at risk for serious misunderstanding, alienation and unequal treatment from the medical system and society as a whole (Institute of Medicine, 2003).

SOCIAL DETERMINANTS OF ETHNIC IDENTITY

Language

Individuals who are monolingual in Spanish, Portuguese, French-Creole or a Native American language are at greater risk of marginalization in the United States. Language does provide an important level of connection with other people and expression of one own needs. The ability to convey very personal aspects of the inner world is probably the main basis for the formation of positive transferences between Latino patients (regardless of their English fluency) and clinicians. This positive sense of connection of speaking the same language is very important in the development of a solid therapeutic alliance.

The connection that language provides is of greater relevance in poor, monolingual Latino patients, where it becomes a lifeline for identifying important physical and psychological needs and accessing basic social, medical and psychiatric services. The language connection is so important to these patients that they incorporate linguistic bridges—interpreters, bilingual secretaries and mental health support staff—seamlessly and unquestionably into their treatment team. It is not uncommon for patients to call directly these staff members in order to convey a particular problem to the clinician. The relatively easier interaction of vulnerable patients with bilingual ancillary staff reflects that for some of these patients linguistic access is coupled with social and even clinical access.

Social Class and Educational Level

Marginalized Latino patients sometimes may not feel comfortable sharing information with their clinicians because of issues related to power differential, fear of rejection, discrimination, and retaliation. There are other factors that compete with lack of English proficiency as important determinants of social exclusion, such as educational level, income, social power and race. Many Latinos in the United States have already experienced being oppressed and relegated in their countries of origin because of being poor, uneducated and/or having darker skin than the dominant group. Alternatively they may for generations have been relegated to inner-city or rural environments in the United States.

Important aspects of self-perception and self-esteem are shaped by the way individuals are perceived or treated in a society, and by the sense of visibility and power that they may exert in it. Even when faced with caring and warm clinicians (who may be Latinos or non-Latinos), many vulnerable Latinos assume contradictory attitudes toward them. Some patients may show submission while others present suspiciousness. Clinicians may become puzzled by the lack of initiative and excessive courtesy that patients may show, despite efforts to include them in collaborative decision-making. In fact, this could be a reflection of the *simpatía* and *respeto,* widely described as Latino cultural values. These attitudes, however, may also have roots in an introjection of social hierarchies that is enacted in the clinical context (Bullon, 2000), where patients are concerned with again becoming victims of retaliation or relegation by the people in power (white, professionals, educated) in the United States if they were to show signs of rebelliousness or social inconformity.

At times, clinicians encounter situations where underserved or poorly educated Latino patients have great difficulty in expressing questions, concerns or dissatisfaction with their diagnosis or treatment, despite efforts to be respectful and inclusive. These patients frequently verbalize full agreement with treatment and express warmth and gratitude towards clinicians. These same patients sometimes are able to convey their concerns and dissatisfaction to the ancillary bilingual personnel of the clinic or the psychiatric inpatient unit, telling them that they do not want to disappoint or anger clinicians. Because of perceived differences in social status, hierarchy and power differential, patients may feel freer to convey some uncomfortable realities to staff members who they perceive as less dangerous in the event of a disagreement.

Race

In many countries, race is closely related with social class and power. This situation occurs particularly in regions where a large number of individuals from a predominant native race (with darker skin) and who may still use a native language, remain and survived despite prolonged domination by European nations. Even after the political independence of these countries from Europe, the descendants of white Europeans maintained most the political and economic power. In the past few decades, many of these countries have gone through equalizing changes and the representation of these relegated groups has increased. Nevertheless, the effects of discrimination by class and race are still relevant (Bruce, 2007). There are some countries where there is a relatively homogeneous racial make up (Caucasian or Mediterranean European) such as Argentina, in which the dynamics between race and social class may play a secondary role, whereas in other countries the dynamics are much more charged and complicated, such as in Mestizo countries that traditionally had white-European groups in political and economic power (Peru or Bolivia, for example).

The dynamics of race are very different in Latin America and the United States. Depending on the color of skin and physical characteristics, some Latinos may be subsumed as part of more familiar racial categories, such as African American, white, Asian, or Hispanic. In some cases, groups that have been relegated by implicit (but heavy) discrimination in their countries of origin (Mestizo Indian-white, Peruvian Cholo) may feel a relative sense of liberation to be in a country such as the United States where the government explicitly supports equality and where overt expressions of racism and discrimination in the work place, school or media may be penalized. Occasionally, individuals from subgroups that have been heavily marginalized or discriminated against in their country (for example, people from poor rural regions who are mistreated and dismissed by people from the cities) may not feel very comfortable socializing with their co-nationals in the United States, because of fear of being identified as members of those relegated groups and being discriminated against again. Some of these individuals even cover up their accent so their compatriots cannot recognize them in gatherings. The sensitive clinician must be aware of the ramifications that past experiences of oppression might have in the current therapeutic dyad.

Patient/clinician matching in terms of nationality (or even ethnicity) may or may not contribute to the initial development of trust. Sometimes oppressed patients would prefer a white-American non-judgmental clinician, than a clinician who shares his or her background, even at the expense of sacrificing the language connection. Certainly, there is no ideal match, and regardless of the characteristics of the therapeutic dyad (intraethnic or interethnic), the clinician should always include in the clinical exploration and assessment the effect of culture, race, and socioeconomic power differential in the dyad.

Religion

Especially in deeply racially and socioeconomically divided countries (Peru, Cuba, Mexico), Catholic religious iconography (through reiterated versions of the perception of Jesus, the Saints and the Virgin Mary) plays an important role in the unification of the identity of those countries. Examples include *El Señor de los Milagros*, *San Martín de Porres*, and *Santa Rosa de Lima* in Peru, *La Virgen de la Caridad del Cobre* in Cuba, and *La Virgen de Guadalupe* in Mexico. In all these depictions of the religious icons, there are elements of race and socioeconomic status that have the tendency to unify otherwise irreconcilable differences. A black slave in Lima allegedly painted *el Cristo Moreno*—the Black Christ. Martín de Porres, the kind mulatto with a broom, fed the same plate to dogs, cats, and mice. *La Virgen de la Caridad del Cobre* appears to a Spaniard, a Caribbean and an African, at the time when their boat is about to capsize in the turbulent waters of a stormy Caribbean sea. *La Virgen de la Guadalupe* appeared to a native Mexican, Juan Diego, who was able to overcome opposition and disbelief in the Spanish church hierarchy. All these icons unify otherwise fragmented nations, and after migration, continue to be important aspects of social belonging and identification, sometimes independently from the individual's level of involvement in other formal religious practices. It is important to acknowledge that not all Latinos are Catholic. A substantial number are Protestant, Evangelical, Pentecostal or Jewish. For many, religious communities and rituals provide crucial sources of connection and identity.

Plurality

It is much easier to identify and express a Latino identity if the surrounding group is populous, or if the group is given a special status in a community (such is the case of recognizing the Latino Mental Health team with importance within the medical community). Pride results from a combination of solidarity (in contrast to invisibility) with celebratory affirmation.

Sexual Orientation

Because of fear of rejection or punishment, it is not common for Latinos to freely acknowledge their sexual orientation if other than heterosexual. When hosted by a society that in general is more accepting of permutations of sexual orientation, openness ensues. When prominent figures in the media or professionals publicly acknowledge being gay, bisexual or transgendered, idealization may serve a reparative purpose giving comfort to those who secretly yearn for acceptance and love.

THE CLINICAL SETTING WITH LATINO PATIENTS AS A UNIFYING STAGE

Through memory, a person can access a historical continuity of bodily and psychological experiences, of interactions with others and of explanations and significance of events that help to provide a sense of permanence of self through time and space. Individuals make such explorations unconsciously and in constant interaction with the environment. Immigration, biculturality and multiculturality, changes in social status, loss, illness and suffering can be challenges to this continuity. The exposure to a new culture, a new social status or connections, a new relationship with the body or the mind, can produce either a deep fragmentation of the self or provide new opportunities for growth (Akhtar, 1999).

Illness and suffering are also expressed and explained through co-constructed narratives, and particular attention is made to certain internal sensations that are related to distressing emotions. Somatization is a non-specific cultural idiom of distress. Amplification of bodily sensations as a defense is ubiquitous, across cultures, and serves as a way to neutralize negative affects when faced with overwhelming ego demands. Valence is assigned to particular body manifestations and states of mind, and expression of distress can oscillate between the verbal and nonverbal.

Positive transferences can provide an opportunity to build a therapeutic alliance but could give a false sense of attunement upon meeting prospective patients. Consider the following story.

Clinical Vignette 1

A 45-year-old Puerto Rican woman is referred by her primary care physician to see one of the authors for an evaluation of anxiety. Born in Puerto Rico, the patient migrated to the United States when she was twenty years old. In the United States, she completed university-level courses and is currently employed in healthcare. She considers herself bilingual and speaks excellent English with a noticeable Spanish accent. The clinician, an immigrant from a different Latin American country, who lived in yet another Latin American country before relocating

> to the United States, speaks with a strong accent and greets the patient in the waiting room asking if there is a preference to speak in Spanish or English. The patient responds: "It's the same for me, whatever you prefer."
>
> In the office, the patient starts to speak in Spanish and exclaims with a sigh of relief: "I'm glad you are Latino. You know it is not the same with American doctors. I think you'll understand better what I am going through. Do you know what I mean, doctor?" The clinician silently reflects—"Well I don't *exactly* know what she means, because I really do not know her life circumstances, but I *kind of* get what she may mean when at least she feels that I may be in a better position to see her perspective."

What are the cultural determinants that trigger an automatic positive transference when there is linguistic or other ethnic affinity? In this case, patient and clinician are from different countries and diametrically different backgrounds. They certainly share a common language, but with different accents, pronunciation, enunciation and possibly do not use certain words the same way. What are then the characteristics that unite them?

Clinicians encounter individuals with illness and suffering, and are in a unique position to observe with admiration the poignant ways they deal with threats to the integrity of the self. One of the ways patients deal with this threat is by returning to familiar and old versions of the self. Notions of illness and health or actions that promote the return to a state of wellbeing that were initially prescribed in the household or in the community are recalled and if possible, accessed. Maternal language, verbal expressions, and non-verbal language such as gestures and body language that are considered reassuring, soothing or empathic by the individual's native culture are sought after. If these activities are available to the individual, they can provide a deep sense of connection and relief.

It is then not unusual for a Latino patient to express relief when he or she learns that the clinician being referred to speaks Spanish or is Latino, even though the patient may be fluent in English. When this happens, there is an immediate positive parental transference with the fantasy that one will be nurtured and is "a little bit closer to home." Even though it is true that emotions could be expressed with more comfort in the language in which one grew up and memories experienced, and the ability to express in the maternal tongue could be very important in the healing process, the Latino clinician should be very cautious in accepting the immediate transference of understanding better the Latino patient as a truism. There may be in fact a greater danger for not seeing the blind spots (Comas-Diaz and Jacobsen, 1991) that clinicians that belong to other cultural groups would question more easily. The Latino patient–Latino clinician is a dyad of endless complexities, which is a situation that itself reflects the multiple variations of the Latino ethnic identity.

We have had some of the most moving clinical experiences that illustrate the complexity of ethnic identity and social struggles of vulnerable Latinos when participating as leaders of psychotherapy groups. In group therapy, we have witnessed patients' efforts to develop attachments, affiliations, and a common identity by taking advantage of every possible connection within grasp. Both authors have experience leading psychotherapy groups composed predominantly of Latina women living in poverty, many who are single mothers and face medical problems, probably one of the most disempowered subpopulations of Latinos and of American society as a whole. Group process is initially characterized by general guardedness. As group members begin to share their experiences, fears, wishes and greatest concerns, they become aware of certain key shared values around family, children, relationships, religion and preservation of health. Gradually, by describing the different words and phrases that are used to communicate distress, and by getting affirmation from the group that they have been effective in conveying thoughts and emotions, the patients become more aware of their own worldviews and therefore of their identity. They educate each other with "what they mean with such and such word or phrase." For example: "Oh—by *pena* you Colombians (or Cubans) mean embarrassment, while we Puerto Ricans mean sadness" or "it is funny that for you in Mexico, *coraje* means anger while for us Dominicans it means bravery." The experience of being listened to in a non-judgmental way by the other members and the clinician allows for the review of their beliefs and their fears of medical and psychiatric treatment.

One observes in these groups a plethora of shared experiences that transcend geographical boundaries, such as *marianismo* manifested by great concern with being good mothers and providing for their children, struggles in dealing with the problems of parenting, ambivalence of feelings toward family including warmth but also of frustration and anger toward those in jail, away pursuing university studies, or in combat.

Patients' contempt for men in general for the way they treat woman coexists with desires to find a caring partner. The frustration of not having been able to learn English compounds anger for being mistreated for being unable to speak English. These groups are characterized by expressions of physical warmth that surface naturally as members begin to connect and form reparative attachments. Common expressions of empathy include words such as *hija* (sister), or *mi amor* (literally, "my love"; and also, "dear," or "darling") when giving advice. Blessings are also frequent and even on occasion prayers spontaneously start, especially if a group member or loved one is gravely ill. There are expressions of nostalgia for the motherland and also of relief to be in a country where "at least I have the basics." There is shame in some and narcissistic entitlement in others for being on welfare. The sentiments "I feel very good in this group, even though I am full of sorrows, I feel that at least here I am somebody" are commonly expressed. Warmth and gratitude are directed toward the group leader. By placing emphasis on similarities rather than differences, our patients solidify their common bonds and decrease their feelings of alienation and inefficacy. This, in turn, leads to greater respect and a common Latino identity.

CONCLUSION

As members of a hyperdiverse society, it is our clinical duty to recognize the characteristics of the different groups that amount to such diversity. Even though categorization of groups based on their ancestry, cultural background and socioeconomic status is complicated and not free of danger (such as oversimplification and stereotyping), we should not shy away from making an effort to try to better understand who we are as clinicians and patients. Although we live in a mixed society in which values and costumes are in constant flux, in which different groups share changing values and customs as expressions of the self, we cannot ignore that the culture and society in which we grew up continues—in different levels for different individuals—to serve as a frame of reference that influences the way we see and experience the world. Latinos, in this sense, have some common characteristics such as history, geography and language. However, they differ greatly in terms of social and economic status, place in society, and racial background. These multidimensional determinants will result in a plurality of individuals, some with common and many with different views of the world. It is important that clinicians prioritize identifying sources of inequalities in Latinos who are most vulnerable to be oppressed and alienated by society at large. Education has been considered the great equalizer, and in fact, in many aspects, it is. Poorly educated Latinos have a lesser degree of exposure to options and lesser knowledge and access to resources. Social and economic power allows people to chose or change environments and access treatment in a relatively organized and planned way. In this chapter, we reviewed challenges in explaining who is a Latino in the United States, emphasizing the constant need to try to answer this question, not only for Latinos but also in a way extending the question to other ethnic groups in society. Finally, we want to affirm that clinicians should not take for granted cultural similarities and differences, in particular when working with patients vulnerable to alienation and mistreatment. The disenfranchised and oppressed deserve priority when they are provided with safe and culturally sensitive treatment.

NOTES

1. See also Saulny, 2011.

FOUR

Latino Gender Roles

April Fallon and Pedro Bauza[1]

Gender identity and the gender roles we come to embrace are important components of how we view ourselves and others. They shape our idealized self and influence our desires, assumptions and behaviors in friendships and with intimate partners. While we value the influence of biology and physiology in the development of gender, culture and family are significant in the construction and internalization of gender roles.[2] Gender shapes our social interaction; likewise our culturally prescribed gendered relational dances solidify and modify our intrapsychic structures and perception of reality. As Harding (1986) in her book, *The Science Question of Feminism,* has suggested, "In virtually every culture, gender difference is a pivotal way in which humans identify themselves as persons, organize social relations and symbolize meaningful natural and social events and processes" (18).

In this regard, there are three distinct frameworks for understanding gender (Wharton, 2012). *First* is the individualistic approach, which emphasizes schemas, traits, and emotions. In this lens, gender is created by biology, and matures through the development of cognitive and affective intrapsychic structures. It is considered part of the self acquired through socialization (e.g., Bem's 1981 gender schema theory) and identity development (Juni, Rahmim, and Brannon, 2001), stable, but modifiable as we move through life. The *second* framework views gender as being created through social interaction and is contextual. Chodorow (2005), a relational analyst, posits that the basis of identity comes from individuals experiencing relational transactions of connecting, separating, and reconnecting. Identity is "shaped through contradiction, conflict and compromise formation" (1112). The *third* framework considers the development and maintenance of gender to be rooted in the structures of social organizations. This approach views gender as embedded in a "system of relational practices" existing independent of individuals and occurring at all levels of social structure (Wharton, 2012). Taken together, these three frameworks suggest that gender is a multi-level phenomenon, revealed in the states and traits of an individual, in the social processes and practices in which they participate, and in the social institutions in which they live. While all of these approaches foster understanding and have merit, we are most interested in gender as both a trait and a relational process. In this paper, we focus on Latino gender roles through the intrapsychic and interactional lens, recognizing that identity and role are ensconced in macro-structural cultural traditions.[3] We broadly characterize these roles and examine how their internalization may affect psychic functioning and influence the psychotherapeutic process.[4] We begin by examining stereotyped gender role terms of the traditional immigrant Latin culture, defining terms such as *machismo* that have become common parlance, but which mean different things to different people. With an example, we next highlight the interlocking dance of men and women in the maintenance of gender role. In our third section, we present case material which reveals the complex ways that defined gender roles unfold in a psychodynamic treatment. Our final section is an examination of several issues related to gender roles in Latin culture that may arise and impact treatment.

LATINO GENDERED LANGUAGE AND ITS CONTEMPORARY USE IN AMERICAN CULTURE

Language is the most highly developed and complex form of symbolism (Hayakawa, 1972). It conceptualizes and defines reality in specific terms and more subtly in the manner of expression. The use of language can be viewed as a symbolic action (Burke, 1968), and in doing so, has the possibility of unconscious, symbolic and differential power (Bourdieu, 2005; Weininger, 2014). In the past several decades, we have seen a plethora of books and studies that have examined the relationship of language and gender; many have proposed that the connection reinforces a differential power to each gender (Eckert and McConnel-Ginet, 1992). This connection between language and gender and its potential relationship to power is salient in the most commonly used Latino gender role terms. In this section, we examine the terms *Macho, Machismo, Caballerosidad, Marianismo, and Machista* as a backdrop to the understanding of how language becomes a backdrop for culturally endorsed gender roles.

Macho is a masculine term derived from the Latin *masculus,* meaning male. In Spanish history, the term has been used to depict an ideal male role and includes bravery, strength, leadership and wisdom. In the 1970s, the term "*Machismo*" began to appear in literature to describe the patriarchal nature of Latino male-female relationships and sometimes it was used more specifically to refer to the supremacy of men over women and the more valued male. *Machismo,* however, can mean different things (Mirande, 1997; Miville, 2013). Torres (1998) defines it as "the complex interaction of social, cultural and behavioral components forming male gender role identity in the sociopolitical context of the Latino Society" (16).

The term implies a cultural expectation that men will be respectful and honorable in their relationships with others, especially toward women (Miville, 2013). Under this definition, a man is supposed to provide for the home and honor his spouse and family. Such a role would be expected to facilitate balance between men and women. Alternatively, *machismo* can be seen as a term that represents male dominance, more specifically over women. This version of *machismo* has derogatory implications rather than connoting a tone of honor and respect. Some propose historic origins of this pattern of interaction (Goldwert, 1985). Goldwert proposes the Spanish conquistadors imprinted a "hypermasculine Hispanic role" (1985, p. 162) for men in the societies they conquered in America many centuries ago. At the same time, he proposes, women identified with the submissive role the Native Americans took. The dominant male or *macho* has been part of Hispanic society for a long time and has, to some extent, been carried on through Latino cultures. Of course, if there is a dominant figure, there will be another that yields, in this case—women. In contemporary American culture, both *Macho* and *Machismo* have come to connote the negative aspects of the term—violence, aggressiveness, and oversexedness (Torres, 1998).

Caballerismo or *Caballerosidad*,[5] a Spanish word for horseman, historically referred to the upperclass gentleman who owned the horses. It has come to refer to the more positive and chivalric aspects of Latin American manhood—honor, responsibility and bravery. Studies suggest that many Latin American men understand their role to include respect for women and their autonomy, and politeness and protection and nurturance of the family (Quintana, 2014; Arciniega, et al, 2008). *Caballerosidad* is viewed as the positive idealized construct, whereas *Machismo* is identified as predominantly negative, backward, and degenerate; however, there remains a patriarchal base in both terms.

Traditionally, women's passive and accepting attitude toward a male-dominated society was considered noble. This noble role is the female counterpart of *machismo* and has been termed *marianismo*. The concept of *marianismo* portrays women as innocent figures that are pure and obedient; they alone, almost exclusively, are expected to foster affection in families. These defining characteristics originate from the Virgin Mary and could be summarized with the following quote by a man in Marie L. Miville's book, *Multicultural Gender Roles*: "a woman has that capability of nurturing, of giving without expecting anything back" (103).

Another aspect of *marianismo* is the idea, and even expectation, that women have access to emotional and affective aspects of life. The man's role is usually perceived as one of action. Traditionally in Hispanic culture, if a man thinks of his internal aspects, he does so in the context of action, as in how he can solve a problem, whereas a woman would be expected to be in touch with her emotions. At the same time, if someone is perceived to be in touch with their emotions, this person will likely be associated with femininity and vulnerability. Even though *machismo* and *marianismo* are supposed to complement each other, these gendered terms describe and reinforce a differential set of expectations for duties and relationships between men and women.

GENDER ROLES WOVEN INTO THE RELATIONAL AND CULTURAL FABRIC

The above descriptions suggest clear role demarcation with compatible interlock. To understand what a woman's role is or can be necessitates examining what men are and the range of how and what they could be. A "separate, but equal" principle is often used to defend the utility of this norm. Yet, as Wharton suggests, "some forms of masculinity or femininity are more socially valued than others" (2012, p. 6). For Latino women their gendered role prescribes being in relation to the family, in particular their men and children. The cultural institutions of marriage reinforce both men and women accepting, participating and contributing to these roles. However, blaming pure male domination of female victims in a villainous characterization is unfair, as women, too, intricately participate (knowingly and unknowingly) in this waltz to maintain the status quo. The example below makes salient the support for the macho role by women.

In Hispanic weddings, the bride's family traditionally pays for the wedding. Although this family was quite wealthy, the family (and father in particular) did not spend money on things that were not of necessity. Nevertheless, the wife had gotten his permission to plan a wedding fitting of their social standing. The mother paid close attention to every detail of the wedding and the father approved the expenses incurred. When the calligrapher presented the invitations to the bride's mother, she became quite distressed. The calligraphy font that had been chosen was such that the first initial of the mother's name was larger than the first initial of the father's name.

The bride's mother returned to the calligrapher and insisted the invitations be made anew with the name of the father of the bride showing a larger first letter than her own. The calligrapher attempted to explain that it was the result of font style that had been chosen, and could not appreciate the request, which would be in her opinion an additional unnecessary cost. The bride's mother, arguing for the absolute necessity of redoing all invitations despite the cost, told the calligrapher in exasperation, "He is the one that pays for the wedding and he is the man. The first letter of his name must be bigger than mine."

At first glance, the request appears consistent with a traditional public viewing of the family with the father receiving top billing and more public prominence as the one responsible for the family, and the mother remaining in the background. Such was the level of awareness of the anxious mother of the bride. Yet, extended family was also aware of the complexity of this event. The wife had revealed to her close relatives how she had always resented her husband's absolute control over all expenses. Thus expressions of this discontent may have found voice in her insistence on new invitations. Her decision to spend additional monies without consulting her husband could be rationalized that if such a mistake were left unfixed, it could humiliate her husband; she wanted it corrected so that no humiliation would be experienced by him. Yet, this decision without his consultation permitted her control over what and how money was spent. Given his conservative approach to spending money, this independent decision allowed her to consciously fix a potential breach in the gender role status quo, at the same time allowing the legitimate expression of unacknowledged anger. This was confirmed by other interactions that occurred over the years in this particular marriage. These *macho-marianista* practices had been passed through the generations. The bride's mother was raised in such a traditional household where the assignment of these relational values were commonplace. However, even within this traditional arrangement, those outside the family recognized the more subtle methods used to obtain some power and perceived control in a relationship.

THE MULTIPLICITY OF FACTORS AFFECTING GENDER ROLES

Our defined terms capture the historical background and the contemporary generalities of Latino/Hispanic male-female relationships with each other. However, the language and description is often stereotypical and static, rather than nuanced and revealing in multi-layered complexities. The terms suggest a homogeneity that does not exist, as there are multiple and conflicting expressions of gender. For example, while some use it to honor the nature of the connection between others, it is often used in a derogatory manner and as an accusation of a prejudicial attitude. Specifically, one female might call another female a "*machista*" if she exhibits behavior that supports notions of men's superiority, used in the context of social consensual validation and reminding all that certain behaviors and beliefs are morally reprehensible.[6] How these roles play out in terms of behavior is the result of more than simply the broad ethnic identity. Within the Latino group, there are different countries of origin and distinct racial groups whose cultural heritage impact this dynamic interplay of gender roles. Immigration and generational status, as well as responsibilities for extended family here in the United States and in the country of origin affect how gender identity is perceived and gender roles are behaviorally manifested. Social class, economic status, and education also play a significant role in the definition of gender roles and acceptable behavior within each of those roles. For example, being a provider is an important component of the family dynamic. Yet, unemployment for Latino men is higher than for non-Latino men (Bureau of Labor and Statistics, 2014). When Latino women are able to equally find employment, psychological stress and the traditional identity and role congruity[7] is threatened. When identity is threatened, this psychological stress can result in increased aggression and violence (Acevedo-Midgette, 2008). Drinking, gambling, aggression, and promiscuity are the common ways of reclaiming *"dignidad"* and *"hombria"* (Torres, 1998).

Although race, ethnicity, geographical location, generation, and social class are often analyzed separately from gender, they are all inextricably and invisibly interwoven in our lived experience. Membership in one, such as social class and generation of immigration, may influence the expression of perceived appropriate gender expression. In the case that follows, we can see how generational immigrant beliefs influence overt cultural expression despite earlier and internalized attitudes of proper gender behavior. This second-generation Latina woman is presented to highlight how issues and conflicts around gender identity and gender roles can affect functioning. This too, is an example of how generation, social class, cultural history, and community complicate and initially obscure her conflicted internalized issues of gender.

The Case of Marie-Maria

Maria, a twenty-six-year-old college student, presented with moderate depression and anxiety. Previous medication had resulted in only slight improvement and with the encouragement of her physician she sought psychotherapy. Although quite intellectually gifted, her college grades were mediocre. She began college at eighteen, but unable to find a direction, had taken a number of semesters off ostensibly to find one. Now, in her final semester she felt a certain panic about her future. She vacillated between wishing to have a traditional life like her parents and wanting to obtain a graduate education. Although she was quite unhappy, reflecting upon her issues in therapy in the first six months was very difficult for her. Eventually, we were able to discover her fear of betrayal by discussing family issues to an outsider. However, issues were not discussed with the family either.

What haltingly unfolded in therapy was a history of both sets of grandparents who had immigrated for political reasons, leaving behind a great deal of wealth and starting over in a lower-middle-class city neighborhood among others who spoke the same language. The parents' marriage was strongly encouraged by their respective families and hopes were pinned on the couple for future wealth. Both sets of grandparents were very proud of their heritage and felt that other Latinos in the neighborhood were not of the same social standing and sophistication as they. Her father excelled in school and eventually started his own business and settled in an area away from the old neighborhood, which was almost exclusively Europeans who had been there for generations. Her mother was in charge of caring for the children, although they, like others in their area, had a nanny until they were adolescents. Sometimes the mother helped the father in his business. Although the parents were bi-lingual, there was strong emphasis at home to speak English.

The patient's birth certificate listed her name as Maria, named after her great grandmother, but her parents referred to her as Marie. This Americanization of name was done with her brother also. She and her older brother were equally encouraged to be good students. During Maria's high school years, her mother went to college; although she expressed interest in attending a professional school, her father convinced her mother to get a degree that would help him manage his office. No country of origin holidays were celebrated at home. However, when her family visited her grandparents, she described stepping into another world and time, where her silent assimilated parents spoke Spanish and their emotional expression broadened. Yet when returning to their home, her parents with an air of superiority would often make disapproving remarks about those still living in the old neighborhood, clinging to their old ignorant ways.

Marie never thought about her cultural heritage in high school as her parents seemed to wish to blend into the white American community in which she lived. Both children attended private school. Neither child overtly rebelled during high school. When Marie was a senior, her brother returned from college and announced that he was gay. Both parents were upset—her father was more overtly angry while her mother cried frequently. There were angry exchanges, expressions of shame and threats to disown. She felt both parents withdraw from her as well. Her brother had not returned home since then. Marie felt that despite her father's anger and threats, his son's announcement broke his spirit, and he became more withdrawn from everyone after this announcement.

Marie looked forward to college, to get away from the despondency and gloom that overtook her parents' home. Although she could perceive no clear danger, there was a palatable fear that had been passed from grandparents to parents and to her that there would be untoward harm if their past was discovered, so that both parents took pains to sanitize their home and demeanor of any evidence of their heritage. During college, Marie pursued her own quiet rebellion and began to refer to herself as Maria and attend Latino social and interest groups at college, which she hid from her parents. She became sexually active, which she knew would have upset her parents if aware. She considered a potpourri of majors, but could not choose. Whereas earlier both parents had espoused an equalitarian status for her and her brother, her father now overtly discouraged her from careers in engineering or architecture, which he said was because the skills required for success were not her strengths. Maria perceived that his disapproval stemmed from the "maleness" of the career.

She changed her major study several times, first to English literature, then education and finally to music with intermittent efforts to pursue pre-med and business. Her mother was as bright as her father and had wanted her own career, but Maria's grandparents and her father supported her role primarily as mother and wife. Maria got the impression that her mother might support her interest in a career, as she would encourage Maria privately to do more with her life. However, in family discussions her mother was silent, unable to voice support for her daughter. Maria felt that her father adored her for her cute and feminine characteristics, and she had become a very beautiful woman. He voiced his desire for her to embrace a role as a wife and mother and the importance of occupying a job until a good man of her stature was available.

After college graduation, she did not take a job and stayed at home increasingly depressed and anxious. For the next year, she felt a darkness and emptiness in her life. Her appearance began to vary widely. She cut her long hair into a buzz cut. Her dress changed from colorful and figure accentuating to black and curve minimizing. Her thoughts about what to do with her life changed wildly. At one point, she applied to engineering school, then later for pre-med. After a few weeks of classes she would withdraw into a solitary depression and stop attending class. This alarmed her parents. This period of acting out was intertwined with tirades in therapy against her parents. She expressed anger at her mother for her passivity and lack of support. She would rage against her father for what she perceived as the haughty arrogance of a *machismo* man. For a long time in therapy, she externalized her internal conflicted partial and fragmented gender identifications by raging against her parents. At one point, she plotted revenge against her parents by fantasizing an announcement to them of her newfound bisexual status and her desire to team up with her lover to open a car mechanic service. However, similarly to her mother, she could not express any of her views directly to either parent. With them, she was passive and silent about her feelings.

As Maria was pushed to recognize these conflicting roles as her own, treatment sessions became stormy as she projected these shifting percepts onto the female therapist. As she increased her understanding and conscious awareness of her conflicted views of the "appropriate" gendered self, her parents' explicit and implicit messages and her desire to please them, she began a slow path to define interests and multiple identities. While there are many interesting aspects of this case, in this chapter we focus on both the influence of culture and immigration as they impact issues of gender identity and gender roles.

To the community in which she grew up, Maria's family passed for white European heritage; her parent's slightly discernible accent was attributed to their city upbringing. Their desire to assimilate, not to seek out others from their ethnic group with whom to socialize, and their abandonment of their foods and traditions in the home was not uncommon for that generation; they believed that total assimilation would help their children be accepted as American. They did not entirely immerse themselves in American culture as the parents never had any close friends in the community and socialized only superficially with other business associates' families and employees. Maria came to view this behavior as representing their distrust of people outside the family, the "Americans." The parents did not differentiate their children's education as both children were sent to private and elite secondary schools and college. Maria did not think of her father as "macho" because she did not associate him with many of the stereotypes portrayed in the media. He was mild-mannered, rarely raising his voice or expressing strong emotion, a characteristic often attributed to Latino men. The family home was not filled with visits from extended relatives or expressions of strong emotion. There were few artifacts that might reveal their heritage.

She had thought that her parents were seemingly disparaging of their Latino heritage. They eliminated all outward appearances of their heritage, and expressed derogatory comments toward those who continued to embrace the culture. Yet, she began to recognize their ambivalence. They gave her a Spanish name, despite only referring to her by the English equivalent. In the period of her second separation-individuation, she adopted her Spanish name in everyday life and began to identify and associate with other Latinos. In doing so, she was asserting her individuality as well as an aspect of her cultural identity that had been denied, yet present all along.

Although Maria's father did not appear to exhibit the stereotyped Latino (*machismo*) characteristics while she was young, once she reached maturity, he became more outspoken about them in relation to her behavior. Her mother exhibited *Marianismo* characteristics, but was quite ambivalent about it, wanting to complete college, wanting to be a professional, privately pushing her daughter toward "male" professions. Maria had internalized the pervasive, stable and gendered interactions of her parents. Her mother set the example of a passive spouse who was deferential to her husband on almost all matters both in and outside the home; he was the captain and she was the first mate. These early internalizations of appropriate and traditional gender roles remained deeply embedded and quiescent during her early years in terms of her parents' stated expectations and were only acknowledged consciously much later in their wishes for their daughter's future. While her father had provided equal education for both children, he expected that Maria would embrace foremost the role of wife and mother. Maria acted out this conflict in her vacillation of desiring and pursuing a professional identity, in her dress and personal care, and in her relationships with men.

She explored identification with various professions as a proxy for her lack of clarity in gender role. What unfolded was a young woman very confused about the role and identity that a woman could and should embrace, and the multiplicity of gender identities within her. She could neither identify with her mother's desire for a career nor reject it. In a sort of doing and undoing, she would start on a professional path and then set up her failure to achieve. She felt that both parents loved her, yet devalued her as a woman. Despite her father's desire to provide her opportunity, she felt objectified and pigeon-holed by him. But she had internalized her mother's own self-doubts and passivity and felt her father's critical view of a woman who exceeds beyond a support role to her husband and the glue that holds the family together.

The parents never challenged each other directly and rarely fought openly, but their deep differences on the subject of gender-appropriate behaviors were apparent through their projections of appropriate gender roles onto Maria. Likewise, Maria could also not express her anger or her preferences to her parents directly. Initially, it was expressed as vacillating preference and behavior. Her rejection of her feminine appearance by adopting a boyish, asexual look in hair and dress seemed to be another expression of gender identity confusion—a rejection of both her mother's and father's idealized image and role for her. Later in therapy, issues of gender identity emerged in the elaborate revenge fantasies about "sticking it to her parents" in an announcement of her bisexual identity.

Unlike either parent, as Maria's depression lifted, she was verbally passionate and emotional in her expression. With no good role models for managing conflict and developing a solid identity, she was unable to contain the conflicting and multiplicity of identities within her. As she became more conscious of her proclivity to act rather than explore the underlying conflicts, she became more consistently and consciously defiant of her view of the traditional role. She experienced pleasure in the open and outward defiance of her parents and felt it countered, separated and liberated her from the oppressive silence of both her parents.

The task in therapy was to explore the deep and conflicting schisms and role conflicts within her. While some may see gender consistency and coherence as an ideal, perhaps a more realistic goal for Maria would be to recognize and tolerate the ambiguity and sometimes inconsistency that these early and conflicting internalized percepts may cause. Maria needed to recognize the past and present pressure of her parents' projected idealized gender roles. She then needed to own the schisms in these identities that she had internalized, and author a way to negotiate these conflicts.

The above case reveals the complex nature in which internalization of a multiplicity of conflicting gender roles may affect intrapsychic functioning and satisfaction in relationships. As in the previous example, gender can be intertwined in the presentation of psychopathology. Notions about appropriate gender behavior can impact what the patient presents, as can be seen in the next case of Tomas. We see here, too, how prescribed notions of relational interaction may affect the patient's interaction with the therapist.

The Case of Tomás: "A llorar pa" maternidad'

Tomás, a forty-five-year-old Hispanic man living in the United States for many years and married to an American woman, was evaluated at a mental health clinic. During the initial evaluation, he reported episodes of hallucinations to the female psychiatry resident. He had been in prison years before and described struggling with auditory hallucinations. He did not have delusions but talked about how "crazy" he was. He spoke in a very animated fashion, with a rapid rate of speech, frequent hand gestures, and made sexually charged comments. His rapid speech, reports of past hallucinations, and hypomanic hyper-sexualized demeanor led to a diagnosis of schizoaffective disorder. As he was not very fluent in English, he initially was assigned a female therapist of Hispanic descent who spoke fluent Spanish.

In therapy, Tomás frequently made explicit sexual comments about the size of his penis and his sexual prowess. This was uncomfortable for the therapist, but she never said anything, as she wanted him to feel like he could speak his mind in therapy and felt that he was testing her ability to accept. Although he did not report hallucinations throughout this time, the grandiose and sexualized demeanor persisted. The female therapist eventually left the clinic and Tomás was reassigned to a male Hispanic therapist.

Tomás sometimes talked to the male Hispanic therapist about beautiful women he saw on the street as if they were his prey. However, he never spoke to the male therapist about the size of his penis, nor did he talk about his sexual prowess. Instead, he seemed to want to engage the therapist as a peer. In one particular session shortly after being assigned to the male therapist, Tomás talked about a woman he saw on the way to the clinic. He detailed specific body parts he found particularly arousing. The therapist saw this interaction as a wish for reciprocity. The therapist held eye contact, but remained silent. Tomás changed the subject and did not talk of those sorts of thoughts again. What gradually began to emerge after that session was a more serious and vulnerable Tomás. He no longer presented this macho façade and there was no psychotic or hypomanic behavior. Instead, what eventually became apparent was Tomás's deep sadness over the regret he felt about past mistakes and personal losses.

His demeanor and conversation turned from hypersexual and over-animated to very somber, with an atmosphere of loneliness.

Tomás spoke about his previous involvement in crime, drugs, and alcohol and his estrangement from his family. His most significant regret was the lack of contact with his adult son. He would talk about his son with nostalgia. The first time he cried in treatment was when he told the therapist his son had called him during the holidays. He yearned for another telephone call from his son. He no longer wanted to engage the therapist in conversations about sexy women. If he spoke about women, it was about his wife and how he appreciated how she cared for him. It started to become evident that Tomás felt very depressed at times mainly as a function of his sense of rejection and failure. He required frequent reassurance and asked the therapist for direction regarding his relationships with his loved ones. There was a definite contrast between this man in treatment and what had been documented by the previous clinicians. Tomás also admitted he was not taking the antipsychotic medication that was prescribed. He did not seem like a man with a psychotic illness nor did he seem like a man with a mood disorder. Rather, this was a man deeply disappointed with his life.

Tomás's treatment had definite limitations. He showed little introspection and his expression of issues was concrete; his treatment was not analytical in a traditional sense. He kept appointments only sporadically and would come to the clinic mostly when he was distraught with life circumstances. The depth of the therapeutic relationship was limited by this. His sadness would dissipate once he felt supported in therapy or when his circumstances improved, but reflection about the mental process behind this was mostly absent. Also, his initial presentation to the clinic was characterized by an apparent mood disorder and psychotic symptoms, which was very different to the clinical picture seen later. The *machista* internalized template that shaped his understanding of gender and gendered relationships influenced the evolution of his presentation at the clinic.

"A llorar pa' maternidad," is a saying that roughly translates to, "if you cry, you belong on the maternity ward." It's a version of the saying "boys don't cry," with an additional element. This particular saying is used as a type of threat for boys when they cry. The saying attempts to humiliate the boy with the idea that only women cry. It also suggests that having feminine characteristics is denigrating for boys and men, with an under-

lying presumption in the saying: that women are weaker than men. This socialization has an impact on the way people relate in a society where *machista* values are common. This saying summarizes, in broad terms, the template Tomás had for relating to his emotional world and people.

For Tomás, asking for help at a mental health clinic was not a straightforward process. He had to surpass cultural barriers first and did so in layers. Hispanic males have been known to have difficulty reaching out for mental health services as it causes considerable internal conflict (Diaz de Chumaceiro, 1996; Toro, 2012; Yamamoto and Acosta, 1982). A psychotic male is someone to be feared for his craziness, more macho than as someone depressed or dissatisfied with his life. For a man with traditional *machista* values, requesting and/or accepting help for his emotional world would imply he is vulnerable and even feminine. This of course, would be shameful. His cultural makeup influenced his treatment in other ways as well.

Although the clinic administration was attempting to be culturally sensitive in this assignment, the assignment of an older Latino male to a younger Latina therapist was humiliating and upset this patient's understanding of gendered relations. The patient's explicit sexual comments to the female therapist were a verbally aggressive attempt to rebalance the relationship with the therapist on his terms. He expressed aggression and a wish to dominate women in the form of inappropriate sexual comments. Not only was this aggression, but he was using the macho role to overcompensate for his narcissistic vulnerability, typical of *machista* males (Diaz de Chumaceiro, 1996). His perception was a cultural expectation that a macho man sexualizes his interactions with women (Goldwert, 1985; Rodriguez, 2011; Satow, 1983).

Tomás's approach to relationships with women, at least in fantasy, was one of domination through sex. He, as many men with traditional *machista* values, had fantasies about conquering women sexually and expecting them to submit. In this arrangement which is "characterized by dominance-submission dynamics" (Diaz de Chumaceiro, 1996, p. 558), emotional intimacy is not possible. Such an internalized relational dynamic would emerge in the therapeutic relationship with a female therapist. A lack of awareness of this cultural dynamic may lead a female therapist to feel disrespected and denigrated, assuming that it is only characterological in origin. Unaddressed, it is likely to lead to an inauthentic relationship. Given the strong gendered roles of some first generation Latinos, female and male therapists would have different challenges when working with someone like Tomás, but a goal may be to help him develop flexibility in his perception of women and in the way he relates to them. The female therapist will very likely have to work through the sexually charged aggression, which may take the transference form of a "Madonna-Prostitute dichotomy" (Kernberg, 1995, p. 154). At times, Tomás may view the female therapist as the prostitute, collecting money from him for her services, or he may see her as the Madonna-like figure that he must protect and receive nurturing from.

With a male therapist, a male patient with *machista* values would very likely try to engage the therapist initially as a peer. We might hope that we could help the patient identify more with adaptive aspects of his gender role, supporting the positive images of *machismo*, or *caballerosidad*, such as "*respeto*," honoring self, family, and others in society. These aspects of *machismo*, which are more consistent with *caballerosidad* or chivalry, have correlated with an increased sense of responsibility and increased sense of affiliation in society (Torres, 1998).

In reviewing the material, the therapist's silent response was a turning point in the therapy, which led to deeper material. However, in retrospect, even though Tomás did not talk about women in a derogatory fashion in treatment again, he may have felt chastised by the therapist's silence, knowing not to talk about this, but not aware of why. Instead, exploring these comments could be used to understand the patient's fantasies regarding women and his view of the Madonna-prostitute dichotomy. This exploration would model respect for the patient view, at the same time encouraging a deeper reflection of the concrete material. As this patient attended the clinic only sporadically when in distress, a therapist would need to accept an ego supportive approach that would allow exploration and encourage curiosity. In doing so, Tomás might come to accept his emotional needs more readily and be less influenced by the *machista* voices within him.

In Tomás's case, culture and gender conspired to have him present with an inaccurate picture of his psychopathology. In retrospect, the reported hallucinations were most likely exaggerations, possibly fabrications, he made to conceal his pain and need for help. Psychotic symptoms were never suspected or reported to the male therapist and it was clear Tomás was not compliant with his medications. Tomás did not feel the need to dominate the male therapist as he did with the female therapist.

It is because of this that he eventually revealed his suffering, once he started working with the male therapist. To him it was less humiliating to be vulnerable in front of a man as opposed to a woman. Tomás's progression in treatment may have taken a more direct course had he not had *machista* values or if the initial therapist had been able to identify his initial aggressive presentation as culturally bound.

In the final section, we wish to present how the internalization of the passive female-appropriate gender role may impede a Latino woman who consciously desires to adopt a more gender-equal position in American society.

INTERNALIZATION OF *MARIANISMO* AND CULTURAL CLASHES

Second generation immigrants are often caught in the clashes between cultural values. They grow up absorbing the relational dynamics of their parents, yet often function and exist in a cohort of diversity where values differ. This might be particularly true when it comes to family values such as divorce. The Catholic religion and Latino culture collude to deter separation and divorce. For example, a thirty-five-year-old 1.5 generation Latina married woman presented for treatment with complaints consistent with moderate depression. It soon became apparent that the woman had considerable distress around her husband's many affairs. She felt that her husband (also 1.5 generation Latino) appeared to care deeply about her and had indicated that these meant nothing to him. After much pressure he agreed to stop this behavior. However, his affairs continued. He came to a session once with his wife, but was not willing to continue in couples' therapy, and when pushed, would defend his behavior.

About eight months into treatment, the patient decided to leave her husband. Out of respect (and perhaps a wish for support), she went to her mother-in-law to report her son's infidelities and her intention to divorce. The patient knew that her mother-in-law's own marriage had been riddled with having to tolerate her husband's many mistresses over the years. Although aware, she perceived her mother-in-law not to be distressed or angry about the situation and had rationalized that her husband had provided well for the family. Now with her son following after his father as a role model her advice to her daughter-in-law was, "Yes, he has had other women and will have more over the years, but that is the way it is. You will always be the one he loves the most and he will provide for you and his family." Indeed, her father-in-law had always been otherwise respectful of his wife and involved in family life. Her mother-in-law indicated that she had become very involved with the church and this activity and the grandchildren had provided meaning for her life. She encouraged her daughter- in-law to do the same.

The patient continued in therapy, unable to leave her husband, but refusing to stay; she vacillated between depression and anger, verbally raging against the *machistas*, including her mother and mother-in-law. "*Todos son unos putos*!" (*translated*: "they are all male whores"). She also would denounce the males in her community, including her respected father-in-law and her husband, "*malditos machistas*" (*translated* : "damn male chauvinists"). She worried that she would not be strong enough to face the familial-cultural condemnation that she anticipated if she attempted to divorce. Her friends strongly encouraged her to stand up for herself and refuse to be a doormat. This seemed to be an irresolvable conflict where the patient focused on external factors for staying or leaving. Certainly, the reality did and does play a role in decisions and psychology. There was a clash between the traditional Latino values of family and the American acceptance of individualism. Had she been "back home" there may have been more ongoing support to remain married. However, she had been exposed to the freedoms and perceived equality of the American woman, but did not want to abandon traditional identification and values and cultural community support.

Even though the patient explored and understood her conflicting worlds, the elucidation of the external factors affecting her reality did not ameliorate her depression or aid in the resolution. The therapist was able to observe and remark to the patient that reliance on her external reality to change was putting the patient in a passive role, perhaps not dissimilar from the passivity of *Marianismo* that she so strongly rejected. Chodorow (2005), although not specifically referring to Latino women, highlights the "self-perpetuating cycle of female deprecation in which mothers transmitted to their daughters their own anxieties and conflicts about femininity" (1116). By becoming aware of her own internalized *marianismo* attributes handed down and instilled in her psychological make-up for generations, this patient was able to recognize her own collusion in the process. Examining the *marianismo* and *machista* within allowed her to evaluate her internal endorsement and condemnation of these values and the effect that leaving would likely have on her own self-construct.

CONCLUSION

Hispanic cultures are heterogeneous; our intention is not to predetermine the reader's ideas about gender roles that Hispanic people might have. However, based on our clinical experience, our personal experience, and a review of the literature to some degree, the framework that defines core gender concepts are shared. In this chapter, we discussed the language that describes traditional gender roles in Hispanic cultures and illustrate how these terms define reality and can influence an individual's identity. The cases discussed are examples of how these cultural characteristics can manifest in psychotherapeutic treatment. They help us better understand how to identify and work with gender related issues of Latino/Hispanic patients, which can be a centerpiece in treatment.

There are class, ethnic and education differences in how gender identity and gender roles emerged for Maria and Tomás. His internalized gender roles affected what he presented and the relational dynamics with the therapist. Tomás seemed to embrace the norms and relate to others in a social construction of men's and women's roles. Maria was more fragmented and conflicted and affectively charged in her identification and disavowal of her gender. Issues of role congruity—that is, differences in the implicit and explicit messages and norms—were an important part of her exploring the multiplicity of gendered identities that she held. While characteristics of Latinos/Latinas have been concretized in language, the value of one gender over the other and dominance/submission paradigm is not unique to their cultures. As Harding (1986) has suggested, "in virtually all cultures, whatever is thought of as manly is more highly valued than what is thought of as womanly" (18).

NOTES

1. We wish to thank Nereidin Feliciano, Ted Fallon, and Rao Gogineni for their valuable suggestions on the topic and manuscript.

2. There are differences of opinion about whether gender role is determined primarily by biology or constructed socioculturally. It is beyond the scope of this paper to address these issues.

3. Such role expectations may influence cultural practice. Femicide is an example of gendered roles that underlie a cultural practice (Russell, 2011). This has become such a problem in Latin American countries that Carmen Moreno, Executive Secretary of the Inter-American Commission for Women of the Organization of American States has called it the principal problem for women in the region (Lissardy, 2013). Acceptance of "*machismo*" that defines and allows for the unequal power structure between men and women has been identified as a significant contributor. While we will not examine explicitly the cultural violence of *machismo* or how it impacts formal law and informal norms, we will look at how some aspects of Latin American gender roles affect individuals.

4. In this broad picture that we present, we recognize that we are guilty of massive stereotyping. We apologize for these generalizations and suggest that they are best used as a cognitive shorthand in appreciating how these perceptions impact both Latinos and non-Latinos. We encourage their use only when the personal interaction supports their validity and discard them when data presents otherwise.

5. Although these terms are often used interchangeably, we are told that the latter term is Spanish and the former, even though not a Spanish word, is sometimes used in the US (Feliciano, April 6, 2014, personal communication)

6. The commonplace use of these Spanish-language gendered terms in the US is quite interesting in light of the fact that many feminists and sociologists have demonstrated how most Eastern and Western societies express gender inequality in family, work, belief, education and so on (Risman and Ridgway, 1997). Their attachment to the specific Latin identity may be more an expression of subtle Latino prejudice in the US. For example, in the Pew Global Attitudes Project (2010), there is no difference in the belief of the value of education between boys and girls in countries such as the US, Spain, Argentina or Mexico.

7. Role Congruity Theory implicates the importance of acknowledging the spoken and unspoken norms that society upholds and equally those we explicitly embrace and implicitly endorse.

FIVE

The Role of Religion and Spirituality among Latinos

Amaro J. Laria

On March 13, 2013, an unprecedented event took place—for the first time in the history of the Catholic Church a Latin American, native Argentinian, was elected Pope. Born Jorge Mario Bergoglio, Pope Francis assumed the highest rank in the Roman Catholic Church, a very influential role, not just as a religious leader, but also in world politics. This notable event serves perhaps as an illustration of the significance of spirituality and religion among Latinos, which influences their psychosocial experience and characterizes their global identity. But, the role of religious/spiritual (R/S) beliefs and practices among Latino cultures is a complex and multifaceted one. The significant diversity among Latinos with regard to their racial, ethnic, and cultural characteristics is reflected in their diverse R/S beliefs and practices. These beliefs and practices have a significant impact on the values, norms, and socially accepted behaviors of members of the various Latino groups. Moreover, besides the R/S traditions that can be traced back to the richly diverse cultural roots of Latin American countries, new beliefs and practices are also acquired in the process of adaptation to US society. In other words, understanding the evolution of R/S beliefs and practices among Latinos in the United States requires an examination of their cultural history, as well as their psychosocial experience living in the United States.

RELIGIOUS AFFILIATION AMONG LATINOS IN THE UNITED STATES

Roman Catholicism has been the dominant religion of all Hispanic countries influenced by their Hispanic heritage. In the United States, however, the number of Latino Catholics appears to be undergoing a significant decline. In a recent 2013 survey, only 55 percent of Latinos reported Catholic affiliation (Pew Research Center, 2014). This means that common generalizations made by US mainstream members about Latinos based on their presumed Catholic affiliation, even if we assumed that these generalizations were accurate, would only apply to about half of Latinos.

In addition to the 55 percent of Latinos who report a Catholic affiliation, about 22 percent of Latinos in the United States identify as Protestants (Pew Research Center, 2014). The largest Protestant affiliation is Evangelical or born-again (16 percent of Latinos; 73 percent of Latino Protestants), many of whom are Pentecostals (29 percent of Latino Protestants). Thirty-eight percent of Latino Protestants describe themselves as either Charismatic or Pentecostal Christian. The next largest group of Latino Protestants is Baptists (19 percent of Latino Protestants). Approximately 3 percent of Latinos identify as "other Christian," the largest group among these being Jehovah's Witnesses (2 percent). About 1 percent identify with "other faiths" (e.g., Judaism, Islam, Buddhism), and 18 percent do not identify with any religion (Pew Research Hispanic Center, 2014). On the basis of these findings, since 80 percent of Latinos report some type of Christian affiliation (Catholic, Protestant, or "other Christian"), and only 55 percent of these identify as Catholic, a more accurate characterization of US Latinos is as a predominantly Christian, rather than Catholic, group. Besides Christianity, a minority of Latinos report other types of religious affiliations. Judaism is practiced by some Latinos, especially from countries that received a large influx of European Jewish immigrants, such as Argentina, Brazil, Mexico and Chile. In addition to the religious traditions brought from Latin America, some Latinos have adopted new religions while living in the United States, including Islam, Buddhism, and spiritual practices associated with non-traditional or alternative movements.

Looking more closely at the relationship between religious affiliation and various sociodemographic variables reveals some interesting differences among Latinos. Older Latinos—50 years old and older—report a higher level of Catholic affiliation than younger Latinos—18–29 years old (64 percent vs. 45 percent, respectively). Latinos with a higher educational level are less likely to report a Catholic affiliation—48 percent among those with at least some college vs. 64 percent among those with less than a high school education. Latinos born in Latin America are more likely to report a Catholic affiliation than US-born Latinos (60 percent vs. 48 percent). With regard to nationality, Mexicans report a higher level of Catholic affiliation than non-Mexican Latinos (61 percent vs. 47 percent). Protestant affiliation tends to be higher among Puerto Ricans (29 percent) and some Central Americans (37 percent among Salvadorans) than among Mexicans (18 percent) and Cubans (17 percent). Those reporting no religious affiliation tend to be younger, more educated, and more likely to be US-born (Pew Research Center, 2014). With regard to religious switching, the three most common reasons reported by Latinos who switched religions include 1) just gradually drifting away from the religion (55 percent), 2) stopped believing in the teachings of their childhood religion (52 percent), and 3) found a congregation that reaches out and helps its members more (31 percent). This last reported reason is important to consider in light of some of the adaptive functions of R/S for US Latinos that will be discussed later.

Although religious affiliation tends to be an important element of the general cultural identity of Latinos, one must go beyond religious identification to examine various measures of significance and active religious practice, which allows for a deeper appreciation of the role of religion among Latinos. In this regard, we find some interesting differences when comparing the two major religious affiliations among US Latinos—Catholics and Evangelical Protestants. Eighty-five percent of Evangelical Protestants report that religion is very important in their lives as compared to 65 percent of Catholics (Pew Research Center, 2014). Evangelical Protestants also report a higher frequency of worship service attendance than Catholics—71 percent attend services at least once weekly vs. 40 percent of Catholics—and praying outside of worship services at least once daily—84 percent of Evangelical Protestants vs. 61 percent of Catholics. Despite these differences, it is clear that religion plays an important role in the lives of most Latinos.

OTHER TRADITIONAL FOLK SPIRITUAL PRACTICES AMONG LATINOS

Given the mix of Amerindian, African, and European ethnicities in Latin America, a variety of R/S practices reflecting the intermingling of this ethnic and cultural diversity evolved in Latino cultures. One set of traditions derives from the syncretism of African and Catholic practices, with a lesser influx of Amerindian elements. These include *santería* and *palo mayombe* among Cubans (Cabrera, 1992) and *brujería* and *gagá* among Dominicans (Rosenberg, 1979). Among these, *santería* is the most widespread among Latinos in the United States. This religious practice is a syncretism of African (primarily Yoruban) traditions and Catholicism. It involves an elaborate pantheon of deities called *orichas* or *santos* (saints) who are believed to exert influence over all elements of life. Most frequently, *orichas* are called upon to intervene in matters related to health, wealth, and social relationships, especially those of a romantic nature. The practice of *santería* has spread from Cuba to other Latin American areas, such as Puerto Rico and the Dominican Republic, as well as to major US cities, where it includes converts from diverse Latino and non-Latino groups.

Some indigenous traditions common among many Latinos are subsumed under the generic label *curanderismo*, and include a variety of folk-healing practices primarily of Amerindian origin (Harwood, 1981). *Curanderos* (indigenous folk healers) of various sorts are commonly sought as part of their help-seeking regimen by many Latinos, especially those of Mexican, Central American, and South American origin. *Curanderos* tend to utilize a complex array of herbal remedies to exert influence over forces of the spirit world, again, most often intervening with matters related to health, finances, and romantic relationships. The term *chamán* (English shaman) is often used interchangeably with *curandero* in some regions. Another spiritual practice popular among some US Latinos is *espiritismo* ("spiritism") (Harwood, 1987). The primary roots of *espiritismo* date to nineteenth-century European spiritist movements. In Latin America, given that *espiritismo* and other Christian and African religious practices share beliefs with regard to the existence of a spirit world, these often became intermixed, resulting in a variety of syncretic folk-healing practices. Some of the countries that received a significant influence of *espiritismo* are Argentina, Brazil, Cuba, Puerto Rico, and Venezuela. In

Latin American countries with large native indigenous and/or African-descent populations, like Brazil and Cuba, *espiritismo* was mixed with practices reflecting those cultural influences, while in countries with a more dominant white European presence, like Argentina, it maintained a more traditional European flavor.

These practices have been stigmatized as primitive both by members of Latino cultures and US mainstream society, resulting in gross negative stereotypes in relation to involvement in them. This often causes reluctance among some practitioners of these R/S systems to openly discuss their beliefs and involvement, especially with those outside their cultural group. Although beliefs and practices associated with these R/S traditions are often quite relevant to beliefs about health and illness, these topics will be generally avoided in encounters with health care providers, who are generally presumed to be unaccepting of these traditions. Such assumptions are often accurate, given that the unfamiliar or exotic appearance of these practices may lead many to pathologize them. Unfortunately, such exaggerated stereotyping prevents a full appreciation of the supportive and health-promoting functions that some of these practices often provide for their practitioners.

The actual prevalence of indigenous folk-healing practices among US Latinos remains unknown. Earlier surveys yielded inconsistent findings (Hohmann et al, 1990; US Department of Health and Human Services, 2001). In a more recent survey (Pew Research Center, 2014) only 14 percent of Latinos reported having sought help from a *curandero, chamán*, or *espiritista*. With regard to a more general belief in spirits and interactions with the living, 57 percent of Hispanics reported a belief in spirit possession, 47 percent believe that black magic was performed either on them or on someone close to them, and 42 percent believe in the possibility of communicating with either spirits or saints. These beliefs vary by religious affiliation, with a greater number of Evangelical Protestants than Catholics reporting beliefs in spirit possession (80 percent vs. 56 percent) and black magic (58 percent vs. 42 percent). By contrast, more Catholics than Evangelical Protestants believe that they can communicate directly with either spirits or saints (46 percent vs. 36 percent). However, given the subsuming of spirits and saints in the survey, it's unclear how these reports would differ in relation to communication only with spirits. There are also some differences with regard to country of origin, with Salvadorans reporting a significantly greater belief in spirit possession

(73 percent) than Dominicans (63 percent), Puerto Ricans (60 percent), Mexicans (55 percent), and Cubans (51 percent). Thus, although indigenous folk spiritual-healing practices are used by some Latinos, one must avoid overgeneralizing about their prevalence. Assuming that the findings from the recent Pew Research Center (2014) survey provide an adequate representation of actual practice (only 14 percent of Latinos reported actual involvement in a traditional spiritual practice), an appropriate generalization to make is that a minority of Latinos in the United States actively engage in these practices.

NEGATIVE STEREOTYPES ABOUT LATINOS AND RELIGION/SPIRITUALITY

Despite the idealized notion of a "melting pot," US mainstream culture has been shaped predominantly by white Anglo-Saxon Protestant ("WASP") values. In a society where mainline Protestant values represent the dominant culture, it should be no surprise that negative stereotypes exist about other religions. The history of anti-Catholicism in the US dates back to influences from the sixteenth-century Protestant Reformation in Europe brought by immigrants to the United States, especially those from England and Germany (Ellis, 1956). The fact that Catholicism became associated later on with many poor and working-class immigrant groups that came to the United States (e.g., Irish, Italians, Polish, German, etc.) only served to reinforce the negative stereotyping even further. According to historian John Higham, anti-Catholicism in the United States represents "the most luxuriant, tenacious tradition of paranoiac agitation in American history" (Jenkins, 2004).

Latinos are often the object of significant negative stereotyping in the United States, given their assigned social categorization as a minority, or non-mainstream, group. Given that a large number of Latinos either identify as Catholics or, as discussed earlier, are wrongly presumed to be Catholics, actual or presumed religious affiliation represents one more aspect of difference among Latinos, which reinforces their minority status in US culture. Common negative traits stereotypically assigned to Catholicism by dominant WASP culture include authoritarianism, guilt-promotion, submissiveness, hyper-morality (in particular with respect to rigid sexual taboos), and primitivism associated with symbolic religious paraphernalia like praying to religious images of saints, among others. Projecting these exaggerated rigidly conservative values onto non-dominant Catholic groups serves the clear function of reaffirming the supremacy of WASP dominant values of autonomy, self-reliance, gender egalitarianism, rationality, liberalism, and self-determination. But, as is the case with most stereotyping, once we look closer we tend to find that intra-group differences greatly overshadow any real inter-group differences. In addition, inter-group differences tend not to be as pronounced as depicted in the exaggerated stereotypes. For example, Protestant values, like those of most religions, certainly have their fair share in promoting hyper-morality, sexual taboos, and guilt. By contrast, other more positive aspects of Catholicism, such as the strong value placed on humility, selflessness, and open displays of charity toward those who suffer, tend to be underemphasized, especially when critically examined through the lens of a Protestant-dominant society.

LATINO CULTURAL VALUES INFLUENCED BY RELIGIOUS BELIEFS

Eighty percent of Latinos report Christian religious affiliation (55 percent Catholics, 22 percent Protestants, and 3 percent "other Christian"). Therefore, it seems reasonable to assume that Christian values have a significant influence on values held by most Latinos. If we focus more on the commonalities rather than the differences among the various Christian faiths, these are characterized by an emphasis on selflessness, humility, compassion toward the suffering of others, and an encouragement to display good-willed "Christian" behavior toward others. Thus, when viewed from this more general lens, Latinos share significant Christian values with US mainstream culture.

An important social phenomenon to consider is the intersection between religion and social class. In the United States, mainline Protestant religions (e.g., Methodist, Presbyterian, Episcopalian) are more common among affluent groups, while Catholicism and some particular non-mainline Protestant denominations (e.g., Evangelical, Pentecostal, Baptist) tend to be more common among members of working and lower socioeconomic groups (Kosmin and Keysar, 2006; Religion in the Free Market). Thus, values attributed to differences in social class oftentimes become implicitly associated with religious affiliation. For example, US mainline Protestants often display an attitude of superiority in relation to

Catholics. By contrast, in Latin American countries Catholicism tends to be more dominant among members of mainstream and more affluent groups, while some of the Protestant denominations (mostly non-mainline Protestant ones), tend to be more popular in the lower social class groups. Thus, with some Latinos, the reverse phenomenon is commonly observed, in that Catholics may display an attitude of superiority in contrast to some of the Protestant denominations, which are often stereotyped as more backward from the Catholic-dominant perspective. Of course, it is important to note that mainline Protestant denominations (e.g., Methodist, Presbyterian, Episcopalian) are the ones typically associated with affluence in the United States, while non-mainline Protestant denominations (Evangelical, Fundamentalist, and Charismatic) tend to be the ones associated with lower class groups both in Latin America and the United States. But, given that Catholics represent the dominant group in Latin American countries, interestingly, similar negative stereotypes of Protestants are often endorsed by Catholics in Latin American countries as those held by Protestants toward Catholics in the United States. For example, Latino Catholics often regard Latino Protestants as more rigid in values, hyper-moralistic, guilt-promoting, and more primitive in religious practices. Thus, values that stem from differences in socioeconomic status become intermixed with differences in religious values.

One particular value that has been often cited in reference to Latinos is *marianismo*. *Marianismo* is a term that was popularized, primarily in the US Latino social science literature, to describe particular values and behaviors displayed by Latina women that were hypothesized to emulate traits typically associated with the Virgin Mary in the Catholic religion (Stevens, 1973). The major traits assigned to *marianismo* are submissiveness to male dominance (i.e., *machismo*) and sexual purity (i.e., *virginidad*). According to this conceptual theoretical model, the expectation that female virginity will be maintained before marriage is primarily influenced by Catholic values regarding sexual purity. The value of female sexual abstinence is highlighted to an extreme level in the notion of the Virgin Mary's immaculate conception. However, despite the apparent general acceptance of *marianismo* as a valid cultural value by some US Latino social scientists, the term has been criticized as paying insufficient attention to underlying socioeconomic factors (Navarro, 2002). It has also been criticized as originally developed from observations of Mexican women, and thus, having questionable applicability to other Latino groups (Altheus-Reid, 2006). In addition, the term has rarely been used outside of the social science literature and it isn't commonly recognized by most Latinos.

Another value associated with *marianismo* that is commonly attributed to Latinos is that of supporting a traditional household where the husband is the primary provider and the wife takes care of the home and children. In contrast to this popular misconception held about Latinos, a recent survey found that the vast majority of Latinos (79 percent), regardless of religious affiliation, report that a more satisfying marriage is one in which both husband and wife work and both help take care of the children (Pew Research Center, 2014). Only a small number (18 percent) reported preference for a marriage in which the husband works and the wife stays home to take care of the house and children. Although such non-traditional views are reported by Latinos of the two most common religious affiliations, a greater number of Catholics report the non-traditional view of marriage than Evangelical Protestants (82 percent vs. 68 percent). Only 15 percent of Catholics express preference for a traditional marriage in contrast to 29 percent among Evangelical Protestants. Another important consideration that challenges the usefulness of the term *marianismo* is the fact that values associated with *marianismo*, if present among some, would only apply to Catholics, who represent 55 percent of US Latinos, and a small number of Protestants. Only a minority of Latino Protestants who were raised Protestants (29 percent) believe that the Virgin Mary was the mother of God. Another measure of traditional values of gender roles among Latinos assessed in the Pew Research Center (2014) survey was the belief that the husband should have the final say in family matters. While the majority of Catholics disagreed with this statement (67 percent disagreed vs. 31 percent agreed), the reverse was found for Evangelical Protestants (53 percent agreed vs. 43 percent disagreed).

Other core values of Latino cultures are very much reinforced, probably in a reciprocal fashion, by Christian values. For example, Latinos place great value on family, with a strong sense of family-centeredness that goes beyond the nuclear family to also include the extended family. In addition, Latinos, in general, have a strong socio-centric orientation that reinforces the need to prioritize collective over individual goals. An illustration of these values is the common practice to have aging grandparents living at home with their children and their families and the tendency among many Latinos to discourage elderly residential placements. It is also common for adult children and grandchildren, primarily women, to become the primary caretakers of aging parents and grandparents. Another cultural value that's rooted in R/S beliefs among Latinos is that toward *compadrazgo* ("co-fatherhood" or "co-parenthood"), a term that defines the relationship between the parents and godparents of a child, established through baptism. In many Latino cultures individuals connected through a god-parenting relationship, termed *compadres* ("co-fathers") or *comadres* ("co-mothers"), establish a very close bond and are welcome into the family system, even in the absence of a direct biological link. The moral charge that defines a god-parenting relationship goes beyond the traditional religious role of serving as a spiritual sponsor or mentor to a child. Typically, godparents agree to assume responsibility for a godchild in case a tragedy occurs to the parents that prevents them from taking care of the child. Although this moral charge often takes on a more symbolic role, it's also oftentimes applied. Thus, in case of the death of parents, godparents are typically among the likely candidates, with other family members, to take care of the orphaned children.

Other Latino values that are influenced, at least partly, by Catholic and other Christian values include the high regard for *respeto*. In most Latino cultures, the notion of *respeto* takes on a stronger connotation than in its English translation "respect." For Latinos, *respeto* bears a stronger moral dimension referring to a deep sense of honor—a sort of high value of the need to pay respect to our and others' core human dignity. This high moral value associated with *respeto* is clearly reinforced by Christian/Catholic values that regard each individual being as something special and sacred. This notion is captured in the following Bible citation: "Don't you know that you yourselves are God's Temple and that God's spirit lives in you?" (1 Corinthians 2:16). Related to the notion of *respeto* is the reverence toward parents and, in particular, the role of the mother among Latinos, which takes on an almost sacred quality. There are numerous popular references in Latino cultures that reflect and reinforce the idealized appraisal of all mothers as pure and unconditionally loving and sacrificing—again, at least partly modeled after the Christian image of Virgin Mary.

GENERAL FUNCTIONS OF RELIGION/SPIRITUALITY

Much has been written about the function of R/S beliefs among all cultures worldwide. A comprehensive analysis of the functions of religion and spirituality universally goes beyond the scope of this chapter. Nonetheless, a brief reflection on some of the general functions that R/S beliefs and practices appear to serve universally can set the stage for a closer look at the role of particular R/S beliefs and practices among Latinos, in particular US Latinos.

The universal prevalence of a wide variety of spiritual and religious traditions across all of the globe's cultures throughout history suggests a universal adaptive function of religious practices for humans. At a very basic level, R/S beliefs provide us with theoretical explanatory models for some of the most fundamental enigmas associated with our core human essence and that of the natural world. R/S beliefs provide us with theorized explanations for a wide realm of open questions related to our core human experience, which, if left unanswered tend to provoke intense anxiety. These include the function of pain and suffering, our mortality and its associated discontinuity of experience, the painful disconnection from our loved ones, the question of life after death, and the enigmas associated with the basic nature of space and time, among others. R/S beliefs provide us with theorized explanations to these basic questions, which can help appease anxieties associated with confronting such basic universal enigmas. Holding on to these beliefs allows us to maintain a sense of control in the face of otherwise wild and uncontrollable natural phenomena. Moreover, spiritual beliefs, given their very categorization as "spiritual," suggest the belief that a "spirit" or non-material/non-physical part of our human essence continues to exist after death. Belief in a spirit world helps us transcend the apparently senseless finality associated with death and the subsequent decay of the physical body. The notion of a spiritual "afterlife," which is common to most religions, also helps us appease fears associated with the unavoidable impending death that awaits us all, and maintain a sense of continuity of experience and connection with loved ones after death.

Another universal adaptive function of R/S beliefs and practices is serving as a core coping mechanism in the face of stressful psychosocial experiences. Religion and spirituality have helped humans throughout history cope with intensely painful experiences, such as plagues, famine, war, genocide, and natural disasters, among others. An illustration of this is the adaptive function of Jewish religious and cultural traditions as an essential coping and survival mechanism throughout the group's history. Jewish R/S beliefs and practices have played a central role in promoting a sense of group endurance and cohesion in the face of the severe adversity and risk of annihilation experienced during the genocide of millions of Jews. Most R/S traditions endorse a belief in a brighter future, which promotes hope, stability and resilience in the face of a disheartening present reality.

All religions endorse some form of moral dogma that defines right and wrong and establishes the standards for discerning acceptable (i.e., "moral") from unacceptable (i.e., "immoral") behaviors. At a larger macro-social level, like with societal regulations and laws, this serves an adaptive function to help control the behavior of individual members of a society, which in turn promotes social order and stability. From a psychoanalytic perspective, at an individual intrapsychic level it serves the healthy ego function of helping contain the wild, untamed impulses of the id. But, religious values also often serve the superego function of excessive censoring and suppression/repression of natural wishes and fantasies. Externalizing or projecting this censoring function onto religious moral codes can help relieve some of the internal tension that results from this intrapsychic conflict.

Freud and Jung provided some of the most influential psychoanalytic thinking regarding the functions of religion for humans. They also diverged sharply on their views regarding the adaptive nature of these functions. For Freud, religion served as a defense mechanism against the fears and anxieties associated with living in a chaotic disordered world. Moreover, he suggested that the ritualistic nature of religious practices represented a sort of obsessional neurosis in an attempt to defend ourselves against the intrapsychic turmoil caused by these inner fears and anxieties (Freud, 1907; Gay, 1995). He also suggested that the image of God emerges unconsciously emulating a paternal figure that's associated with providing protection and order in the face of adversity and chaos (Freud, 1918; Palmer, 1997). But, for Freud the ultimate goal was to rid ourselves of this primitive defense and transcend such an obsessional neurotic state. By contrast, Jung regarded religion as an integral and essential healthy aspect of our human psyche. For Jung spirituality and religion functioned as a basic medium for representing core archetypes that humans share throughout history via a universal collective unconscious (Palmer, 1997). Thus, he saw the image of God as serving as a core archetypal representation of our innate need to attain a state of transcendence in an attempt to understand the meaning of life and our purpose in the universe, what he termed the *nunem* or divine (Jung, 1958). Although these classical psychoanalytic theories on religion have been critically analyzed and challenged in more contemporary psychoanalytic writings, as well as in cultural and religious studies, elements of Freud's and Jung's theories have permeated contemporary lay and professional views of the universal functions of R/S beliefs and practices.

THE FUNCTIONS OF RELIGION/SPIRITUALITY FOR LATINOS

The Role of Religion in Latin America

Clearly, like with any cultural group, there are some adaptive functions associated with the role of spirituality and religion in Latino cultures. Looking at the history of Latin America, R/S beliefs and practices have served an important function to help individuals cope with many of the adversities faced in the various Latin American countries. Throughout history, Latin America has clearly had its dose of intensely stressful psychosocial events, such as plagues, poverty, famine, wars, civil and political violence, political oppression, and natural disasters, among others. R/S beliefs have served an important function as a coping mechanism to help buffer some of the severe physical and emotional pain and suffering associated with these events. However, at times, R/S values have also been used as justification for ambitious social and political agendas. Colonialist expansionism in Latin America was characterized by the illegal acquisition of lands and goods, mass killings of indigenous populations, and inhumane oppressive measures like slavery. These actions were oftentimes justified "in the name of God." In fact, the Catholic Church played a dominant role in the colonization of Latin America. The unwarranted religious indoctrination of indigenous populations in Latin America was an oppressive social practice imposed on the natives by the colonizers, and justified by them on the basis of offering the natives an opportunity for spiritual salvation.

Today, there are many religious missionary groups, primarily Christian, actively working across Latin America, like in many other areas of the world. Besides their religious activities, these groups typically carry out community development projects in disadvantaged communities. There are often controversial views held by the local communities regarding these groups given their clear religious agenda. It's important to appreciate the invaluable contributions that these missionary groups make, especially in impoverished communities, often participating in building schools, health clinics, and other projects to promote adequate nutrition, clean water, and sanitization. Nonetheless, these groups tend to operate based on a strong self-righteous "religious-moral" conviction that they're carrying out an invaluable mission, not just social, but religious, which not everyone shares.

Religion and Spirituality among US Latinos

There are two basic facts about Latinos living in the United States that are essential to keep in mind in conducting a psychosocial analysis of their experience living in this country. The first one is that Latinos are categorized by US society as a "minority" group; in fact, they are the largest minority group (which sounds almost like an oxymoron). At a purely definitional level, the "minority" label seems appropriate in describing the socio-demographic characteristics of groups that have limited access to a society's basic resources, primarily wealth, education, political power, and health. Latinos, as a general group, fair worse than white US mainstream members in many important markers in all of these realms. But, one can also challenge the questionable usefulness of grouping all Latinos into one general category, especially given that Latinos prefer to identify themselves in reference to their nationality (e.g., Mexican, Puerto Rican, Cuban, Salvadoran, etc.), rather than as a generalized cultural group (Pew Research Center, 2012). At the level of social awareness and consciousness, the "minority" label bears a negative connotation of being socially deprived, lacking, or "less than"— obviously, not a good thing. But, regardless of the lack of cultural relevance this label may have for Latinos themselves, the fact that US society assigns this label to them affects how they are perceived by the mainstream society, and consequently, their psychosocial experience living in the United States.

The second important fact to keep in mind about Latinos is that, although the majority of Latinos living in the United States are US-born according to the US Census Bureau (2013), Latinos still represent the largest group of immigrants to this country. Moreover, most Latino immigrants to the United States come from low socio-economic backgrounds and come seeking to improve their financial status. Thus, Latinos, like most socio-economic immigrants, lack some of the basic resources and marketable skills required to succeed in the United States. A vast body of literature documents the negative psychosocial aspects associated with the migration experience, such as loss, disconnectedness, uprootedness, isolation, marginalization, and limited access to societal resources (Akhtar, 1995; Berry, 1990; Suárez-Orozco, 1995, 2002). But, ironically, being born in the United States doesn't appear to serve a protective function for Latinos; in fact, some studies suggest that it seems to pose more of an additional risk factor, what's often referred to as the "immigrant paradox," "Hispanic paradox," or "Latino paradox" (Franzini et al., 2001; Gallo et al., 2009). In other words, the limited "social capital" associated with socio-economic immigrants that limits their access to society's resources doesn't seem to wash away with subsequent generations born in the United States. In fact, it seems like the opposite happens; US-born immigrants appear to lose some of the protective factors associated with their culture of origin that help buffer the challenges of the cultural adaptation process. These two facts about Latinos—their ethnic minority categorization by US mainstream members and their socio-economic immigrant status—are essential to consider in analyzing their experience living in the United States. Besides the stressors associated with the migration experience, in particular for socio-economic immigrants, an assigned minority label represents an additional psychosocial risk factor that interferes with the otherwise healthier cultural adaptation process in subsequent generations born in the United States.

Clearly, the general experience of many Latinos in the United States is characterized by significant psychosocial stress. As a group, Latinos in the United States have some of the lowest levels of educational achievement and socio-economic indexes (as revealed by various relevant measures like median family income, poverty level, unemployment, and rates of uninsured/underinsured) (US Census, 2013). In addition, Latinos are often the victims of racism, prejudice and discrimination in the United States. R/S beliefs and practices serve an important function for Latinos in the United States to help them cope with the significant adversity they face as an ethno-cultural group. Participation in R/S activities serves an important protective function providing a supportive community for many Latinos. The significance of this supportive role is highlighted in findings from a recent survey mentioned earlier in which one of the most common reasons that US Latinos offered for switching religious affiliation was finding a congregation that reached out and helped more actively (Pew Research Center, 2014). The social support provided by religious communities helps buffer some of the negative effects of social isolation and marginalization that so many Latinos experience. It also promotes a sense of solidarity and group cohesion. Active religious participation can reinforce a feeling of acceptance and belonging as a cultural member of a local community, thus promoting a sense of positive "cultural self-esteem." This counteracts the negative social valuation provided by US society to members of so-called minority groups. While societal valuation of minority individuals connotes being "less than" mainstream group members, there is no "minority" labeling in a religious community. God, who is regarded as more powerful and influential than the larger US society, accepts all individuals equally without distinction of class, race, or culture. Thus, R/S beliefs and practices serve to reinforce an individual's worthiness, regardless of culture of origin, race or social class. The lacking social valuation associated with minority group membership is counter-balanced by a positive appraisal from God, which promotes personal and cultural self-esteem.

The lacking "social capital" that characterizes socioeconomic immigrants and minority group members leads to a psychosocial experience of social neglect. At an individual level, we well know that neglect is one of the most pervasive forms of psychological trauma that an individual can endure. A particular characteristic of neglect is its inherent invisibility, as compared to other more visible forms of trauma and abuse (e.g., physical or sexual abuse, combat, violent crimes, etc.), which often makes neglect difficult to identify and intervene against. Similarly, the social neglect that many immigrants and minority group members experience directly or indirectly pushed into the margins of society can be regarded as a form of passive-aggressive violence or collective trauma. Healing the consequences associated with an individual's exposure to traumatic experiences requires a relational context characterized by safety, connectedness, and validation in order to counter the detrimental effects that result from lack of safety, disconnection and invalidation. Applying an individual trauma model to a collective level, R/S beliefs and practices can provide an important supportive context to help buffer some of detrimental effects from the social neglect experienced by many Latinos living in the United States.

LATINO UNDOCUMENTED IMMIGRANTS, MORALITY, AND THE DISCOURSE OF "ILLEGALITY"

An illustration of the social neglect and collective trauma experienced by many Latinos in the United States is the case of undocumented Latino immigrants, who are commonly referred to as "illegal aliens" or simply "illegals." There has been an actively enforced campaign for many years in the United States to arrest and deport undocumented individuals, the large majority of whom are Latinos. Although it's difficult to argue the importance of respecting a country's migration laws and regulations, attitudes and behaviors acted out against undocumented Latino immigrants in the United States have gone disproportionately beyond the obvious consequences that can be expected from committing a legal violation by entering this country without proper authorization. Violent raids against undocumented Latinos in the United States, mostly while working in factories, have been routinely carried out with blatant violations of basic human rights. These violent acts are typically regarded by many US mainstream members as, simply, justified actions against individuals who break the law. Scores of undocumented Latinos have been handcuffed and shackled, simply for lacking documents of legal residence in the United States. The type of force and measures routinely used by law enforcement agents against undocumented Latinos during raids for a civil violation would be considered unconstitutional if these were committed against legal US residents. Most US mainstream members ignore the fact that residing in this country without having obtained proper documentation—legally referred to as "undocumented presence"—is a civil, not a criminal, offense. The use of handcuffs and shackles in cases of civil violations, ironically, represents itself a violation of US civil rights. But, given that undocumented individuals don't have any "civil rights" while living in this country, their rights are routinely violated without their ability to properly defend themselves.

I was personally involved in humanitarian efforts to assist victims of a 2007 raid in New Bedford, MA, in which 361 workers, mostly women, were detained while working at a factory (ironically, one that manufactured backpacks for the US military). Over 300 US Immigration and Customs Enforcement (ICE) agents used violent measures to arrest and detain the workers, often mocking and humiliating them in the process. Many of the workers were mothers who were separated from their children for days, simply because they couldn't provide proper documents confirming legal authorization to reside in the United States. The detained included many nursing mothers of infant children. These mothers, who warned officials that their children would be at risk if they abruptly ceased nursing their infants without the required gradual weaning, were asked to provide evidence that they indeed were nursing their children. Obviously, the only way a woman can produce such evidence without an infant present is demonstrating they have lactating breasts. Many of these women had to undergo the intensely humiliating and dehumanizing experience of showing ICE officials that they were indeed in a lactating state. We were told stories of officials, oftentimes female, mocking them in the process of producing such evidence. There were cases of infants who became severely dehydrated because their mothers were detained for days before being released. In one such case, a pediatrician, after having evaluated one of the babies, furiously contacted ICE officials on behalf of the infant's critical health condition to intercede for the mother's release. I, personally, co-led a support group with two of my graduate students for some of the victims of the raid and their relatives. In the group sessions, we heard numerous stories of blatant violence and abuse committed against the workers. Many group members displayed clear post-traumatic stress symptoms, often recounting in tears the intense individual and collective traumatization and demoralization they experienced during the raid and their subsequent detention. But, what was perhaps most disturbing about these events was the general silence and lack of general public reaction to the events. We participated in various activities coordinated by community organizations that provide social and legal assistance to Latinos and immigrants. Yet, outside the active involvement within this small circle of local agencies, there was a general indifference to these events from mainstream members and organizations. The general reaction appeared to be one of, not just impotence given the inability to effect any changes, but in fact, having no sense of a moral responsibility to do so. Most regarded these events as, simply, unavoidable consequences of breaking US federal immigration laws.

An iconic image that stayed with me from these events was that from signs in protest demonstrations that followed the raid that read *"We may be illegal, but we're still human; we still have our basic human dignity."* In fact, one of the most common themes that emerged in the support group that we led was the intense shame the group members felt finding themselves in handcuffs and shackles. I vividly remember one group member saying, "When I saw myself with my hands and ankles shackled it reminded me of those images of violent criminals that one sees on TV; we're decent people who just came to this country to work hard and earn an honest living to provide for our families back home; we aren't violent criminals" (quote paraphrased and translated from original quote in Spanish). When a country at large looks the other way while a group of predominantly hardworking individuals are traumatized and stripped of their basic human dignity, it's hard to think of a better example of social neglect.

R/S beliefs and practices served a core protective role during these events. If a group's basic human dignity was being disregarded by the host society, God respects and values everyone's dignity without distinction according to ethnicity, culture, race, minority labeling or legal residence status. While working directly with traumatized victims of the raid, we often heard individuals make reference to God as a source of hope and faith that things would ultimately be fine. Local religious groups assumed a leading role in providing direct instrumental support and services to those affected by the raids. On the day of the raid, a Catholic church in the proximity of where the events took place, and which had a large Latino membership, opened its basement 24 hours a day as an improvised shelter for children who were leaving school or day care centers and had no parents or relatives to pick them up. Many of the children, whose mothers were detained, had fathers who worked multiple jobs and long hours, so schools and day care centers were unable to communicate with many of the children's fathers or other relatives. The church also provided essential social services, with church volunteers flocking to the scene to help facilitate communication with law enforcement agencies to obtain information about the detained, and, in particular, to advocate for those whose children had no guardian available. The church quickly joined forces with other local agencies, in particular a local Catholic social services agency, as well as agencies that provided legal services. During the subsequent days and weeks, this Catholic church became the central site to provide assistance to those affected by the raids. The church basement became an improvised shelter, food pantry, communication center, and primary site where the affected received direct legal and financial assistance, as well as psychological counseling, which we assisted with. The support group that we ran was made possible through collaborative efforts with the church and the Catholic social services agency. They helped us find a place to run the group sessions and recruit participants. The priest-in-charge at the church allowed us to make an announcement to the congregation about the support group after Sunday mass. These religious organizations also played a central role in some of the political advocacy initiatives that were organized later on to denounce the blatant violations by US ICE officials, and to demand changes to federal guidelines for more humane practices in carrying out raids.

The case of undocumented Latino immigrants in the United States serves as an example of the subjectivity that's associated with context-dependent definitions of morality. Individuals who risk their lives to migrate to the United States as a result of the severe despair they endure from poverty in their countries of origin, in general, see themselves morally justified to overlook a country's migration regulations in order to cope with their critical situation and seek basic resources for their family. These individuals know that following the appropriate procedures to request legal authorization to enter the United States will be useless, since they're ineligible for such authorization given their low socio-economic status. Thus, they typically see themselves as having no choice but to engage in a desperate measure as their only hope out of their precarious situation. Within their local morality, while they understand that their actions violate US immigration laws, they tend to feel supported by God under a greater universal moral code. Thus, while a society persecutes and demoralizes "illegal" individuals who break their immigration laws, R/S beliefs counter these demoralizing effects by providing a moral justification to individuals possessing a strong sense of human dignity and responsibility to provide for their families.

THE PARAPROFESSIONAL SERVICE PROVIDER ROLE OF RELIGIOUS AND SPIRITUAL PRACTICES

R/S practices among US Latinos serve other important functions beyond strictly religious ones. Latinos often seek assistance for personal emotional matters from R/S leaders. Given the limited availability of adequate resources to meet the particular social and mental health needs of the

Latino population in the United States, R/S leaders often serve as sort of paraprofessional counselors and psychotherapists. Whether a Latino individual may seek help from a Catholic priest, a Pentecostal minister, or an *espiritista,* these R/S leaders typically share important demographic characteristics with them, including culture, language, race, socioeconomic status, and R/S worldviews. They represent natural support systems that are available within the local community. The culture-syntonic nature of these resources promotes a higher accessibility and utilization of services, as well as a greater likelihood that help-seekers will follow recommendations and participate actively in their "treatments."

Besides the general lack of availability and accessibility of health care and social services for the Latino population, Latinos also tend to underutilize these services, even when they are available and accessible. Latinos often complain about services being too bureaucratic and impersonal, which causes them to feel misunderstood by, and distrusting of US mainstream service providers. By contrast, R/S leaders tend to be members of their community, and typically perceived as more personally engaging, trustworthy, and available than mainstream providers. The individual seeking help from a priest or healer doesn't have to wait months for an appointment and there are no forms to fill out, complex health care insurance procedures, or other impersonal bureaucratic measures. Given the shared culture and language, R/S leaders can communicate more effectively and are typically perceived as warmer and more personally engaging. In addition, the shared worldviews shaped by culture and R/S beliefs lead to overlapping explanatory models of a presenting problem. Advice or suggestions given by R/S leaders may exert a higher degree of influence than those offered by less trustworthy US mainstream service providers.

SOME PSYCHOANALYTIC CONSIDERATIONS OF THE ROLE OF RELIGION AND SPIRITUALITY AMONG US LATINOS

Many Latinos who migrate to the United States come from social backgrounds characterized by poverty, as well as by social and political violence. Some Latino immigrants have endured traumatic experiences before migrating to the United States, and many of them already had a marginalized experience in their Latin American countries of origin. In addition to these pre-migratory psychosocial risk factors, the migration experience itself is often characterized by loss, uprootedness, disorientation, isolation, and a loss of social status. Latinos arrive at a new sociocultural setting where they're suddenly assigned an unfamiliar social label as "minorities," often becoming the direct object of racism, ethno-cultural prejudice and discrimination. These social experiences, regardless of an individual's personal history, can represent significant challenges to one's core sense of identity and self-esteem. Individuals who have endured negative personal and social experiences before migrating to the United States are in an even more vulnerable position as they confront the challenging psychosocial experiences associated with the migration and cultural adaptation process.

From a psychoanalytic frame extrapolating from individual to social experience, we can describe the reception to many Latino immigrants by mainstream US society as providing a general negative valuation, a sort of collective negative "social mirroring." With time, prejudicial stereotypes and attitudes toward Latinos may eventually become internalized as negative introjects, which can significantly affect some individuals' sense of identity and self-esteem. R/S beliefs and practices can serve an important protective function to counter some of the detrimental effects of the negative social messages received from the host society. Applying a Kohutian self-psychology psychoanalytical frame one could say that religious communities often serve as a sort of "holding environment"(Winnicott, 1960) or "nurturing context," (Kohut, 1971, 1977) at a collective societal level, to help buffer the negative effects associated with migration, cultural adaptation and ethno-cultural prejudice. This holding environment can play a crucial role in buffering the negative aspects associated with an intrapsychically fragmenting experience characterized by loss, uprootedness, confusion and isolation. Thus, R/S communities provide a sort of positive social mirroring to counter the negative social mirroring by the larger society. Again, this can serve an important protective function helping individuals maintain a sense of internal cohesion, identity preservation, and a positive self-esteem. At a psychosocial level this can promote a strong sense of cultural self-esteem, which, in turn, may interact in a reciprocal self-reinforcing relationship with individual self-esteem.

Although the functions of the psychoanalytic notions of mirroring and a holding environment are conceptualized primarily in the context of an individual's formative developmental years, they seem to bear some relevance, even in the case of adults, as applied to the post-migration adaptation process. The migration experience often causes a sort of developmental regression given that adult immigrants are suddenly confronted with new challenges to their core sense of identity and self-esteem, which may be reminiscent of identity challenges they faced during their earlier development. Things that are taken for granted in one's culture of origin are suddenly questioned and challenged in a new setting where the familiar rules of the game have suddenly changed. Immigrants often describe their experience analogically as feeling like they need to learn how to walk and talk (often literally speaking) all over again—a sort of developmental regression triggered by a marked cultural transition. Limited English proficiency poses significant challenges in basic communication, which may feel like one is regressively communicating as a child. Like young children, adult immigrants often communicate using very basic language and may need assistance from other adults, or even from their own children, to facilitate communication. The latter case creates an interesting role reversal in family dynamics, which also challenges adults' sense of parental competence. Thus, the migration experience can be conceptualized as a formative experience in an individual's social development that bears much similarity with individual development. The situation described previously in which a local church became the central setting that provided shelter and basic humanitarian services to a traumatized group of undocumented Latinos after the New Bedford raid serves as an excellent illustration of a holding environment or safe haven in the midst of a fragmenting traumatic collective experience.

Attachment researchers and theorists have elucidated the effects of particular characteristics associated with various parenting styles on child development (Bowlby, 1969; Ainsworth, 1978). There is also evidence that these effects during childhood development tend to be long-lasting and play a significant role in shaping adult personality styles. The experiences of Latino immigrants in the United States, as emphasized throughout this chapter, are often characterized by traumatic loss, separation and disconnection. Again, extrapolating from an individual to a social developmental model, these characteristics often lead to insecure attachments styles, such as anxious, avoidant, ambivalent or disorganized (Ainsworth, 1978; Main and Solomon, 1990). By contrast, in the Christian religions practiced by most Latinos, God is generally characterized as a responsive, unconditionally loving and caring figure. From an attachment developmental perspective, God provides the ideal recipe for a secure attachment relationship. Thus, R/S communities often take on the role of a sort of surrogate nurturing stable home base with which individuals can develop a secure bond.

RELIGION AND POLITICS IN LATIN AMERICA AND US LATINOS

Religion has had a close relationship with politics in Latin America, like in most parts of the world. The Catholic Church played a central role in the colonization of Latin America, which included expansionism and the oppression of indigenous populations. Symbolic testimony of this is evidenced in the numerous Catholic churches and cathedrals that were built on top of sacred temples built by indigenous populations throughout Latin America. Many Catholic priests were among the original *encomendados*, who were commissioned *encomiendas* by the Spanish crown that included land and natives, and where the natives engaged in forced labor (Calero, 1997). Thus, the Catholic Church had a significant involvement in the promotion of slavery, first of native indigenous populations, and later on of imported African slaves. Nonetheless, there was also evidence of some tension within the Catholic Church regarding this role. An illustration of this are the writings of Bartolome De Las Casas, a Spanish Dominican friar who was one of the earliest European settlers in the Americas, and who lived and worked in Mexico and Guatemala. De Las Casas initially participated in the *encomienda* system, but later gave up this role to become the most well-known figure denouncing the church's unfair colonial practices and injustices committed against the indigenous population (Clayton, 2012).

Another example of the close relationship between religion and politics in Latin America is the Liberation Theology movement. This movement emerged throughout Latin America in the 1950s and 1960s in reaction to the disheartening widespread poverty and social injustices pervasive in the region. The coining of the term "liberation theology" is attributed to Gustavo Gutierrez, a Peruvian priest who worked actively helping the poor. In his book, *Theology of Liberation*, Gutierrez (1971) denounced the social injustices that led to poverty, describing them as some of the worst sins committed against humankind. In the Liberation Theology movement Christian teachings are applied to the socio-political reality of poverty and injustice in Latin America. In fact, from the movement's perspective, Jesus Christ is regarded as perhaps the most well-known social activist given his active involvement in helping the poor and others marginalized by society (Boff, 1978). The Liberation Theology movement makes a call for spiritually and religiously justified political action against the social injustices in Latin America, what is referred to as "orthopraxis." Thus, the movement emphasizes the need to take action, rather than simply promoting dogma or orthodoxy. Although the Liberation Theology movement has been controversial within the Catholic Church and some have denounced it as an appropriation of religious principles to promote a Marxist political dogma, it has fueled an influential social and political force in many Latin American countries, including Brazil, El Salvador, and Uruguay, among others.

In the United States, there are interesting associations between religion and socio-political views among Latinos. A recent large-scale national survey (Pew Research Ctr., 2014) found that, although the majority of Latinos report a Democratic political affiliation, a greater percentage of Evangelical Protestants (30 percent) report a Republican leaning in comparison to Catholics (21 percent) and those reporting no religious affiliation (16 percent). Similarly, with respect to social views that in the United States are strongly linked with political partisanship, as with the case of abortion, a significantly higher number of Evangelical Protestants (70 percent) express more conservative views against abortion than Catholics (54 percent) and the religiously unaffiliated (35 percent). Interestingly, despite the widespread stereotypical assumption that most Catholics hold anti-abortion views, the survey shows than only approximately half of Latino Catholics support these. With regard to same sex marriage (another social opinion associated with political conservatism vs. liberalism in the United States), a greater number of Latino Catholics support rather than oppose same sex marriage (49 percent vs. 30 percent), in sharp contrast with Evangelical Protestants, who predominantly oppose it (19 percent support it vs. 66 percent who oppose it). Moreover, according to the survey, the majority of Latino Catholics feel that priests should be allowed to marry, that women should be allowed to become priestesses, and that the Catholic Church needs to do more about the sex abuse scandals. These findings confirm the inaccuracy of exaggerated stereotypes held in the United States about Latino Catholics as endorsing extreme conservative values. Clearly, spirituo-cultural values and religiosity among Latinos is a complex realm that transcends the simplistic categorization typically portrayed in caricatured cultural stereotypes.

CONCLUDING REMARKS

In the process of completing this chapter, I had a psychotherapy session with one of my patients, which I would like to share, as it serves to illustrate some of the main ideas discussed. Mariela is a woman in her 40s from Guatemala who came to see me with her two daughters, feeling distraught in the midst of a family crisis. During a trip she had recently taken to Guatemala with her husband, her two daughters and her thirteen-year-old stepdaughter (her husband's daughter from a previous marriage), the stepdaughter announced unexpectedly that she wouldn't be returning with them back to the United States. Instead, unexpectedly, she had decided to stay in Guatemala with her biological mother. The father approved of his daughter's decision to stay with her mother in Guatemala, and also suddenly announced to Mariela that he wanted to get divorced from her. It appeared as if the husband was considering a potential reconciliation with his ex-wife (his daughter's mother) and had decided to leave Mariela and return to Guatemala to reunite with his ex-wife and daughter. All of this came as a complete surprise to Mariela, who hadn't seen any of this coming. Her husband traveled back with them to Massachusetts, but announced that he would stay at home only temporarily until he made arrangements to move out. He also announced that from that point on, he would not continue to provide any more financial support to Mariela and her daughters (whom he had never legally adopted) because he had to save money to move. Mariela came quite distraught in the midst of this family crisis, dealing with the impending break-up of her marriage, the abrupt separation of her daughters from their stepfather (they had been living together for three years), and feeling desperate about their impending financial situation. Despite the fact that she worked two jobs and her teenage daughter had a part-time job, they would be unable to keep their home without her husband's financial contribution.

When I inquired about potential sources of support, Mariela explained that she had no relatives in the area who could offer them any instrumental support because all of her extended family lived in Guatemala. She also reported having no close personal friends locally. But,

Mariela is a very active participant in the Jehovah Witness religious faith. She attends bible study meetings several times weekly, and had assumed a leadership role in the church's public ministry, actively involved in community preaching and other missionary activities. When she described her situation to fellow church members, she received very close personal support from them during such a crisis. Despite the church's limited financial resources, the members organized a fundraising initiative to offer her some financial assistance. In addition, church members offered her other forms of instrumental support, such as providing her information about community social and legal services agencies that she could consult with regarding her rights in this situation. Obviously, I offered Mariela whatever emotional support I could within my limited role as her psychotherapist; yet, I felt rather helpless finding myself unable to provide her more instrumental support. The support I could offer her through our psychotherapeutic work felt minimal as compared to the more direct emotional and instrumental support she received from her fellow church members. As I tried my best to express words of empathy, Mariela replied: "Don't worry, doctor, I have a very strong faith in God, and I know he's going to help me get through this tough situation with my daughters; I know once we get past this storm, things will be ok." These words reminded me of the positive cognitive restructuring that we often find ourselves hoping to attain with our patients. But, coming from such deeply rooted religious beliefs appeared to carry so much more weight than what I could have hoped for from a simple cognitive restructuring intervention. My efforts trying to instill a sense of hope in her throughout this crisis were humbled in the face of the strong faith granted to her by her religious affiliation.

This chapter emphasized the need to contextualize existent biases with respect to the role of religion among Latinos in the United States from the perspective of a US Protestant–dominant culture. Looking closely at the multiple factors and complexities with regard to what defines religiosity and spirituality among Latinos, one can appreciate the need to look beyond a simple religious affiliation in order to attain a deeper understanding of the role of religion in Latino cultures. R/S beliefs and practices among Latinos have had a significant role in shaping the history of Latin American cultures, often making it quite challenging to separate religious from political agendas and socioeconomic realities. R/S beliefs have also helped shape particular values that are typical of many Latino groups, even when these may be displayed outside a religious context, as in the case of *respeto* and the reverence paid to the role of *la madre* (the mother). Moreover, some of the functions of R/S practices in the cross-cultural adaptation process of millions of US Latinos were discussed, as illustrated in the above vignette. Perhaps a way to iconize the legacy of Christian values in Latino cultures is found in the basic theological virtues of Catholicism, namely *fe, esperanza y caridad* (faith, hope and charity). These values can be quite adaptive in promoting resiliency and maintaining a basic sense of human dignity in the face of adversity caused by poverty, illness, violence, political oppression, and other forms of human suffering.

SIX

Passion, Morality, and Resilience in Movies about Latino Immigrants

Salman Akhtar and Maria Elena Aguilo-Seara

The emerging genre of "ethnic movies" for and about immigrants seems to rest upon three premises: (i) that there is an emotionally significant difference between the immigrant's original culture and the culture of his adopted land, (ii) that the immigrant suffers from a psychic bifurcation which pulls him in the opposite directions of nostalgia and assimilation, and (iii) that the epigenetically unfolding developmental epochs (and the neurotic conflicts attendant upon them) often get intertwined with genuine "cultural conflicts" (Akhtar, 2011) to the extent that the two might be inseparable for all practical purposes.

It is with such orientation that we offer a psychoanalytic discussion of three "ethnic movies" pertaining to Hispanic-American immigrants. One involves newcomers from Columbia, the other involves those from Mexico, and the third involves those from Cuba. Each movie depicts the condensation of intrapsychic and reality conflicts and the nuanced play between personal anxieties and cultural dislocation. Our aim in presenting this material is to highlight how idiosyncratic and emotional variables invariably lurk underneath the more comprehensible societal dramas of our lives. We hope to enhance the reader's empathy with this particular group of immigrants to the United States.

Before initiating the main text of our discourse, though, we must enter a few caveats. *First,* we must acknowledge the inevitable element of personal bias in the selection of the movies discussed here. As cinephiles, we are familiar with a large number of movies pertaining to the American Latino population (see Akhtar, 2011, 233–242) but we selected these particular movies for their evocative qualities, plot, developmentally oriented concerns, and deft use of extrapsychic-intrapsychic conflation in the course of life. That making a selection of this sort involves highly subjective elements goes without saying. A *second* caveat pertains to the fact that we are not social anthropologists. While we are somewhat familiar with the cultural matrix of our protagonists, we might have missed its finer hues and shades; our emphasis is essentially psychoanalytic. *Third,* we do not possess knowledge about the personal backgrounds of the writers and directors of these movies. On the one hand, we are aware that a movie differs from a poem (or a painting, for that matter) in being a product to which many, many individuals contribute and therefore lacking knowledge of its writer or director might not diminish an interpretive effort. On the other hand, factors of a personal nature do play a role, especially if the writer and/or director has made a series of moves with overlapping themes. Keeping their personal background in mind can then enrich the interpretive effort. *Finally,* in focusing upon the psychodynamic aspects of the three movies under consideration, we might appear to give short shrift to the socio-political undertones of the plot. Being firm believers in the "principle of multiple function" (Waelder, 1936), we do bring up this dimension toward the end of our contribution. We therefore urge the reader to bear with us till then. It is with these caveats that our discussion of these three movies should be approached.

ABANDONMENT, EMPTINESS, AND SURVIVAL: *ENTRE NOS*

Directed by Gloria La Morte and Paola Mendoza, the searingly painful *Entre Nos* (2009), takes place in Queens, New York, and revolves around a mother, Mariana, and her two children, Gabriel Jr. and Andrea, as they reunite with her husband, Gabriel Sr., after moving from Colombia. The film is sad, dark, and replete with themes of poverty, lack of resources, and hunger. And yet, there is a redeeming and hopeful quality to it, as we shall demonstrate in our discussion. The story focuses on the psychosocial dilemmas consequent upon immigration from a foreign country as well as the financial and emotional strain that comes with the process.

Initially, the film begins with Mariana making empanadas for her children, husband, and her husband's two friends. Gabriel Sr. leaves the family for a night out in the city. After that night, Gabriel Sr. returns to tell the family that he is planning on moving to Miami and will have the family join him later. The family is shocked by this change, but they say goodbye, trusting that they will be reunited soon.

Shortly after their father leaves, the children attempt to assimilate with "local" children as they play kickball in the streets. Mariana, meanwhile, is desperately calling her husband to find out if he has arrived safely and to go over the next steps that the family should take to be reunited. After all, she moved the family from Columbia to New York to be united with her husband. Each phone call and voice message that is not returned ultimately drives Mariana to visit one of Gabriel Sr.'s friends to gather further information. In visiting this friend, Mariana learns that her husband has left her for good and has no plans to return to see the family or have them join him. In desperation, Mariana attempts to gather all of the money the family has to fly them to Miami but comes up short with the money for the tickets. Mariana shares with the children her plan to go to Miami as soon as possible. The children ask, "What is going on with Papi?" She can only answer, "I do not know." Frustrated and angry, Mariana did not know what to say further to the children.

Mariana feverishly attempts to sell more empanadas in an effort to earn enough money for their flight but has no success. Upset and frustrated with the situation, the children often ask Mariana if she is mad at them because she is no longer joking and smiling with them. Mariana attempts to find work as a seamstress but is denied the opportunity when her potential employers discover that she has two children. After much effort, Mariana finds work as a dish washer, but she now has to leave her children at home while she is away at work. During the day, the children sneak out to play with the other kids in the neighborhood. Unfortunately, the children are caught and Mariana argues with her son, who was supposed to be caring for his younger sister. In response, he begins to yell and argue back. The situation they are in is becoming increasingly stressful.

In an attempt to distract the children, Mariana brings them to the movies, but quickly realizes she does not have enough money for the three of them. While the children enjoy the movie, she remains outside watching as a couple uses a grocery cart to pick trash and acquire a stockpile of cans and bottles. After following the couple, she notices that the cans are taken to a recycling center where the couple is given money for their work.

Soon after her discovery, Mariana embarks on an adventure with her kids, stealing a grocery cart from a store and attempting to earn money. Despite being happy at having learned a new way to earn money, the family is soon locked out of their apartment and discovers that Gabriel Sr. had skipped out on three months of rent—not just one. Threatened with police action if she does not pay the rent immediately, Gabriel Jr. quickly runs into the apartment to take basic items for his family. The family had to run to live in the street. Pushing all they own in the grocery cart, Mariana takes the children to a park to play and forget about the stress in their life. While attempting to sleep on a park bench, the children voice their fears, but it is Andrea, the little girl, who tells Mariana that she is "super mom" and will take good care of them. Cold and alone, Mariana watches over her children as they sleep on the park bench.

Finding food from local friends and food kitchens, they began to think of the next step for survival. As they find money to rent a hotel room, the children are hungry and split a bag of chips. A dirty bedroom with graffiti blasted walls is all the family can afford—and the children split a chip bag, licking the bag inside and out for the last crumbs. Speechless and in shock, Mariana sits still in utter disbelief.

On the streets one night, the family finds some empty boxes on the steps by a train, where they all lay down and try to fall asleep. Gabriel Jr. looks at his mother and asks why they left Colombia, to which she responds, "Because of your father." Even though exhausted, he decides to continue the job of collecting empty cans to help the family earn money while his mother is sleeping. Dirty and disheveled, he looks through a fence at the other children in school, wishing he could one day be there. After spending his day collecting cans, Gabriel Jr. comes back with money.

A man now enters Mariana's life. He recommends the family to his friend who rents out rooms. They eventually work together and decide to make the money to live in better living conditions. Mariana gets pregnant. The family begins to fight and Gabriel Jr. is frustrated with the demands placed on him as well as the ongoing responsibility of always having to babysit his younger sister. The outgoing long-distance phone calls to Gabriel Sr. to either see how he is doing or to yell at him eventually stop and Mariana does not even share with him news of her pregnancy. She decides to terminate the pregnancy.

The landlord who has rented her the room then proceeds to help Mariana terminate her pregnancy with a home remedy since she cannot afford to go to a medical doctor. Exhausted and weak from the procedure, Mariana makes a trip to the church but at the door she stops to think and ask for forgiveness from the Lord, begging for strength. While Mariana is resting, Gabriel Jr. is out collecting cans, trying to earn enough money to cover their rent. Afterwards, as Mariana regains her strength, they go out as a family, collecting cans and finding any means to survive. With time, Gabriel Jr. realizes they are not going to Miami and that his father had abandoned the family. However, in reaching this conclusion, Gabriel Jr. acknowledges how instrumental his mother was in providing the family with strength and protection throughout their very difficult situation.

Time passes. After months of collecting cans and renting a room, life eventually becomes more stable. The last shot of the film shows a cleanly dressed Mariana selling empanadas from her friend's food cart while Gabriel is walking to attend school. The family has survived after all.

Entre Nos is not a movie for the soft-hearted. Its focus upon poverty and hunger can be disturbing to watch. The depiction of children suffering is also difficult to bear. Through empathy as well as by becoming the recipient of projective identification, we feel helpless, ashamed, and desperate. Alternatively, we identify with the brave mother, Mariana, and with the deprived children, Gabriel Jr., and Andrea. We oscillate between hope and hopelessness, between parental responsibility and childlike expectation of support, and between adult strength and infantile weakness. We note how those who migrate to the land of golden opportunity do not always strike gold. We taste the bitter bile of the father's treachery and abandonment of his family. We shiver with empathic resonance at the frequent homelessness of the main characters in the movie. The sustained strain on our egos while watching this movie results in what Khan (1963) has called "cumulative trauma." Our hearts are repeatedly broken and our mourning capacity severely taxed. The empty cans that the family collects to trade in for small amounts of money represent the empty and "dead mother" (Green, 1980) that their adopted country has turned out to be. At the same time, the very fact that these empty cans become a source of income reflects the potential of regeneration and what Winnicott (1969) has termed "survival of the object."

And, herein lies the hidden beauty of *Entre Nos*. Despite profound adversity, soul-wrenching hardship, and shocking betrayal by her husband, Mariana retains the dignity of effort and the devotion of a mother. It is her dedication, faith, and perseverance—in essence, her mental health—that ultimately sees the family through the seemingly unending saga of despair. Plodding along, holding her head high, making pragmatic decisions even if they go against her religion (e.g., getting an abortion), and never giving up on her maternal role, Mariana becomes a "tutor of resilience" (Cyrulnik, 2008, 24) for her two children. In turn, they identify with her inner strength and try to be helpful to her and to each other. The dialectics of reciprocal concern and love wins over the anguish of material deprivation. The children, though often lacking food and a safe place to sleep, never feel unloved by their mother and this helps them grow up well. Fascinatingly, as the movie ends and the credits begin to roll, we are informed that the characters had been based on real people and that the two children grew up to be successful adults. In fact, it was Andrea who actually created the original documentary on her mother's life on which the movie *Entre Nos* is based.

COMING OF AGE, SEX, AND MONEY: *QUINCEAÑERA*

Quinceañera (directed by Richard Glatzer and Wash Westmoreland, 2006) is a colorful lark of a movie which bustles with manic energy and hilarity even when it deals with the serious matters of conflicted sexuality, economic rivalry, religion, and teenage pregnancy. The movie focuses on a Mexican American family from Echo Park, Los Angeles, as it struggles with a highly stressful coming-of-age celebration of its teenage daughter, Magdalena. This involves her *quinceañera* (literally, fifteenth birthday), as she transitions from a young girl to a woman. The movie also explores the conflicts of Magdalena's gay cousin, Carlos, who is facing ostracism by his parents.

The movie begins with Magdalena's cousin, Elena, and the celebration of her *quinceañera*—with Elena dressed in a beautiful gown, riding in a fancy limousine and surrounded by her beautiful family and friends. The pomp of the religious mass, professional photography, and formal dancing is followed by the young kids breaking free and celebrating with family and friends over traditional Mexican food and music. Magdalena is given special attention from a young man at the party, whom she acknowledges, but does not let the young man distract her. Meanwhile, Elena's mother speaks with Magdalena's mother and graciously offers to alter Elena's dress for Magdalena to wear on her own *quinceañera*.

As Magdalena's family struggles over finances, Magdalena realizes that they will not be able to buy her a new dress for the *quinceañera*. She, however, cannot let go of the desire to rent a Hummer limousine. This too is out of her family's reach. The ensuing financial struggle is just one of the many battles for Magdalena. Coming from a strict, traditional, and highly religious Mexican American home, Magdalena's father is outraged when he learns that she is pregnant and the boyfriend gone. His anger is amplified when Magdalena insists that she did not have sexual relations with her boyfriend.

Fascinatingly, her gynecologist confirms this and attributes the pregnancy to the "accidental" traveling of sperm from her thigh into her vagina while she and her boyfriend were "fooling around." Nonetheless, Magdalena is kicked out of the house by her father. She moves in with an elderly uncle, Tomás, who helps unify her and her cousin, Carlos, who has been ostracized because of his homosexuality. The three build a life of humor, mutuality, and sensual comfort that is in stark contrast to the harsh anti-instinctual stance of Magdalena's religious father.

It is not until the death of Tomás that the family is finally reunited. With another life event bringing the family together, Magdalena's father begins to listen to her and feel that there must have been a "religious reason" for her pregnancy. In the end, after significant emotional development on the part of both Magdalena and her father, she has her *quinceañera.* To her delight, she finds herself with all the items she had originally wished for, including a new dress and the beautiful Hummer limousine.

The film explores a few key elements common to the Hispanic/Latino community through various symbols and experiences. The film depicts the struggles and hardships that a second-generation Mexican American family endures while attempting to adjust to the culture of the United States. In this particular area of Los Angeles, one can see the gentrification process occurring, as areas which once consisted of abandoned shops and vandalized buildings have transitioned into bodegas and quaint apartments. Throughout the film, there is a focus on the various cultural aspects that are crucial to the Hispanic/Latino community—such as the Catholic religion, culinary traditions, and the emphasis upon family as the focal point of concern. Each character struggles with the idea that Tomás would be their patriarch and keep the family united. Moreover, regardless of whether the family is faced with hardship or partakes in celebration, the various aunts, uncles and cousins are constantly present to support and help each other in any way possible. Examples of this include Elena's mother offering to alter Elena's dress for Magdalena; the collaborative family effort in preparing for Magdalena's *quinceañera;* the mutual love and support as the family mourned the loss of Tomás; and Magdalena's *quinceañera,* which culminated in celebration and the new dress and limousine that Magdalena so desperately wanted, but could not afford.

The importance of Catholicism is underscored by the film's depiction of pervasive religious décor within the home and of the importance of prayer to the family. Another aspect of Latino/Hispanic culture emphasized throughout the film is the concept of "tradition," which manifests itself in everyone's love of Mexican music and food, as well as their deep regard for family ancestors. Photographs of the family across various generations, as well as Mexican food and music, can be observed in numerous scenes of the movie.

Quinceñeara portrays a traditional Mexican American family that is vastly different from the American culture it is trying to assimilate into. The Mexican American family is portrayed as traditional, colorful, and highly fertile through the depiction of religion, vivid color schemes, numerous relatives, large families, and even Magdalena's ability to conceive a child without intercourse. On the contrary, the American family is portrayed as progressive, bland, and infertile through the depiction of a homosexual couple that lives in a house with neutral color schemes, minimalist décor, and few photographs giving hints of their heritage.

The essence of *Quinceñeara* lies in the conflation of the usual adolescent dilemmas of sexuality, rivalry with peers, and consolidation of identity (Erikson, 1950; Blos, 1967; Kieffer, 2013) with the intergenerational struggles in an immigrant family. This condensation of the expectable conflicts and the cultural disharmony between immigrant parents and their offspring (Akhtar, 2011) is depicted in diverse realms. One pertains to money. For immigrant parents, especially those from poorer nations like Mexico, money might have been a motive for moving to the United

States. However, the affectualized acquisition of material goods during the early post-migration period often settles down and nostalgic longing for the "old country" (actually a retrospective idealization) takes its place. The situation with the first generation born in the United States is different. They have higher baselines and bigger dreams; Magdalena's wish to be driven to her coming-of-age celebration in a Hummer limousine (itself a caricature of affluence) is a case in point. Ordinary phase-specific competitiveness of adolescence finds a cultural idiom of expression here. Her wish is not only to be like her wealthy cousin, Elena, but to outshine her financially strapped parents, especially her mother who, surely, had not gone to her *quinceneara* in a chauffeur-driven oversized limousine.

This brings up the powerful oedipal undercurrent to the movie. A daughter's blossoming into a young woman tests the father's oedipal restraint and exerts a civilizing influence upon him. Renouncing any claims to her body strengthens the incest barrier in the father's mind and adds to his capacity for humility. The daughter, on the other hand, has to work through her erotic desire toward the father as well, and this takes time. In *Quinceneara,* we witness a father who is deeply uncomfortable about his daughter's transition into womanhood and comes down too hard upon her. And, we see a daughter, Magdalena, who is a bit hurried (for the oedipal underpinnings of hurry, see Akhtar, 2015) in actualizing her oedipal child fantasy. Not only are these "positive" oedipal themes evident in the movie, the negative oedipal scenario also finds its place. This is the tale of Magdalena's cousin, Carlos, who seems to be an avowed gay man but turns out to be only going through a phase of negative oedipal regression. His trial homosexual encounters (with the "American" gay couple) as well as his basking in the warmth of elderly uncle Tomás give ample testimony to such an assertion. Interestingly, the gratification provided by these experiences results in a psychic shift toward identification with Tomás's phallic generativity and paternal cadence.

Yet another realm in which the adolescent struggle is depicted pertains to religion. Magdalena's father is deeply religious and, being Catholic, devoted to the Virgin Mary. Mercilessly teasing of this faith is the fact of his daughter's sex-less ("immaculate"!) pregnancy which he, of all people, refuses to believe. Here the old and new—the Virgin Mary and Virgin Magdalena come crashing at each other. Religion and science combat each other in the form of the believing father and the reassuring gynecologist of Magdalena. Can the old be true? Can the new teach us about the old? We are left wondering! Would Magdalena have found such a sexual freedom and/or such a remarkably informed physician had the family not left their little village in Mexico? Here we see both the pros and cons of immigration and their complex interplay with adolescent turmoil.

PSYCHOLOGICAL TWINNING, HOMOEROTICISM, AND AGGRESSION: *MAMBO KINGS*

Mambo Kings (directed by Arne Glimcher, 1992) focuses on the lives of César and his younger brother, Nestor, as they journey from Cuba to the United States in the 1950s to become the next top mambo players. As the film begins, César is caught up in a physical altercation as he discovers that Nestor's girlfriend, Maria, has married his enemy in order to protect Nestor from harm. César, angered by this, promises Maria that he will protect Nestor from the pain of a betrayal, keep it a secret, and take him to America.

After a lengthy journey to the United States, César and Nestor make their way to their cousins' home in New York City, where they are met with family and, of course, tons of Cuban food. Children are running around as they celebrate the arrival of César and Nestor. At this dinner, César announces it will be he who will network for their business in music while Nestor will create the music. He comes up with the name "Mambo Kings" for their duo. Without hesitation, César requests that everybody present get a jump start on working for César, and says "the shrimp that sleeps gets carried away by a cocktail." César seems full of determination for both himself and Nestor to achieve fame on the Cuban scene.

Soon after this first meal in the United States, César and Nestor head to the Palladium, a local music club in New York City, to hear some of the top musicians in the area. Without rest or hesitation, they want to see their biggest competitors and begin their own networking campaign. The Palladium is filled with glitz and glamour, as well as a number of music moguls scouring the scene for new talent.

They draw the attention of the "right people," and soon César and Nestor are asked to play and perform at various music venues. As they begin to build a name for themselves, César and Nestor obtain part-time employment at a meat distributing agency to earn a steady paycheck. Nestor eventually meets a young Spanish woman, Dolores, a local housekeeper, with a very strong work ethic and the aspiration of becoming a school teacher. Upon getting to know her further, he discloses his song, "Beautiful Maria," and how it was written for his former fiancée. They discuss their particular ambitions over coffee and Nestor eventually invites her to see him and César play at the local club.

Within minutes of meeting Dolores, it becomes evident that César is attracted to her and, after a strong and passionate dance, their connection is even more apparent. Despite this clear attraction, Nestor whisks away with this girl. Nestor soon marries Dolores and discovers that they are going to have baby. Dolores soon finds herself sad and confused when once, Nestor calls out the name, "Maria," to Dolores.

The Mambo Kings prevail with accomplishment after accomplishment and even travel to Los Angeles to appear on the wildly popular television sitcom, *I Love Lucy*, and perform with Desi Arnaz. During their stay in California, Nestor is caught having an affair with a woman who resembles his beloved Maria. The situation escalates into a fist fight with César, who proceeds to reveal the truth behind their travel to America and how Maria begged César to take him out of Cuba. Nestor is left bewildered by this information and confused as to why his brother had not shared it with him before.

Tormented by the knowledge that his beloved Maria had sacrificed herself for his safety, Nestor experiences a difficult time in his life. Depressive guilt is now warded off by powerful "manic defense" (Klein, 1935). Nestor begins to feel that he must outshine his brother. He strives to emerge from underneath his brother's shadow, and involves himself with the Mafia to obtain his own music club. Nestor then admits to his wife, Dolores, that, despite the chaos, he has always loved her and states that she should go to school and pursue her passion to become a school teacher.

After the Mambo Kings deliver a beautiful concert at the Palladium, Nestor insists on taking the wheel and driving César and his girlfriend home. The three drive off into the night when Nestor suddenly loses control of the car, collides with a tree and is ejected through the windshield. César is paralyzed and shocked as a result of his brother's death. He finds himself lost and alone to wander a world that he and his brother once thrived in.

Soon afterward, César dedicates his life to Nestor's memory and opens a bar in his honor; Dolores reveals to César that his brother had always idealized him. César responds by saying, "everything I was in my life was because of him." Dolores then suggests that César sing the song, "Beautiful Maria," for him. Filled with passion and resolve, César proceeds to step onto the stage to honor his brother as the movie comes to its end.

Scenes of food and family are laced throughout *Mambo Kings*. The very instant César and Nestor arrive in America, they are greeted with family and an elaborate display of food. When Nestor and César appear on *I Love Lucy*, we see many generations of family members coming together within the home to watch the show and eat Cuban food together. The theme of music and the passion it has for Cuban culture is also apparent from the very beginning, particularly in the heart of Havana, where the characters are first introduced. It is through this theme that their passion allows them to succeed and become successful Cuban musicians in America. The theme of dedication and perseverance is revealed in the film when, shortly after their first meal in America, the brothers head to the local concert hall to begin networking into the business. It is also apparent when César says, "a shrimp that sleeps gets carried away in a cocktail." This quote summarizes the energy and drive one needs in order to follow his or her dreams and become successful in this new country, as it was for the many Cubans before and after them. It also betrays the dread of failure via laziness. Moreover, the fear of being devoured reflects the projection of post-immigration hunger for emotional and material goods.

The film depicts two brothers: César, the elder one, portrayed as assertive, brave, courageous, and physically strong; and Nestor, the younger one, portrayed as truly talented but with feminine qualities. There appears to be a close relationship between the two brothers from the very beginning of the film, where the elder one serves as protector of the other, while the younger one provides talent to the other. Upon immigrating to the United States, the younger one quietly writes the songs that would make him and his brother famous, while the elder one fights and navigates the turbulent waters of the music industry to make them financially successful. The closeness of the two siblings is symbiotic and reminiscent of what Ainslie (1997) has termed "psychological twinship." This, of course, has to come to an end. Fascinatingly, it is the younger sibling who initiates such separation. The older one is not able to be psychologically independent and pretty much "needs" his brother to die in order to break free and embark on his own path.

But why are they so close? We are left wondering since little information about their parents and their formative childhood years is available to us. Any reconstruction, in the absence of such data, is bound to be spurious. What we do know is that women who came between them invariably became a problem for the sibling symbiosis. Maria's love led César to pull Nestor close to himself. Delores took Nestor away but not without César trying to snatch her from him. And, finally, Nestor dies while in the company of César and his girlfriend. What is going on here? What is threatened by these women? An unspoken homosexual bond between the brothers, dare we suggest? Could the subtle masculine-feminine hues of their characters stand for unconscious "top" and "bottom" homosexual positions? One also wonders if the enemy of Nestor, whom Maria married, and César represent the positive and negative oedipal father images for Nestor. One takes his woman away, the other takes him away from the woman. Conceptualized this way, César turns out to be the father of Nestor's negative oedipal complex.

The experience of immigrating and adapting to the United States is also different for the two brothers. The elder one, César, demonstrates more manic defense against the transition and is portrayed as happy, constantly busy, seeking out success through fame and encounters with women. He appears to have no attachments and is in full acceptance of this change. Meanwhile, the younger one, Nestor, continues to ruminate about the loss of his fiancée and his native Cuba. Many times he says throughout the film, "Let's go back to Cuba," in a manner that reveals how he is unable to let go of his motherland (i.e. mother, Maria). Both brothers, in their own way, deal with the mourning of migrating from Cuba.

Mambo Kings is a powerful testimony to the complexity of the sibling bond with all its affectionate glory, hostile rivalry, and not infrequent erotic undertones. It also displays how oedipal themes can be enacted within the sibling relationship and how what appears to be a symbiotic tie is actually a defense against powerful but repressed aggression within the dyad. The theme of immigration adds color to these relational scenarios with the manic energy of denial constantly clashing with wistful homesickness.

SYNTHESIS AND CONCLUSION

Our discussion of these three movies has made it clear that developmentally ubiquitous and intrapsychically unique conflicts often get conflated with challenges posed by immigration. Regardless of whether it is the mother-child bond (*Entre Nos*), the adolescent passage (*Quinceñeara*), or the complex relationship between siblings (*Mambo Kings*), the psychic reality adds nuance to the external reality, and vice versa. The regressive and progressive shifts typical of developmental epochs fuel the oscillation of belonging and alienation in the setting of immigration. Physical accoutrements can often contain, symbolize, and help express these conflicts (Akhtar, 2003). In the three movies under consideration, for instance, inanimate objects that have wheels and move play a very significant role. In *Entre Nos*, a shopping cart becomes the source of the family's survival (they collect and carry cans to recycle in it). In *Quinceñeara*, a similar shopping cart is used by Tomás to sell food; moreover, the Hummer limousine serves as the ultimate symbol of having "arrived" (i.e., having become successful) in the new country. In *Mambo Kings*, it is the large Greyhound bus that carries César and Nestor from the airport to their relatives' home in New York City. All these moving objects symbolize the sojourn of migration as well as the transition from one developmental stage of life to another.

Another element common to these movies (and others of this ilk) is the frequent depiction of food. Now, we know that for immigrants

> food takes on special relevance because it symbolizes the earliest structured link with the mother or mother's breast. Thus, the immigrant may vehemently reject the new country's local dishes and nostalgically seek out foods of his own country. . . . The immigrant may also take refuge in food to ease his anxiety, thus recreating an idealized breast that is generous and inexhaustible, with which he tries to compensate for the many losses incurred during the move. (Grinberg and Grinberg, 1989, 79)

It should also be noted that such "ethnic food," when eaten with gusto in the company of co-nationals, also serves as a memory rite that is highly nourishing for the immigrant. It rekindles good internal objects from the past.

This brings up the importance of family ties which is powerfully endorsed by all three movies. In *Entre Nos*, it is maternal love that keeps things together and becomes the agent of the family's survival. In *Quinceñeara*, it is the older uncle who brings the "exiled" children together during his life and causes the entire family to unite in his death. In *Mambo Kings*, the siblings hold and support each other throughout life even when they compete and fight against each other. In all three movies, redemption from intrapsychic conflict and survival in the face of actual hardship comes from the love and support of the family unit. This unmasks the hollowness of the political right wing's assertion that immigrants have a negative impact upon family values in America. To be sure, the family structure is in trouble here. However, the roots of such breakdown are to be found in the disruptive nature of capitalism which creates false consumer needs, fuels human greed, pulls mothers prematurely away from their infants in order to earn money, lulls people to live their entire lives in debt, and puts a premium on material acquisitions at the cost of family cohesion. The sexual revolution, the institution of no-fault divorce, the growing anomie of urban life, and the widely prevalent cynicism toward government have also contributed to the current cultural meltdown. And, these detrimental vectors have originated in the heart of the white Anglo-Saxon America; they are not brought to the shores of this nation by "Third World" immigrants.

The movies also make an ironical political comment upon the lives of poor immigrants in a rich country. The lure of wealth and success that draws immigrants to this country often does not pan out and even when stability is found, leaving one's home takes an emotional toll.

In presenting these movies and raising these points of discussion, it has been our hope that empathy with Hispanic immigrants would be enhanced. Our elucidation of the cutting pain of loss, the bittersweet sense of nostalgia, the fumbling tenderness of adaptation, and the challenges of leading a bicultural life is directed at both the Hispanic Americans and their non-Hispanic fellow citizens. For the former, encounters with these familiar scenarios might enhance their "mentalization" (Fonagy et al, 2002) and thus improve the ways of dealing with them. For the latter, encounters with these movies (and others like them) might open up vistas of knowledge and understanding of their immigrant brethren. For both groups, such enrichment can be of use at personal, interpersonal, and clinical levels.

SEVEN

Help-Seeking Behavior and Access to Mental Health Care

Félix E. Torres

The umbrella designation of "Latino" encompasses a large number of nationalities, with some overarching similarities—mainly the language origin—yet a myriad of differences. Application of DSM-IV criteria across cultural dimensions can be a daunting process without an adequate understanding of the patient's cultural background. An important caveat in DSM-IV reminds us that "a clinician who is unfamiliar with the nuances of an individual's cultural frame of reference may incorrectly judge as psychopathology those normal variations in behavior, belief, or experience that are particular to the individual's culture" (DSM-IV-TR, 2000). This is especially true when considering the Latino patient.

Latino culture is as varied as the wide-ranging distances from the hot Sonoran desert to the warm Caribbean beaches to the glaciers of Tierra del Fuego. While Latinos share a common language, national and regional differences exist. There are also variations in history, ancestry, heritage, race, ethnicity, beliefs, values, religion/spirituality, family dynamics, and cultural identity. An in-depth evaluation of the specific differences is beyond the scope of this chapter. The reader should nonetheless remember this fact when formulating a diagnosis and providing treatment to a Latino patient.

This chapter will discuss help-seeking behaviors within the Latino population, with a focus on culture-bound syndromes, as well as challenges in the access to mental health care. I will draw from my experience as a psychiatrist in a predominantly Latino neighborhood in New York City and, through clinical vignettes,[1] share my perspective and recommendations for improved delivery of mental health care for Latinos.

HELP-SEEKING BEHAVIORS

Latinos may often be misdiagnosed due to a lack of understanding about certain cultural aspects that may influence their help-seeking behavior. The significant difference in the degree and style of emotional expression between Latino and mainstream American cultures may lead a clinician to qualify a behavior as dramatic or exaggerated (Laria and Lewis-Fernandez, 2006) with the potential detriment of misjudging the presentation and depriving the individual of adequate mental health care. This section describes help-seeking behaviors within the Latino population, including culture-bound syndromes, somatization, misuse and/or abuse of drugs and alcohol, suicidal behavior, and disability-seeking behavior, and provides clinical management recommendations.

Culture-Bound Syndromes

Important in the diagnostic formulation of the Latino patient is the acknowledgment of certain culture-bound syndromes, which may or may not correlate with mental disorders but could nonetheless cause significant distress. Appendix I of DSM-IV-TR describes culture-bound syndromes as "recurrent, locality-specific patterns of aberrant behavior and troubling experience that may or may not be linked to a particular DSM-IV diagnostic category" (898). Culture-bound syndromes experienced by Latinos include: *ataque de nervios* (nervous attack), *desmayo* (falling out or blacking out), *bilis* or *cólera* (rage), *mal de ojo* (evil eye), *brujería* (witchcraft), and *susto* or *espanto* (fright or terror).

The following clinical vignettes help illustrate these culture-bound syndromes:

Ataque de Nervios

Ana, a forty-five-year-old Nuyorican woman, was calmly sitting in her living room when she received a call from a cousin informing her of her brother's death in a motor vehicle accident. Her husband rushed from

> the bedroom after he heard her scream in agony. He found her crying, aimlessly pacing back and forth, shouting, pulling her hair, and hitting her chest complaining of "dying of a heart attack." She suddenly collapsed. The emergency response team found her on the floor, unresponsive, with no major abnormalities in her vital signs. "It is as if she is sound asleep," one of the paramedics remarked. Ana "woke up" as she was being wheeled into the emergency room with no recollection of the events during her *ataque*. She has no known history of mental illness.

Ataque de nervios are characterized by a sense of being out of control. The individual usually returns to the baseline level of functioning, at times with amnesia about the aberrant behavior. While there may be many similarities with a panic attack, these events usually occur as a reaction to a specific stressor and individuals who suffer them rarely experience the classic fear or concern about having additional attacks (as seen with panic disorder) (DSM 899).

Desmayo

> Gloria, a fifty-two-year-old Argentinean woman, suddenly feels dizzy and complains of "a foggy feeling in my head." Her daughter comes to her aid as Gloria plummets to the floor. She repeatedly moans, "I'm blind, I'm blind," while gazing from side to side with her eyes wide open. Her arms fall flaccidly to the floor as her daughter attempts to sit her up. She appears unable to follow commands despite being able to hear. Within minutes, Gloria slowly regains her motor abilities and her vision returns albeit initially "blurry." She is transferred to the emergency room where full cardiac and metabolic work-ups are unremarkable. Brain imaging shows no intracranial pathology. The daughter tells the emergency room physician that her mother "has been going through a lot recently" due to marital problems. She would like for her mother to "start seeing someone." Gloria is referred to the local mental health clinic.

A medical work-up in this situation is essential as the etiology of Gloria's syncopal episode may be as innocuous as a vasovagal event or as serious as hypoglycemia, seizure activity, or cardiopathy, amongst other medical conditions. Only after a thorough work-up is completed and medical causes are ruled out should a psychological process be considered.

Ataque de nervios and *desmayos* may be a call for help or an effort to engage family members or those in the individual's surroundings to provide support during an overwhelming situation (Laria et al, 2006). While the clinician should not readily pathologize the behavior, it is important to acknowledge that individuals with similar presentations may have, or may be more susceptible to, mood, anxiety, somatoform, conversion, or dissociative disorders. An in-session analysis of precipitating and/or contributing events may guide the psychotherapeutic intervention, providing an understanding of the individual's level of frustration tolerance with the goal of strengthening coping skills.

Bilis and *Cólera*

> Manuel is a twenty-eight-year-old Nicaraguan man, domiciled with his mother, with no psychiatric or substance abuse history, who was referred by the mother due to irritability and frequent anger outbursts. He immigrated to the United States as a legal resident three years ago. His grandparents raised him after his mother came first to New York when he was nine years old. Manuel's "anger problems" have been occurring since his arrival in New York City. There is significant resentment towards his mother for having left him in Nicaragua. They only had weekly telephone contact for the sixteen years they were apart "until one day my papers came through and within two weeks I was on a plane here." Manuel feels he has never had a relationship with his mother who now "easily gets on my nerves." He becomes angry and verbally abusive towards her "out of nowhere." While he denies physical abuse, he has been known to escalate on several occasions, throwing things around the apartment and breaking furniture.
>
> Interview yields no evidence of depression, anxiety, psychosis, obsessions/compulsions, or substance abuse. Manuel denies any major dysfunction outside of his unexplainable *cólera*. He states, "It is as if something comes over me and I cannot control myself." Manuel feels physically exhausted after each episode and sometimes has to "sleep it off until the next day."

The terms *bilis* and *cólera* are rooted in ancient Hippocratic medicine and the concept of humors, which in turn is closely related to the theory of the four elements. For a Latino patient, an increase in *bilis* (or bile) is similar to the excess of the yellow bile humor (*chole* in Greek) and the element of fire. The choleric temperament describes an individual with bad temper, who is easily angered and may be prone to mood swings and aggression.

Although not necessarily pathognomonic of a particular DSM-IV disorder, *cólera* may occur in individuals with mood, anxiety, impulse control, or personality disorders. An individual suffering from these episodes of rage would benefit from both individual therapy and anger management groups. The individual therapy should focus on identifying the sources of anger and the underlying triggers and feelings. It can also provide instruction on relaxation techniques such as biofeedback and deep-breathing exercises. Groups may supplement individual sessions with the goal of learning effective anger management techniques in a supportive peer environment.

Mal de Ojo and *Brujería*

> Maria, a sixty-one-year-old Puerto Rican woman, brings her two-year-old granddaughter to the emergency room due to vomiting and diarrhea. She tells the emergency room physician that her neighbor's sister came to her house to visit the girl and gave her *mal de ojo*. While the child was playing on the floor, "the lady gave her a compliment and her *manita de azabache* instantly burst into pieces." Maria already took the girl to the *espiritista* in her *barrio*. She is hoping the doctor would give the child something for the vomiting until "the herbs kick in and the curse is lifted." The girl is actually severely dehydrated and needs to be admitted to the hospital for intravenous hydration.

The concept of the "evil eye" is present in many cultures throughout the world. Children are thought to be most susceptible to these evil forces believed to cause bad luck, disease, and even death. Evil eye is most often attributed to excessive admiration or envy and may be cast onto a person without express malice or knowledge. Amulets, like the *mano de azabache* (or jet claw) bracelet and other charms, may serve as protection against *mal de ojo*. Having the admirer touch the child is also believed to instantly prevent the *mal de ojo* from being cast. Adults may also fall victim to *mal de ojo* and, consequently, attribute their psychiatric symptoms to this supernatural force.

Unlike *mal de ojo*, *brujería* (or witchcraft) is generally believed to be an intentional hex on the person. Described under the heading of *rootwork* in Appendix I of DSM-IV, "symptoms may include generalized anxiety and gastrointestinal complaints, weakness, dizziness, the fear of being poisoned, and sometimes fear of being killed" (902). Removal of the spell usually requires the intervention of a healer.

In Latino mental health, it is important to assess an individual's cultural beliefs, including those about *mal de ojo* and *brujería*. Access to mental health care may be delayed, even in the presence of severe psychopathology, if the symptoms are attributed to either of these forces. Even when mental health treatment is sought, compliance may be affected by outside influences: seeking the assistance of *curanderos* (folk healers) or *espiritistas* (spiritual healers) and potential interactions with herbal remedies. The clinician should always ask the patient and/or family members what they believe to be the cause of the symptoms. When *mal de ojo* or *brujería* are suspected, a non-judgmental conversation needs to follow, addressing the person's spiritual beliefs, not necessarily dispelling, but rather attempting to incorporate them in a "multi-disciplinary" approach. As a result, the patient will be more open to discuss aspects of the "outside treatment" which may hinder improvement and even interact with the recommended management. A complete list of medications, including "natural" and herbal remedies needs to be obtained. Finally, the clinician should not underestimate the supportive nature of the patient-healer relationship, the presence of a therapeutic alliance with the healer, or the power of a spirituality-driven placebo effect.

Susto

Julio is a thirty-year-old Mexican man, with a long-standing history of anxiety, recent onset of mood symptoms, no formal psychiatric treatment, no history of substance abuse, and unremarkable medical history. His primary-care physician was originally managing his symptoms with a selective serotonin reuptake inhibitor (SSRI) but now refers him to the community mental health clinic due to unremitting anxiety and depression over the past 4 months. Julio reports a history of anxiety "for as long as I can remember."

He appears highly impressionable. Most recent increase in symptoms coincides with listening to an Internet radio broadcast about a demonic possession that occurred on Christmas day. Since that time, he has been thinking about "the power of the Devil" on a daily basis. He constantly worries about his family, harm coming unto them, and being "a good Catholic." A previous "bad episode" occurred back in 2001 when his friends dared him to walk through the cemetery at midnight.

Julio's symptoms include ruminative thoughts with religious themes, muscle tension, fatigue, poor concentration, irritability, sleep difficulties, depressed mood, low energy level, decreased motivation, lack of appetite (with a quantified 18-lb weight loss), feelings of helplessness, and social isolation. He denies panic attacks or obsessions/compulsions. He adamantly denies a history of depression prior to this *susto*. He admits he has not been taking the medication prescribed by his physician because "nothing can help me until my soul comes back into my body."

Support, reassurance and psychoeducation were provided. Julio agreed to take the medication "to help me deal with the situation." He returned to the clinic three weeks later reporting a mild improvement in mood and anxiety symptoms. He states, "I feel calmer and can think more clearly."

Susto or *espanto* (fright or terror) is described as a loss of the soul following a frightening event. The individual suffering *susto* may experience symptoms of depression, anxiety and somatic complaints. The presentation may be consistent with a mood disorder, acute or posttraumatic stress disorder, and other anxiety or somatoform disorders. Similar to *mal de ojo* and *brujería*, the afflicted individual may seek the help of a healer to pull the soul back into the body and restore the balance (DSM, 903). In Julio's case, symptomatology is consistent with generalized anxiety and major depressive disorders, both of which responded well to an SSRI. Once active symptoms lessened, therapy could focus on psychoeducation, exploration of contributing stressors and negative schemata, and positive coping skills training.

Somatization

Somatization is the expression of psychological distress by means of unexplained physical symptoms (Lipowski, 1988). Present across various cultures, the process is common in the Latino population (Escobar, 1987). The patient usually seeks medical treatment for different physical ailments. It is not until several rounds of diagnostic work-ups have been completed that the individual is referred to mental health treatment for symptoms "of unknown medical etiology." In psychodynamic theory, somatization is considered an immature or primitive defense. It is regarded as a transformation of psychic pain and distress into bodily complaints as a means to defend against psychological instability. Recent research has nevertheless demonstrated a growing acceptance and validity to both psychological and somatic expressions of psychic distress (USDHHS, 2001).

Empathy and validation of the individual's physical complaints are important during the initiation of treatment (Kirmayer, 1991). By the time the individual comes into contact with the mental health provider, he/she may have grown frustrated after several office visits and tests with no remarkable findings. The patient is likely to be sensitive to rejection, prone to pick up on judgmental cues from the provider, and promptly move on to the next treater in the hopes of finding a resolution to the complaints, yet perpetuating the cycle and prolonging the suffering. Along with support and reassurance, empathic validation can provide the foundation for a meaningful and long-lasting therapeutic alliance. Once engaged in treatment, somatic symptoms that occur in the context of a mood or an anxiety disorder often diminish when the primary psychiatric disorder is managed. A cognitive behavioral therapy approach may then assist in the identification of psychological distress, the development of adaptive coping strategies, and the modification of maladaptive responses and the ensuing somatic complaints.

Suicide Attempts and Parasuicidal Gestures

According to the latest data available from the Centers for Disease Control and Prevention (CDC), suicide ranked as the tenth leading cause of death in 1999 among persons ages 10 years and older, accounting for 36,891 deaths. It was the third leading cause of death among teenagers and young adults (ages 15–24) and the second cause of death in the 25–34 age group. As an ethnic group, Hispanics[2] had the second lowest suicide rate at 5.3 per 100,000 population when compared to Non-Hispanic Whites (13.5), American Indian/Alaskan Natives (12.3), Asian/Pacific Islanders (6.3), and Non-Hispanic Blacks (5.1). While at first glance, these statistics may be reassuring, it should be noted that Latinos attempt suicide with a higher frequency than other ethnic groups, at least in the high school population.

The 2011 Youth Risk Behavior Survey (YRBS) conducted by the CDC was a nationally representative sample of students in grades 9–12 who attended public and private schools. The findings, published in the Youth Risk Behavior Surveillance Summary, show more alarming trends:

- The prevalence of having made a suicide plan was higher among Hispanic (14.3 percent) than White (12.1 percent) and Black (11.1 percent) students.
- The prevalence of having attempted suicide was higher among Hispanic (10.2 percent) than Black (8.3 percent) and White (6.2 percent) students.
- The prevalence of having made a suicide attempt that resulted in an injury, poisoning, or overdose that had to be treated by a doctor or nurse was higher among Hispanic (3.2 percent) than White (1.9 percent) students.

While further studies are needed to generalize these findings to other Latino age groups, anecdotal evidence is consistent with higher rates of suicidal ideation, parasuicidal gestures, and suicide attempts in Latino patients. Self-injurious behavior, like with any other culture, should be taken seriously. The clinician should conduct a complete evaluation with the goal of identifying risk and protective factors, distinguishing static from modifiable risk factors, determining the level of suicide risk, and devising a safety plan. As an individual's risk of self-harm is dynamic, risk assessment should be revisited throughout treatment, as deemed clinically appropriate. A distinction should also be made between the suicidal individual's intent and the lethality of the means used. As defined in the American Psychiatric Association's *Practice Guideline for the Assessment and Treatment of Patients with Suicidal Behaviors* (2003), intent is the "subjective expectation and desire for a self-destructive act to end in death" (p. 9), whereas lethality is the "objective danger to life associated with a suicide method or action" (p. 10). While the lethality of cutting one's wrist may be considerably less than a substantial overdose on a tricyclic antidepressant, the patient's intent to die may be the same or higher.

Research on the efficacy of psychotherapeutic interventions on suicidal behavior is sparse but "clinical consensus suggests that psychosocial interventions and specific psychotherapeutic approaches are of benefit to the suicidal patient" (APA, 2003, p. 10). Regardless of theoretical school of thought or therapeutic approach utilized, a positive and meaningful therapeutic alliance is paramount and may serve as a protective factor against suicidal behavior.

Alcohol and Substance Use

Substance use is highly prevalent among individuals with mental illness. The 2010 National Survey on Drug Use and Health (SAMHSA, 2012) found 4.3 percent of Hispanics in the United States experienced a co-occurring mental illness and substance abuse disorder, a rate similar to non-Hispanic Whites and Blacks. While rates of lifetime illicit drug and alcohol use were lower among Hispanic adults as compared to the national averages, the rate of past month alcohol binge was highest in the Hispanic population (SAMHSA, 2012). The evaluation of alcohol and substance use is an important component of a thorough psychological/psychiatric assessment. Substance and alcohol use may result in substance-induced disorders whereas primary psychiatric disorders may lead to misuse, abuse and/or dependence of certain substances or alcohol as a means to self-medicate symptoms.

Factors that influence substance use in the Latino population include younger age, single marital status, lower education, unemployment, and undocumented immigration status (Alvarez et al., 2007). "*Ahogar las penas*" (to drown one's sorrows in an alcohol binge) may become a maladaptive coping mechanism to deal with these psychosocial stressors. Education about the harmful effects of substance use, including medical and psychological consequences, is important but a discussion about the positive and negative aspects of the alcohol and substance use should drive the intervention. The individual may be drinking as a means to relieve stress or improve mood or may be smoking marijuana as a way to quiet the voices or slow down the mania. Without a good understanding of these motivations, treatment may be jeopardized by continued substance use, sporadic compliance with psychotropic medications during binges, and premature termination of care.

Disability-Seeking Behavior

Latino patients, similar to other ethnic groups, may seek mental health treatment with the purpose of obtaining disability benefits. The patient's prompt arrival at the first assessment session with the thick manila envelope full of disability forms should not detract the clinician from performing a complete evaluation. While the possibility of malingering and symptom amplification needs to be considered, so should the likelihood of the patient having a legitimate mental illness. DSM-IV-TR (2000) recommends malingering should be suspected if any combination of the following is present: (1) medico-legal context of presentation, (2) substantial discrepancy between the claimed stress or disability and the objective findings, (3) lack of cooperation during the evaluation and poor compliance with recommended treatments, and (4) the presence of Antisocial Personality Disorder. Even when malingering is deemed present, the individual's motivation for seeking disability needs to be explored. The clinician must remember that symptom amplification and/or malingering may occur in someone with legitimate symptomatology and whose disability-seeking behavior may represent an adaptation or coping mechanism to deal with the illness. Dismissing a patient's complaint as a direct product of the apparent (or obvious) secondary gain may lead to an undiagnosed mental illness that would in turn remain untreated (i.e., a mood, anxiety, or somatoform disorder). Exploration may also uncover a factitious disorder, wherein the individual assumes the sick role with internal incentives such as attention-seeking, sympathy, nurturance, reassurance, or dependency. If a psychiatric disorder is identified, attempts should be made to engage the individual in treatment. The clinician should inform the patient about a requirement for an adequate amount of time in treatment for a clinical determination to be made (e.g., 4–6 months with treatment compliance to determine response and prognosis). That time should be used to effectively treat the patient, provide psychoeducation about the illness, further explore the patient's motivation for seeking disability (or other identified secondary gain), determine the level of commitment to treatment, improve insight, and strengthen coping skills, self-image and self-esteem.

There may be circumstances when this is not possible. The following vignette illustrates this situation:

"Just in Case"

Rodrigo was a fifty-two-year-old Cuban man, unemployed, receiving Supplemental Security Income (SSI) benefits for "my nerves and my back," with remote history of depression, alcohol dependence with reported sobriety for the past two years, and no prior psychiatric hospitalizations or suicide attempts, who returned to the mental health clinic "to re-open my case." Rodrigo reported a remote history of mood symptoms characterized by depression, low self-esteem, crying spells, feelings of helplessness, irritability, poor appetite, and social isolation. Symptoms preceded alcohol use and worsened as the use became excessive. He gladly reported sobriety from alcohol and being psychiatrically stable for over two years.

He was last exposed to antidepressant medications five years ago. During his last period in treatment, he was poorly compliant with therapy sessions. He attended ten sessions over a span of eighteen months. Rodrigo denied any current or recent problems with depression, sleep, appetite, feelings of hopelessness, or suicidal ideation. He denied any functional impairment. Upon further inquiry, Rodrigo reported returning to the clinic because he was concerned his SSI would be cut off if he did not attend treatment. He recently received a notice for a Continuing Disability Review from the Social Security Administration.

Rodrigo was not open to the possibility of engaging in treatment to further explore his motivations, was not interested in therapy, did not warrant psychotropic intervention, and wanted "my case to be open just in case." He was educated about misuse of psychiatric services. He was welcome to return to the clinic in the event of resurgence of mood symptoms or relapse on alcohol.

CHALLENGES TO ACCESSING MENTAL HEALTH CARE

Latinos are the largest and fastest growing ethnic minority group in the United States. While having a rate of mental illness similar to Whites, Latinos are less likely to receive mental health care. Latinos confront many barriers in their access to mental health care, including stigma about mental illness, inappropriateness of services, language barrier, shortage of Spanish-speaking and/or culturally competent[3] providers, poverty, lack of health insurance, and undocumented immigration status, among other influences. This section examines some of the challenges in the access and provision of mental health care for Latino patients.

Stigma

Some Latinos may fear "*locura*" (literally translated to craziness or lunacy) more than death. The stigma behind mental illness is the biggest challenge to overcome when treating Latino individuals. Social stigma has and will continue to be present despite continued efforts to educate the population about mental illness. Stigma takes on many forms, from discrimination and stereotyping to fear and abuse. At the individual's level, self-stigma, largely driven by societal influences, also has considerable significance within the Latino culture: it is a major obstacle to the access of mental health care as well as to the adherence and compliance once in treatment. Individuals may equate mental illness to inadequacy, shame, weakness, or the inability to take care of themselves or control their feelings. The following vignette highlights this process:

"Psychiatrists Are for 'Locos'"

Carmen, a fifty-eight-year-old Dominican woman, returned to the local mental health clinic for the seventh time in the past ten years. She was severely depressed, with significant decrease in the level of functioning, loss of energy, insomnia, ruminative thoughts about her children's problems, and feelings of helplessness/guilt for "not being able to do more for my children." She stopped caring about her hygiene and appeared slightly disheveled. She was brought to the clinic by her children who also report she has been "talking to herself."

Carmen's current presentation is similar to previous episodes. She was diagnosed with major depressive disorder, recurrent, severe with psychotic features. She does not meet criteria for involuntary commitment as she is not deemed a danger to herself or others and has the support of her family to care for her activities of daily living. Carmen was started on an antidepressant and a low-dose atypical antipsychotic medication and was assigned a Spanish-speaking therapist.

Within three months, Carmen was doing much better. She resumed caring for her grandchildren after school and her own children were no longer bringing her to the clinic. Attendance began to falter and she missed many appointments. The issue was addressed in session. Carmen felt she was back to normal and no longer in need of treatment. She stated, "I am not crazy. Psychiatrists are for 'locos.' I could have dealt with everything on my own but my children forced me to come here." Carmen failed to return for follow-up appointments. She did not respond to several telephone and mail outreach attempts. The case was terminated due to non-compliance.

The Latino patient may regard mental illness as a sign of weakness. It is not uncommon for patients to seek treatment at the height of psychiatric symptoms, usually at the behest of family members who become increasingly concerned about, or can no longer manage, the behavior. Education is paramount. Without the appropriate psychoeducation, patients may continue the pattern of treatment recidivism, lowering her baseline level of functioning with subsequent decompensations. At the beginning of treatment, and with the patient's consent, it is extremely important to engage available members within the patient's support network as allies in the treatment. They may assist with improving treatment compliance, dispense medications, remind client about appointments, and provide progress reports to the clinician. Identified allies should be educated about the nature of the illness, debunking any stigma along the way and highlighting the importance of treatment compliance.

Once the acuity of symptoms has subsided and the patient is clinically suited to tolerate a psychotherapeutic intervention, significant efforts should be made to educate the patient. Clinicians should use the patient's medical history to their advantage, as it would not be uncommon for the Latino patient to have at least one chronic medical illness: hypertension, hypercholesterolemia, diabetes, heart disease, hypothyroidism, and so on. Granted, compliance with the medical treatments for these conditions may also be poor, but Latino patients may be more readily open to discuss their "medical problems" than their mental problems. Mental illness could be likened to one of their chronic medical illnesses. Patients should be educated about mental illness being a medical condition, just like their diabetes or high blood pressure, and should not be regarded a sign of weakness, a punishment for past misdoings or a challenge imposed by a higher being. Just like they would not stop their high blood pressure medication abruptly because "my pressure will get really high and I can have a heart attack," their psychiatric treatment or psychotherapy should not be discontinued without consultation with their provider. A good therapeutic relationship will enhance the likelihood that such a conversation will occur.

For the Latino patient, the onset or recurrence of mental illness may also be seen as an opportunity to renew one's faith and devotion or to reengage in abandoned practices (i.e. attending church, praying, performing good deeds). Some individuals may seek the help of clergy rather than a psychiatrist. I am always reminded of the client who, during our initiation sessions, would mistakenly call me "Padre," after the many years that her parish priest had served the role of a therapist. The patient's spiritual beliefs and the significance of any religious practices should be explored and incorporated into the patient's treatment as elements of culturally competent care.

APPROPRIATENESS OF MENTAL HEALTH SERVICES

Latinos tend to be overrepresented in emergency rooms, psychiatric inpatient units and general medical clinics while underrepresented in the mental health outpatient setting (SG, 2). It is general knowledge that primary care physicians are the number one providers of antidepressant medications in the United States and a primary target of pharmaceutical representatives in their marketing detailing and sampling efforts. This is a great benefit to the Latino patient, who may have limited financial resources, no mental health coverage, and is already engaged in primary care for the management of medical conditions. On the other hand, the patient may be deprived of a more comprehensive mental health treatment to include specialized psychiatric care and individual/group psychotherapy. Referral to a mental health facility may at times be delayed until symptoms become unmanageable and the level of functioning is severely affected.

Even when a patient is referred to specialized mental health services, the provision of care may be affected by the language barrier and a dearth of Spanish-speaking and/or culturally competent providers. No national data exist indicating the language skills of mental health providers in the United States (SG, 2) but a 1999 survey by the Center for Mental Health Services (2000) found there were 29 Latino mental health professionals for every 100,000 Latinos in the population (compared to 173 White providers per 100,000). While the use of interpreters (in person or through telephone language lines) may satisfy administrative demands, translation by individuals lacking interpreter training, mental health knowledge, or cultural competence raises critical ethical issues in the delivery of mental health care to Latino patients. Efforts should be made to promote employment of Spanish-speaking providers, train in-house interpreters, decrease the use of language lines (which are not only costly but impersonal), incorporate telepsychiatry with a Latino provider as an alternative, and implement Latino-oriented services and programs.

Despite our best efforts, a patient's lack of improvement may require a higher level of care as illustrated in this case:

"Natural Remedies"

Angel is a twenty-seven-year-old Venezuelan man with schizoaffective disorder. He was a high-functioning sophomore in college when psychotic symptoms began to surface. Angel's treatment compliance has been problematic throughout his management. Insight into the importance of adequate mental health follow-up is impaired despite recurrent psychiatric deterioration and hospitalizations. During his last visit at the clinic, he broached the topic of discontinuing his medications. He stated he had been thinking about "natural remedies." When asked to be more specific about the type of remedies he replied, "Nothing definite yet. I am just doing my research."

I educated Angel about his illness and the need for continued long-term treatment. I got him to acknowledge the intensity of symptoms and degree of dysfunction when he was unmedicated. While I agreed the ultimate decision was within his power, I explained his choice would be against medical advice and strongly encouraged him to remain on medications. Angel dropped out of treatment after that visit, failed to respond to outreach attempts, and could not be located by a mobile crisis team. He ended up hospitalized within two months due to an episode of psychotic mania. After a long hospitalization, he was discharged to an Assertive Community Treatment team (ACT) with an Assisted Outpatient Treatment (AOT) order granted by a judge (outpatient civil commitment). Angel has been stable over the past eight months. He has enrolled at a local community college and is taking some remedial courses. ACT providers are ready to discharge him back to our outpatient mental health clinic.

Accessibility of Mental Health Services

Latinos face major obstacles in the accessibility of mental health care. Lack of insurance, limited financial resources, incomes below the poverty line, unemployment, and undocumented immigration status may deter patients from seeking care. Undocumented individuals may not engage in mental health treatment for fears of deportation or provider mistrust. Trust issues should be addressed early in the process to reassure undocumented patients that the services are provided free of bias and regardless of their immigration status. The availability of sliding scale fee schedules, based on the patient's income, and referral to medication assistance programs or pharmacies with low-cost generic formularies may decrease the financial burden on the patient, increase the likelihood of treatment retention, and improve treatment outcomes.

CONCLUSION

Latinos represent the largest and fastest growing minority group in the United States. Unified by a common language, Latinos are a heterogeneous group with significant variations in their history, heritage, ethnicity, and beliefs. Understanding culture-bound syndromes and other help-seeking behaviors within the Latino community is important for the delivery of culturally competent mental health care. The clinician should also appreciate the power of mental health stigma, the social challenges in the access to care, the influence and importance of engaging the patient's support network, and the significance of psychoeducation in the treatment of the Latino patient.

NOTES

1. Clinical vignettes derive from my direct patient care. Age, gender, and other demographic information have been changed to protect the patient's identity.
2. The term Hispanic is used by the United States Office of Management and Budget as an ethnicity and may apply to a person of any race. It is one of four recognized racial and ethnic minority groups in the United States: African Americans (Blacks), American Indian/Alaskan Natives, Asian/Pacific Islanders, and Hispanics (Latinos). These categories were developed for the collection of information by Federal agencies (USDHHS, 2001).
3. Cultural competence is defined by the Center for Mental Health Services as "a set of values, behaviors, attitudes, and practices within a system, organization, program, or among individuals that enables people to work effectively across cultures. It refers to the ability to honor and respect the beliefs, language, interpersonal styles, and behaviors of individuals and families receiving services, as well as staff who are providing such services. Cultural competence is a dynamic, ongoing, developmental process that requires a long-term commitment and is achieved over time" (USDHHS, 2003).

EIGHT

Mental Health and Psychosocial Risks in Latino Youth

Andres J. Pumariega, Consuelo Cagande, and Eugenio Rothe

Latinos are the largest minority group and the second fastest growing segment of the population of the United States (after Asian Americans). The Latino population in the United States currently numbers approximately 50.5 million and comprises 16 percent of the total population. It is expected to reach a total of over 100 million by 2050, and many states (Texas and California chiefly amongst them) are shortly about to become majority Latino. Latinos account for over half the population growth in the United States, and the Latino growth rate from the 2000 to 2010 census (43 percent) is over four times that of the general population (10 percent). The majority of Latinos (64 percent) are Mexican American, while the rest are comprised of (in order of population) Puerto Ricans, Dominicans, Cubans, Central Americans, and South Americans (US Census Bureau, 2011). Latinos are growing at such a high rate both as a result of both a higher birth rate and high rates of immigration. The United States accepts the highest percentage of immigrants and refugees of any nation on earth. The total number of immigrants in the United States is estimated at 50 million, with 1.1 million immigrants and refugees entering annually. Approximately 54.6 percent are from Latin America. Approximately 800,000 to 1.2 million undocumented immigrants enter the United States annually, with a net increase of 400,000 to 700,000, once those exiting return to their home nations. An estimated total of 8 to 12 million undocumented immigrants currently live in the United States, with most originally from Latin America (US Census Bureau, 2012).

The significance of the Latino population to the future of the United States cannot be underestimated. The Latino population is providing a significant percentage of future adults in this nation, so the future of the United States hinges on it. At the same time, this population faces mental health and psychosocial challenges that can affect their future adaptation and success. In this chapter, we will discuss key mental health and psychosocial challenges that US Latino youth face, particularly depression, suicidality, substance abuse, and teen pregnancy. We will examine key cultural factors that contribute to these challenges, and possible approaches to address them effectively.

ACCULTURATION AND ACCULTURATIVE STRESS

Acculturation stress is the adverse effect of psychological conflict resulting from the process of acculturation, apart from the physical health and lifestyle effects of acculturation (Berry, 1997). This results from internal conflicts over cultural values (for example, between achievement versus family relations and family loyalty), pressure to assimilate to avoid discrimination and margination, the loss of natural protective beliefs and values, the loss of extended family and kinship social support, especially moving to an individualistic orientation from a family and collective orientation), and strains over changing roles (gender, relational, etc.).

A number of early studies have found associations between higher acculturation/assimilation and risk for psychopathology amongst the children of immigrants. These studies not only support the findings of higher level of mental health problems in second generation immigrants, but also clarify the processes through which these generational disparities arise. Pumariega and associates (1992) found that second generation status, depression, male gender, cultural factors (lack of family cohesion, unsupervised time with friends, no religious ties, media exposure), and school problems were predictors of higher risk of substance abuse amongst Latino youth living along the US-Mexico border. Pumariega and associates (2012) similarly found cultural factors (lack of family cohesion, media exposure, non-supervised time with friends, no religious ties) associated with higher suicidal ideation amongst Latino youth along the

US-Mexico border, but not actual attempts. The findings around suicidality in many ways predicted the higher levels of suicidality found amongst Latino youth in the YRBS (Eaton, et al., 2012). Dihn and associates (2002) found that problem (externalizing) behaviors in Latino youth increased with increased acculturation, with that relationship mediated by parental involvement.

Recent studies have further reinforced the relationship between acculturation stress and psychopathology among Latino youth. Romero and associates (2007) found that bicultural stress was higher for Latino and Asian origin youth, and that it was significantly associated with depressive symptoms after accounting for ethnicity, socioeconomic status, gender, and age. Cespedes and Huey (2008) found that Latina teens reported greater differences in traditional gender role beliefs between themselves and their parents than Latino males, and higher levels of depression mediated by increases in family dysfunction. Lower levels of ethnic identity have been correlated to substance abuse risk, acculturative stress and self-esteem in Latino youth (Zaboanga et al., 2009). Latino youth with higher English language fluency reported greater violence exposure and post-traumatic stress disorder (PTSD) symptoms than those with lower fluency, but no differences by English fluency (Kataoka, et al., 2009). Acculturative stress in Latino youth has been correlated to physiological, concentration, and worry symptoms of anxiety, with perceived discrimination accounting for a large proportion of the variance (Suarez-Morales and Lopez, 2009).

Recent literature has examined the potential role of acculturation in explaining birthrate and health disparities among Hispanic adolescents (Lara and Lewis-Fernandez, 2006). Later generation status appears to correspond with earlier initiation of sexual intercourse and lower rates of adolescent childbearing, while findings related to use of contraceptives are equivocal. Several studies of male and female adolescents (Ebin et al., 2001; Guilamo-Ramos et al., 2005) and of Latinas only (Aneshensel et al., 1990; Landale and Hauan, 1996; Jimenez, Potts, and Jimenez, 2002; Rafaelli, Zamboanga, and Carlo, 2005) report that US-born or second-and-higher generation Hispanic adolescents are more likely to become sexually active or report a history of sexual risk than first-generation adolescents. An analysis of the 1997–2003 National Longitudinal Survey of Youth found that fewer first-generation adolescents transitioned to sexual intercourse before age eighteen and fewer first- and second-generation sexually active teens used contraceptives consistently at age seventeen than third-generation teens. Language was similarly associated with the transition to sexual intercourse and contraceptive practices (greater transition with increased English fluency) (McDonald, Manlove, and Ikramullah, 2009).

A common source of acculturation stress is inter-generational cultural conflict, more recently termed *acculturative family distancing* (AFD). These conflicts are set up by the immigrant youth's greater cognitive flexibility, resulting in rapid assimilation into the host culture, especially their ready adoption of the new language, cultural norms, and particularly new expectations around family roles and limits. In these contexts, immigrant parents have slower adaptation to the new cultural milieu, particularly as a result of greater enculturation and social isolation, difficulty mastering the new language, and fears of new parenting role expectations and of their children's loss of their identification with the traditional culture (and consequently with their family). The conflicts between home and external community environments around cultural norms and values become acted out and these differences lead to inter-generational psychological conflicts. Acculturative family distancing has been reported amongst both Latino and Asian immigrant youth and families, and has been associated with increased risk for youth substance abuse and conduct problems (Szapocznik, Kurtines, and Fernandez, 1980; Portes and Rumbaut, 1996), and more recently, related to depression and anxiety (Hwang, 2006; Hwang and Wood, 2009; Chung, Flook, and Fuligni, 2009).

Sullivan and colleagues (2007) found that integrated Latino immigrant adolescents who maintain heritage culture practices and adopt receiving culture practices reported higher parental involvement, positive parenting, and family support, while assimilated adolescents reported greatest levels of aggressive behavior. Birman and Taylor-Ritzler (2007) found that family relationships mediated the impact of Russian immigrant youth's acculturation stress, in both directions. Martinez, McClure, and Eddy (2009) found that youth and families in high language brokering contexts showed higher levels of family stress, lower parenting effectiveness, poorer academic and emotional adjustment, and substance use in Latino immigrant youth. Trickett and Jones (2007) found that greater youth culture brokering linked to less parental acculturation and more family conflict in Vietnamese immigrants. These findings support concerns about the adverse psychological burdens of placing youth in the positions of being linguistic interpreters and cultural brokers for their less acculturated immigrant parents. Mena and associates (2008) and Zayas and colleagues (2010) found that extended parental separations in Latino immigrant youth are linked to problem behaviors, and separations from mothers are particularly linked to depressive symptoms and suicidality, especially for females.

Acculturative family distancing may also play an important role in Latino teen pregnancy and HIV risk. One of the most widely reported barriers to sexuality communication in Latino families is parental discomfort and embarrassment. Although the reasons *why* parents feel embarrassed are less well understood, some have theorized that generational and cultural differences unique to Latinos in the United States may be partially responsible. For example, many Latino parents were raised in families and cultures with limited to no family communication about sex and related issues. Some researchers also have noted that traditional cultural norms, such as *marianismo,* may encourage women to maintain a "sexual silence," and as a result Latina mothers feel particularly uncomfortable when talking to their children about sex (Flores, Eyre, and Millstein, 1998; Guilamo-Ramos, et al., 2006). Latino adolescents who report feeling close to their parents are less likely to initiate sex at an early age and are more likely to use contraception consistently and carefully (Velez-Prastana, Gonzalez-Rodriguez, and Borges-Hernandez, 2005). These factors obviously play a significant role in the prevention of HIV risk amongst Latino teens (Van Oss Marín, 2003).

FURTHER RISK FACTORS

Epidemiological studies on the mental health of immigrants have been consistent in demonstrating that first-generation adult immigrants have lower levels of identified psychopathology than the mainstream population and their children (Escobar and Vega, 2000; Oquendo et al., 2001). In analyses of data from the Epidemiological Catchment Area, individuals who were less acculturated were found to have a better mental health profile, those with moderate acculturation had medium levels of mental health, and more assimilated individuals had the worst mental health outcomes. Suicide was also less prevalent in the less acculturated group. The following hypotheses have been developed around these findings: a) first-generation immigrants are naturally selected to be a more resilient group, given their decision to emigrate against many odds, with the second generation being "softer" and less resilient; b) first-generation immigrants suppress their mental health needs in order to subsume them below their more basic and immediate needs for personal and material/economic security. Once the second generation is more comfortably established, they can then pay attention to pent-up mental health needs; c) the second generation may identify more readily with the devalued and denigrated concepts of their ethnic identity, adopted from the xenophobic attitudes of the host culture, which may lead to "ethnic self-hate" and higher risk for psychopathology (Escobar and Vega, 2000). However, a fourth hypothesis can be proposed, given the adverse effects of strains on family support for immigrant youth due to acculturative family distancing (AFD), and its impact on adolescent-family relations, supported by a growing body of literature (see below). Added to this fourth hypothesis, mental health services disparities compound these difficulties through delays in timely care and greater degree of acuity of mental health problems.

Additional risk to mental health comes from unplanned teen pregnancies, which put a burden on a young and often weak ego. Whether getting pregnant at a young age itself betrays psychopathology is debatable but the stress of raising a baby with little resources at hand is hardly questionable. Adolescent birth rates among Latinos in the United States are the highest of any racial/ethnic subgroup and have changed little since 2002 (Hamilton, Martin, and Ventura, 2007). More than half (54 percent) of Latina teen moms do not complete high school, compared to 34 percent of teen moms overall (Perper, Peterson, and Manlove, 2010). Of all Latinas who drop out of high school between their sophomore and senior year, 36 percent cite being pregnant or becoming a mother as a reason they dropped out (National Campaign to Prevent Teen and Unplanned Pregnancy, 2010). Additionally, the incidence of human immunodeficiency virus (HIV)/acquired immune deficiency syndrome (AIDS) and other sexually transmitted infections (STIs) are also disproportionately high among young Hispanics (US Department of Health and Human Services, 2006 and 2007; Augustine and Bridges, 2008).

PSYCHOPATHOLOGY

Depression

According to the latest Youth Risk Behavior Survey (YRBS) by the Centers for Disease Control, 32.6 percent of Latino youth reported feeling sad or hopeless every day for two weeks or more over the past year, while 27.2 percent of Whites and 24.7 percent of African Americans reported feeling this way (Eaton, et al., 2012). Though overall epidemiological data does not suggest higher risk for depression for Latinos over other ethnic groups, various smaller studies have pointed to a growing prevalence and risk for depression amongst Latino youth (Cespedes and Huey, 2008), and many show a strong correlation to cultural factors.

Substance Abuse

Substance abuse is a growing problem amongst Latino youth. In overall abuse of illicit drugs, Latino youth have equal rates as Whites, but higher rates than African Americans (Zambrana and Logie, 2000; Eaton et al., 2012), with 10.8 percent of Latino youth ten years and older using illicit substances. However, according to the latest YRBS, amongst the three main racial/ethnic groups in the United States, Latino youth have the highest history of use (73.2 percent) and current use of alcohol (42.3 percent), history (10.2 percent) and current cocaine use (5.4 percent), and history of heroin (3.3 percent), inhalant (14.4 percent), ecstasy (10.6 percent), methamphetamine (4.6 percent), and injectable drug use (2.9 percent (Eaton et al., 2012). Swanson and colleagues (1992) found that the rates of overall substance abuse by Latino youth on the United States side of the US-Mexican border were three times higher than youth on the Mexican side of the border.

Suicide

Suicide is the third leading cause of death in Hispanics ten to twenty-four years old and the seventh cause of death in this ethnic group before 75 years of age, so it is disproportionately faced by youth and could well grow with future generations. The majority of suicides in Hispanics occur among males by use of firearms (Canino and Roberts, 2001). These are troubling statistics, given the already higher rates of homicide and institutionalization amongst youth of color, suggesting that they now suffer from the "worst of both worlds" in terms of mental health. According to the latest YRBS, amongst the main three racial/ ethnic groups in the United States, Latino youth have the highest rates of having seriously considered suicide (16.7 percent), making a plan to commit suicide (14.3 percent), attempting suicide (10.2 percent), and making a suicide attempt that required medical attention (3.2 percent; at least 50 percent higher than whites or African Americans, according to Eaton and associates (2012). Swanson and associates (1992) found that suicidal ideation was three times more prevalent among Latino youth on the United States side of the US-Mexican border than youth on the Mexican side.

Risk factors that affect the rates of sucidality among Hispanics often yield contradictory results. In Texas, Hispanic women had the lowest suicide rates compared to White non-Hispanics and African Americans. Yet, another study found that suicide risk was higher among Hispanic females (Doddakashi, Wilcox, and Hauser, 2003). Family dysfunction and lower socioeconomic status have also been associated with increased risk for suicide among Hispanics, as well as being a victim of physical and sexual abuse (Queralt, 1993; O'Donnell et al., 2004). The use of alcohol and drugs has also been found to increase the risk of suicide among Hispanics, and substance abuse that is co-morbid with depression and being a Hispanic homosexual male also increases the risk (Marzuck et al., 12992; Vega et al., 1993; Rew et al., 2001; O'Donnell et al., 2004).

Protective factors against suicide among certain Hispanic subgroups appear to be related: 1) having a fatalistic view of the world, 2) a passive coping style and 3) moral and religious objections to suicide (Oquendo et al., 2005). However, these findings seem to be more characteristic of individuals of low socioeconomic status, and may not be representative of the totality of the Hispanic population in the United States.

One of the major challenges of cross-cultural research is to disentangle the effects of culture from those of demographic factors such as socioeconomic status, ethnicity and family structure. Culture and socioeconomic status can interact in ways that either exaggerate or mask group differences, but race and ethnicity, income and family structure when taken together, may only partially explain suicide risk behavior in adolescents, including Hispanic adolescents (Blum et al., 2000; Oquendo et al., 2005).

MENTAL HEALTH DISPARITIES

In addition to acculturation stress, services disparities may also contribute to the increasing risk for psychopathology being identified amongst immigrant children and youth. For example, Pumariega and colleagues (1998) found that Latino youth used half as many counseling services as Whites and African Americans, and that first-generation Latino immigrants used even fewer services. Juszczak, Melinkovich, and Kaplan (2003) found that Latino youth used fewer mean visits in school-based health centers. Yeh and associates (2003) found that Latinos and Asian youth showed higher levels of unmet mental health needs than Whites, but parents endorsed fewer barriers to care, with cultural factors influencing parental perceptions of barriers. A result of such disparities may be a high risk of referral of Latino youth to juvenile authorities for behavioral difficulties (Vander Stoep, Evens, and Taub, 1997).

Mental health disparities appear to play a role in the development of mental health problems amongst diverse immigrant populations of children and youth. Martin and colleagues (2003), Snowden, Cuellar, and Libby (2003), and Leslie and colleagues (2003) all found lower rates of prescribing psychotropics for Latino and Asian youth versus for Caucasians. Insofar as psychotherapy services, various studies have found significant disparities in immigrant groups. For example, Pumariega and associates (1999) found half as much utilization of school-based counseling services among Latino youth versus Caucasian and African-American youth in Texas, while first-generation immigrant Latino youth utilized even fewer such services. Bui and Takeuchi (1992) and Lahey and colleagues (1996) found similar lower utilization of mental health services by Latino youth in Los Angeles and in New York respectively. Juszczak, Melinkovich, and Kaplan (2003) found that Latino youth used fewer mean visits in school health centers than African Americans.

THERAPEUTIC APPROACHES

The concept of *culturally competent services* is critical in effectively serving immigrant children and youth and their families. Cross and colleagues (1989) defined cultural competence as the ability to serve people across cultural differences. They identified important provider (awareness/acceptance of difference, awareness of own cultural values, understanding dynamics of difference, development of cultural knowledge, and ability to adapt practice to cultural context of patient) and system characteristics (valuing diversity, cultural self-assessment, managing for the dynamics of difference, institutionalization of cultural knowledge, adaptation of policies, values, structure, and services to better address diverse cultural needs). Both of these are needed in order to effectively deliver culturally competent services.

Applying the Cultural Competence Model

For mental health services, as well as other human services, culturally competent services can be operationalized along different phases of service delivery (Pumariega, Rothe, and Rogers, 2009):

- *Assessment*: This includes assessing the cultural context of symptoms/problems, symptomatic expression, level of acculturation of the youth and family, immigration history and stressors/trauma, context of adaptation, cultural strengths.
- *Linguistic support* is critical for effective service delivery, either through trained and certified interpreters or preferably by clinicians who are fluent in the family's native language and familiar with their culture. The use of family members as interpreters should be avoided at all cost, and least of all the use of an affected child. There should even be caution about using interpreters from the same community as the family, as that may result in a breach of confidentiality within their own communities.
- *Family involvement*: Family involvement is critical. Family therapy needs to focus on inter-generational conflicts, bridging the generational acculturation gap, mobilizing family supports, promoting respect for the traditional family structure while promoting some cultural flexibility on the part of parents and elders with their children, facilitating the negotiation of gender roles, and negotiating confidentiality issues where youth can have privacy but continue to remain engaged with their families without allowing confidentiality to become a barrier to communication.
- *Psychotherapy:* Psychotherapy needs to be practical and problem-solving. It should address immigration traumas and acculturation and ethnic identity conflicts (internal or generational). The use of

culturally specific modalities, themes, or stories may be helpful in addressing these issues.

- *Contextual/systemic supports:* Clinicians should promote and utilize family strengths and community natural supports and, as much as possible, avoid institutionalizing youth or removing them from their families and communities. Ethnically specific programs may be particularly effective if available. Additionally, case managers from the population of origin are needed who can mobilize such community supports and also serve as intermediaries between the immigrant family and the mainstream community agencies (schools, courts, child welfare, juvenile justice, and mental health).
- *Pharmacotherapy,* if utilized, should consider genetic and dietary factors that impact the metabolism of different medications. Clinicians should de-mystify the use of medications, provide effective education to youth and family members, address cultural myths or beliefs that may intersect with the use of medications, but at the same time respect the autonomy and decision by parents and elders around using pharmacotherapy.

Practicing in an Evidence-Based and Culturally Informed Manner

A number of culturally informed evidence-based interventions have been developed to address the special mental health needs of Latinos. For example, Brief Strategic Family Therapy (Santiesteban, et al., 1997), a family-based intervention focusing on addressing acculturative family distancing, has demonstrated significant improvements in addressing youth substance abuse and conduct disturbance, and has been adopted as a NIDA (National Institute of Drug Administration) endorsed evidence-based practice. Culturally Informed and Flexible Family-Based Treatment for Adolescents (Santiesteban and Mena, 2009) is a newer combined family and individual cognitive behavior therapy (CBT) and psycho-educational intervention that runs sixteen sessions twice weekly and combines interpersonal and crisis management skills borrowed from Linehan integrated and culturally relevant materials and themes relevant for Latinos. Cognitive Behavioral Therapy for Traumatic Stress (CBITS; Kataoka, et al., 2003) is a school-based, multi-level CBT intervention (group, individual, psychoeducational) that is delivered by educators and mental health professionals in school settings and addresses acculturation stress and cultural trauma. It has demonstrated significant reductions in PTSD and depressive symptoms. There have also been a number of culturally adapted evidence-based therapies for depression, anxiety, and substance abuse with Latinos. For example, Rosello and Bernal (1999) have made cultural adaptations on manualized CBT for adolescent depression, while Cardemill and associates (2007) have made cultural adaptations for school-based CBT for depression.

Culturally based interventions based on themes and practices from cultures of origin are also utilized to meet the unique mental health and cultural needs of immigrant populations. A number of these have been developed for Latino populations. For example, Cuento Therapy (Constantino, Malgady, and Rogler, 1994) is a culturally sensitive storytelling form of cognitive behavioral therapy using culturally based myths and stories. It has been shown to improve academic performance and self-esteem and reduced anxiety symptoms (Ramirez et al., 2009). Rotheram-Borus and colleagues (1999) adapted the Hispanic media genre of "telenovelas" as part of an emergency room intervention with suicidal Latinas in Los Angeles, resulting in significant reduction in ER recidivism and subsequent suicidal behaviors. The Club Amigas Latina youth-mentoring program pairs Latina college and middle school students with mentee self-esteem, having been correlated to commitment to the program by participants (Kaplan et al., 2009). Adaptation of traditional cultural approaches to services, such as the *promotoras de salud* model of neighborhood health care workers (Grames, 2006) has also been utilized effectively. In the area of teen pregnancy prevention, programs that incorporate Latino cultural values and engage families in improving communication around sexuality have shown greater efficacy (Vexler and Suellentrop, 2006).

CONCLUSION

Immigration has been a traditional characteristic of the US national identity. However, future success is more dependent on this unique characteristic than ever in history. Immigrants, particularly immigrant children and the children of immigrants, are the nation's future citizens. Meeting their developmental, educational health, and mental health needs reduces margination, improves the overall social and community climate, and makes immigrants stakeholders in the future of the nation. Meeting the adaptational needs of immigrant children and families minimizes future health, mental health, and social welfare expenditures. Furthermore, immigrants comprise a major portion of the future US workforce, and meeting their health and educational needs maximizes the nation's potential for productivity and success.

NINE

Individual and Sociocultural Dynamics in the Treatment of Latino Patients

Ricardo Ainslie

The Civil Rights Act had a profound impact on all aspects of the American experience. This is especially true for those Americans from historically marginalized communities such as Latinos, who in many parts of the Southwest were subject to the same Jim Crow laws (and their underlying attitudes) that were targeted at the African American community. In what follows I present clinical case material from work with a Latino man in an effort to illustrate psychological experiences that simultaneously operate at two different registers: individual and collective experience. This material helps orient us toward the importance of understanding a broader sociocultural context when thinking about our patients, whatever their racial or ethnic background. I draw particular attention to the understanding of psychological experience as constituted by multiple registers that operate simultaneously. These include social and historical contexts, dimensions that infiltrate psychological processes in conscious and unconscious ways, in addition to the more familiar individual and family psychodynamics that we use in framing our understanding of our patients.

A CLINICAL ILLUSTRATION

Jaime (a pseudonym) was a Latino man in his late thirties whose primary presenting concern was that he and his girlfriend were not getting along. He felt very in love with her; in fact, for the first time in his life he was considering marriage. However, though initially equally enthusiastic about the relationship, his girlfriend had developed reservations due to his excessive drinking. While drunk he tended to act out in a variety of ways, such as becoming impulsive and verbally aggressive toward her and others. Jaime sought therapy at her strong urging, clearly aware that his behavior was threatening a relationship he did not want to lose.

While both were successful professionals, their lives growing up were a study in contrasts. Jaime was Latino and had grown up very poor, living in a public housing project in a large city for most of his childhood. Jaime's girlfriend was White and from a middle to upper-middle-class family. In her late thirties, she had attended a respected university and was successful in her work. Her path to college had been a seamless transition from high school, whereas Jaime had worked after high school before attending junior college and then a four-year institution. She had never dated anyone who was not of her cultural background or social status. Since high school, Jaime had dated White women almost exclusively.

Patient's Ancestry

Jaime's parents were both of Mexican ancestry and he had grown up in a neighborhood that was nearly 100 percent Latino. Jaime had a brother that was two years older. His mother's family had been in the United States for many generations and all were more or less acculturated, even if their economic circumstances remained on the social margins. Everyone from his maternal line was, at best, working class. None had attended college; in fact, several had not graduated from high school. No one in his mother's family spoke Spanish with the exception of the occasional Spanish word inserted into family banter. The maternal family identified themselves as Americans even as they held on to some aspects of Latino culture: they ate Mexican food with regularity, they followed celebrities such as Eva Longoria and Selena, they were nominally Catholic, and so on. There was a great deal of family dysfunction on the maternal side of the family. The kinds of chaos that often marks the lives of poor, urban dwellers in communities of color were rife: divorces, children born out of wedlock, drug and alcohol addictions, welfare, unemployment and prison sentences. Those that held steady jobs worked at low-paying positions offering no future, such as groundskeepers, custodial staff, and low-skill employees for the city.

Jaime's father and his four uncles had been born in Mexico. Spanish was their primary language although all had learned English in the United States with the exception of the paternal grandparents who remained monolingual Spanish speakers. The older uncles spoke an accented English, while the younger siblings were fully bilingual. With respect to the father's family, then, there were clearly differing degrees of acculturation, with the younger uncles more comfortable bringing aspects of American culture into their world and, presumably, into their identities. His two youngest uncles had served in the US military.

The paternal line of Jaime's family was significantly more successful than his mother's side of the family: They owned small businesses (landscaping, auto repair) and one worked at the Post Office. Jaime's father worked as a foreman in a warehouse. Though some had been divorced, in general there was more stability within their families. All of their children had graduated from high school and many had attended junior college or four-year colleges, though Jaime was the only one of his cousins to have earned a masters degree. It is evident that the cultural context within Jaime's immediate family was defined by a complexity that, while not altogether atypical, frequently eludes formulations about Latino culture which often represent it in homogenous, monolithic terms.

Immediate Family

When Jaime was seven years old his father developed a serious medical condition that made it impossible for him to work. He went on permanent disability. Prior to the father's illness, the family had barely managed on his modest wages. They now fell into abject poverty and moved into a public housing project in a neighborhood rife with gangs, drugs, and violence.

Throughout Jaime's childhood, there was significant conflict between Jaime's parents. Though not physical, the arguments were often violent, with doors slammed, objects broken, and voices raised. In the cramped quarters of their small home and later in the housing project, Jaime and his brother were constantly exposed to these arguments, inducing a chronic fear that their family was about to disintegrate. After numerous separations, Jaime's parents divorced when he was nine years old. Jaime continued to live with his mother at the housing project, where she had a series of boyfriends, some of whom stayed for extended periods although the relationships were always tempestuous. These men had no interest in fathering the boys and on occasion physically mistreated them.

Outside of his home, Jaime was harassed by the local gangs and sometimes beaten up. Leaving his apartment was always a fear-inducing experience and the fact that he was invested in school only made him more of a target. Jaime managed to remain in school, in a social environment where dropping out was a common occurrence. He credited this to school counselors who engaged him, supported him, and helped him navigate the terrain. They became surrogate parents; his mother was minimally involved in his schooling.

After high school Jaime moved out of the projects and supported himself with low-skill jobs. A year later, he started attending junior college, where he excelled. For the first time he met fellow students who were from more middle-class backgrounds. It was also the first time he had Whites in his classes. He did well, transferring to a four-year college and eventually earning a bachelor's degree and then a masters degree in a technical field. He had a capacity to engage others and that included enlisting mentors who believed in him and looked after him, much as his counselors had done throughout his school years.

After leaving home, Jaime had almost no contact with his mother or her relatives. However, even though he'd only seen them episodically, his father's family had felt like a source of support throughout his childhood and they remained an important part of his life. He frequently spent holidays in their homes, for example.

SOME THEORETICAL POINTS

In working with Latino patients there is a great deal of variation in the way in which culture is framed as a set of constructs that organize a patient's identity. Each patient's family constellation, as well as issues such as the character of the community where the patient grew up and the family's social class, shape how cultural variables are brought into the consulting room. These variables play an active role in shaping a Latino patient's identity and are likely to shape transference-countertransference variables, the patient's expectations about treatment, and the comfort with which a patient engages the therapeutic process.

Winnicott (1967) has given us a rich theoretical base from which to understand the role of culture in psychological experience. This experience runs deeper and is more profound than can be surmised from descriptions of sociocultural characteristics. Winnicott describes the ways in which the mothering object infuses the parent-child interactional space with cultural elements that infiltrate and give shape to psychological experience from the very beginning of life. Everything that can be said about an infant's experience exists within a cultural medium that initially is simply felt, existing outside of the realm of language or reflection.

Culture is embodied in people's lives in infinite forms and variations. Beginning with the specific sounds of the "maternal" language, the scent of regional foods and plants, dominant weather patterns, music, religion, and characteristic modes of interaction such as conventions about social distance within a community (see Akhtar, 1995), all influence the intersections of culture and subject. These are just some of the forms that culture takes and some of the ways in which culture is insinuated into our lives as psychological processes (Ainslie, 1995, 1998). Winnicott's formulations readily lend themselves to considerations of race and ethnicity, although these are not specific foci within his theorizing.

The work of psychologist Stephen Quintana (1998) helps us understand the relationship between cultural forces and individual identity from a different, if related, perspective. In a series of studies, Quintana has mapped out the developmental trajectory within which children begin to establish an awareness of and attitudes toward members of other racial and ethnic groups, including how they develop the concept of themselves as members of a specific ethnic group. His research, and that of others, indicates that already by the age of four, children have established concepts of race and ethnicity. One of the findings that Quintana (1998) reports is that children's early racial and ethnic cognitions tend to be pro-White even though, for ethnic minority children, these attitudes may not necessarily become crystalized in the form of poor self-esteem. In addition, children as young as four show racial preferences and, for White children, racial prejudice appears quite high between the ages of five and seven before it begins to level off. The critical element here is to emphasize that, in keeping with psychoanalytic formulations that theorize cultural variables as deeply important in relation to identity, the work of Quintana and other psychologists documents the presence of ethnicity and race as active constructs for children beginning from a very early age. Relatedly, psychoanalysis has long theorized that experiences that shape a child's early life tend to contribute to personality development in deeper, more profound, and more enduring ways (Erikson, 1950). Thus, this research gives us reason to believe that race and ethnicity are powerful organizers at both conscious and unconscious levels by the time a child has entered the pre-school years.

Vamik Volkan's (1997, 2004) work adds to our reflections from a different level of analysis. Volkan focuses on how cultural elements and shared historical experiences are incorporated within group identity processes while also helping us to conceptualize the relationship between individual and collective identity, teasing out the interplay between these two aspects of identity processes. Volkan theorizes that individuals carry collective identity elements as ever-present, implicit structures. These become activated or more salient at times when group identity is under threat or mobilized for other reasons. Volkan uses two frameworks for organizing collective experience in relation to group identity, what he terms "chosen traumas" and "chosen glories." Chosen traumas are those adverse collective experiences that have helped forge a group's identity. Examples include the role of the Holocaust in Jewish identity, or the role of slavery in African American identity. For Latinos of Mexican descent, a chosen trauma might be Mexico's loss of 50 percent of its territory following the Mexican-American War. That territory became the American West and Southwest. These were geographic areas where Mexican culture, conventions, and language were once the foundations for social life. As a result, Mexicans became foreigners in their own lands (and in many instances their lands were forcibly taken from them). The schools attended by their children now punished them for speaking Spanish. In addition to being targets of generalized violence (Montejano, 1987), in the Southwest Mexicans were also frequent victims of lynching. There were nearly 600 documented lynchings of Mexicans or Mexican-Americans between Reconstruction and 1928 (Carrigan and Webb, 2003; Delgado, 2009). This collective history represents a chosen trauma for Americans of Mexican ancestry.

Like chosen traumas, chosen glories are shared collective experiences of a positive variety that become elements in the formation and affirmation of collective identities. Often these may take the form of patriotic holidays, such as Bastille Day in France, the Fourth of July in the United States, or Cinco de Mayo in Mexico. Patriotic fervor and a feeling of belonging to a group often draw from the matrix of emotions associated with chosen traumas or chosen glories. However, what is important about them is that they are components of identity and they tend to be intimately associated with the elements of identity that are linked to racial and ethnic ancestries.

These theoretical perspectives are useful in our understanding of clinical work with Latino patients (indeed, with all patients) because they require us to formulate their concerns in ways that include relevant cultural frames of reference. But Volkan's contributions are especially valuable as a way of theorizing how aspects of individual and collective identity are deeply linked. We all live within the psychological spaces created by these cultural and socio-historical circumstances just as much as we live within the psychological spaces shaped by familial circumstances.

Latinos represent a very diverse group with many different developmental contexts—indeed, with different chosen traumas and chosen glories organizing collective experience. For example, for a Cuban American, the experience of her family's 1959 exodus from Cuba may be a salient part of her psychological experience, and these attitudes may shape the patient's political identifications and reactions to current political events (say the Mariel boatlift of the 1980s, or the saga of Elián Gonzalez, the Cuban boy who was returned to Cuba in 2000 in the midst of great controversy). But beyond political encounters, a Cuban American will draw from a variety of cultural reference points that differ substantively from, say, those that shape the experience of individuals of Mexican ancestry. For the latter, the organizing principles may be events and experiences that mean nothing to a Cuban American.

Altman (2006) notes that the legacy of racism leads to ongoing social and economic outcomes that become built into language, culture and values. For Mexican Americans, the Southwest represents a collective wound, a chosen trauma. They live their lives within a particular historical and cultural context that is densely psychological if often unconsciously so. They grow up surrounded by names and landmarks that refer to a time when Mexico (and Mexicans) governed the space within which they live. There may be historical landmarks such as churches or other pre-Anglo structures that form part of the community's architectural identity. Spanish street names in their communities are pronounced in

English. Individuals of Mexican ancestry may now have American names, and if they have Spanish names their teachers and even their families may pronounce them "in English." In this sense, the experience of a collective trauma is all around one, yet simultaneously negated. Those historical and cultural facts are inescapable and ever-present, but not necessarily felt as emotional processes that live within one's subjectivity unless something activates their awareness. For these reasons, living in the Southwest may imply living in a perpetual state of tension derived from an ambivalent relationship toward the historical-geographical fact that this was once Mexican territory. It makes the region both home and a place of dislocation, and, in that dislocation, it is also a zone of experience that may evoke collective humiliations, collective depression, and collective rage, among other reactions.

Viewed in this way, we might argue that the notion of chosen trauma is excessively narrow, for it privileges specific historical experiences. While obviously important, such experiences gain power because of their broader social and psychological *sequelae*. The emotional aftermath of devastating historical and socially transformative events spreads deeply and may have many manifestations, including legacies of racism, marginalization, and poverty, as Altman (2006) describes. Those create profound psychological effects for generation upon generation that may be thought about in sociological terms without adequate consideration of their historical origins and their psychological underpinnings. These perspectives are related to the concept of cultural holding (Parens, 1998). They also reflect Layton's (2006) ideas about what she terms the "normative unconscious": that is, "the psychological consequences of living in a culture in which many norms serve the dominant ideology" (p. 239)

The processes being described are exceedingly complex and it would be reductive to assume that how these elements exist within personality structure is homogenous or uniform. Quite the contrary is true. Further, for people of Mexican ancestry living in the Southwest, aspects of identity are drawn from a post-cataclysm cultural space which is infused with both White and Mexican dimensions. These become deeply inscribed in ways that are ultimately related to, but distinct from, the contributory cultural strands of "White" and "Mexican" cultural elements.

BACK TO THE CLINICAL MATERIAL

Returning to our case illustration, the theoretical ideas that have been presented can help us understand my patient's particular concerns in a more nuanced way. Over the course of two years, I initially saw Jaime once a week, then twice a week for a year-and-a-half, and again once a week as his therapy was winding down. As noted, his presenting concern centered on stresses in his relationship with his girlfriend. He feared that he might lose her. In fact, he had come to therapy largely at her urging. Thus, the initial therapeutic alliance centered on the crisis in this important relationship. He had no prior therapeutic experiences and the culture of therapy was quite foreign to him. To his knowledge, no one in his family had ever received psychological treatment.

In part because of the fact that we had certain cultural features in common (see below), I felt an easy affinity with him. I respected the trajectory of his life, especially given that he had grown up in a very poor urban context. I sensed that there were significant strengths that had allowed him to transcend the chaos of his background, especially the chaos of his family. That dimension of his personality interested me.

His transference to me was positive and I was folded into the cluster of representations formed from positive mentoring figures that had nurtured him and looked after him throughout his life. It was also comforting to him that I, too, was of Mexican ancestry (that was evident from my first name a well as from Google searches from which he gleaned bits and pieces about my Mexican background). In this way, he felt a degree of camaraderie with me. He assumed that, like him, I had navigated the currents of a White-dominated society as a person of Mexican ancestry. Akhtar (2006) describes the technical problems associated with such a circumstance—specifically, that it lends itself to countertransference complications, including the danger of "nostalgic collusion" between the analyst and the patient. I was aware of these countertransference potentials throughout our work together.

Jaime was heavily defended and not innately psychologically minded. The very concept of a talking therapy was awkward for him. He was more inclined toward being analytical, with the mindset fitting the stereotype of, say, a computer geek that conveniently allowed him to keep emotional material at a safe distance. He was initially expecting direction, suggestions, and advice (the mentorships of his youth, young adulthood, and, later, in the context of his professional career, were the templates that he drew from in coming to see me). His approach to the problems that he presented was that they were obstacles to be solved rather than experiences to be understood and mined for exploring his feelings or potential motives. The idea that his presenting concerns might point to the ways in which his parents and his childhood experiences might be activating conflicts in his present life was not an easy construct for him to grasp initially.

The crisis in his relationship with his girlfriend deepened as his acting out persisted. His girlfriend was both insistent on, and supportive of his therapy; but she was also increasingly leery of his outbursts, which led her to begin to question the future of their relationship. She seemed to know very little about his ethnic and cultural background. By the time they'd met, he had succeeded in building a professional career, becoming part of a cultural framework which was very familiar to her, but which had been largely absent from his own background. Since completing college he had lived almost exclusively in a White world. In addition, their social life as a couple was White, his professional life was primarily White, his close friends were White. In fact, in conscious and less conscious ways, Jaime tended to view Whites and White culture as the yardstick for success. At one point he noted that "for some reason" the fact that his girlfriend was White made her more desirable in his eyes. He had not dated Latina women since high school.

Yet, at the same time, he subverted himself in this relationship by drinking to excess and becoming belligerent. His girlfriend complained that he became a different person, saying that he became "crass": He made crude sexual remarks and he became loud and exhibitionistic. He also became aggressive, argumentative, and demeaning toward his girlfriend, poking fun at her and putting her down in front of their friends. He tended to minimize these behaviors, chalking them up to the alcohol, thereby rationalizing his behavior away. The fact that he did not otherwise drink a great deal, or that there might be long intervals between these incidents, was used to buttress his view that this was a circumscribed, rare issue. He found it very difficult to stop and reflect on what was going on internally for him and why he might be behaving in this way.

A common trigger for these incidents involved his feeling vulnerable because of social situations. The social milieu in which he travelled was very mainstream American business culture. As noted, their friends were almost entirely White, middle class, college educated, and professionals. He was often the only non-White person in the group on social outings. While it appeared that he was well liked, in the course of our work he was able to begin to reflect on the ways in which he felt different from his girlfriend and his broader social and professional group.

One might argue that Jaime experienced significant cultural disidentification, given the extent to which he lived in a "White" world and given his self-imposed distance from his family. However, to the extent to which disidentification was present, it was largely unconscious. The distance was also driven by the exigencies of the world in which he was actually living (an urban, predominantly White professional environment). Yet, there were vital, important ways in which he felt nourished by his familial and cultural background. His father's family was very important to him as an emotional resource, even though he rarely saw them, and within the view of his father's family he was admired as one who had most managed to become successful in mainstream terms among his siblings and cousins. This represented a kind of collective familial mirroring that helped fuel his accomplishments. Though his contact with them was inconsistent, he knew that they were there should he need them.

During the course of his treatment, we explored his angry ambivalence toward his mother, an ambivalence derived from her lack of maternal warmth and from her preoccupation with herself at the expense of the needs of her two children. As a child, it had been commonplace for him and his brother to be left alone in the family apartment while their mother went out on dates and for the boys to never know if she would return that night. She was also harsh and excessive in her discipline. We traced the links between this history and his pattern of relationships with women who were narcissistic, controlling, and ungenerous.

His relationship with his father had also been marked by distance and emotional disengagement, but his father was not abusive and overall his father was far less emotionally toxic than his mother. Though he spent most of his time with his mother as a child, and there was no standing visitation schedule, when he saw his father following the divorce his father took the boys to parks, or the zoo, or otherwise made plans even though his physical condition limited the father's physical activity. He was a man of few words, and not comfortable in the least with his emotions, but he was not hostile toward the boys. It was my impression that Jaime's successful engagement with mentors in school and later in his professional life drew, partly, from these comparatively more "usable" paternal representations. These themes were reflected in the transference.

Jaime's relationship with his girlfriend at times activated maternal conflicts: he scanned their interactions for evidence that she was disinterested in him, or that she was being self-centered. However, he felt closer to her than he'd ever felt to anyone prior to now, a feeling that truly frightened him. My impression of her was that she was well-meaning, that she appeared to really care about him, but also that she lacked a very complex understanding of his cultural background, including his childhood growing up in poverty. However, he contributed to that by finding it difficult to tell her about it in any depth. He preferred not to discuss it at all. The painful feelings about his childhood and his family made him prone to keeping things to himself. It was partly a choice he made, but it was also largely part of unconscious defensive processes of isolation and denial that helped protect him from depression and shame.

The psychodynamics motivating his efforts to keep his familial history at a remove were multifaceted. There was a powerful element of shame related to growing up in the public housing project, primarily focused around his mother's promiscuity from which he and his brother were not shielded, in addition to the myriad other ways in which she was dysfunctional and inadequate as a maternal figure. There were also the traumatizing experiences of chronically feeling vulnerable and scared within the neighborhood, given the frequency with which he'd been attacked, belittled, and bullied as a child by other children and, as an adolescent, the local gangs. These experiences formed a pool of conscious and unconscious psychological pain that had required all of his emotional resources to contain and survive. A lifetime of effort had been involved in defending himself against these emotions as a matter of psychic survival. It was a stance that had translated, in the context of his relationship, into a silence about his family background save for the faintest of references. For Jaime this stance was ego-syntonic; it felt normal to him, and it went unquestioned.

However, woven into this same fabric was a set of broader sociohistorical elements that were easily and readily fused with the specific psychological experiences of his childhood. There was a convergence or isomorphism between the conflicts of his childhood as they related to his experience of shame, devaluation, and hostility, and the position which people of Mexican ancestry had historically occupied within the larger social context: marginalized, devalued, and objects of hostility. A great deal of psychological strength had been required to transcend those forces and continue working in school, and, after his studies were finished, to live in what was essentially a White world.

Meeting His Family

A year and a half into their relationship Jaime had met his girlfriend's parents and extended family, but she had not met a single person in Jaime's family. She brought this to his attention, fearing that signaled a lack of commitment on his part. In response, he accepted an invitation for them to attend Thanksgiving dinner at the home of one of his paternal uncles.

He felt anxious as Thanksgiving approached. When I asked what he feared about the visit, he answered that he was not sure how his girlfriend would react to finding herself in a very Latino cultural context. Even as she was reassuring, indicating that she was looking forward to meeting his family, he felt increasingly distressed about the holiday. Illustrating Layton's (2006) "normative unconscious," he worried that she would find them "low class," not recognizing that, within these fears, was a self-representation: he feared that she might reject him both because this was his familial history and because this was his cultural history as well. They were hidden evaluations formed by part of his psyche and they were highly conflictual.

The impending visit provided the impetus for bringing a great deal of this cultural material into the treatment as it related to his general sense of vulnerability. It formed part of his associations as he thought of all the reasons he felt anxious about her actually coming into his extended familial world and the cultural domain that held him and his extended family. This reflection with his therapy did not take the form of a sociological or historical lesson. Rather, it was linked in a more organic and spontaneous way to his specific anxieties and ideas as to what those anxieties might mean.

CONCLUDING REMARKS

In this chapter I have sought to illustrate the ways in which individual and collective frames of reference might be understood in clinical work. Jaime's identity was not only shaped by the conflictual and non-conflictual components of his childhood and his family life. Rather, these were "held" within a cultural space, including the socio-historical context of his community and the place of people of Mexican ancestry within that context. The latter are powerful forces with deep psychological implications. The idea of Whiteness within American culture (Altman, 2006) is related to Layton's (2006) notions of the "normative unconscious." Within a therapeutic context, they speak to how both therapist and patient engage the clinical process and psychic elements that may be assumed and therefore evade reflection. Such evasion may mean that, in the best of cases, important aspects of a patient's experience go unexamined. However, such evasion may have a more pernicious impact if it means that the therapist unconsciously imposes dominant frames of reference upon the patient.

In the present case, a critical moment in the treatment (Jaime's impending introduction of his girlfriend to his family) became a vehicle for exploring a psychological register in which social and collective identity processes intersected. Individual psychodynamics, including self and object representations, were significantly populated by both domains of experience. His fear that his girlfriend would experience his family as "low class" was simultaneously a reference to the collective experience of most people of Mexican ancestry living in Texas as objects of racism and devaluation. However, it was also a statement regarding his fear of rejection in a person for whom experiences of rejection were extensive and painful. His sociocultural legacy was thus intricately intertwined with his personal conflicts. Careful analysis of such condensation is necessary in clinical work with bicultural patients like Jaime.

TEN

On Being a Latino Psychotherapist in the United States

Solange Margery Bertoglia

I was born and raised in Latin America. I did my medical education there and then came to the United States for psychiatry residency training. People do not readily assume that I am Latina, since my name reflects a European background, and my skin tone and features go along those lines. This "disguise" is certainly not unique. Latinos have a wide range of phenotypical presentations and names that might not reveal Hispanic roots. This "disguise," though, has proven to be an added element to my experience as a Latino therapist in the United States. It allows people to freely speak their minds on how they feel about Latinos without censoring what is politically incorrect. Latinos themselves speak freely in Spanish, thinking that I am blissfully unaware of what they are saying. This circumstance has made me acutely aware of the erroneous cultural assumptions and generalizations that are made about Latinos. Latinos themselves make the mistake of identifying their own personal values and experiences as that of all Latinos.

Latinos are a diverse group of individuals with different languages and dialects, mores, historical backgrounds, races, religions, and traditions. Latino patients cannot be clustered as a homogeneous group and neither can Latino therapists. There are the differences that come from being raised in different countries, but most importantly the differences that arise from having different personal stories, including different migration journeys. Lillian Comas Diaz (2005) wrote about "becoming a multicultural psychotherapist." She was born in Chicago to Puerto Rican immigrants. The family moved back to Puerto Rico when she was a child and she was immersed in a culture of magic realism where her grandmother, a folk healer, became a central element of her development. In her article, she explains how living on a small island with colonial status and attending the university during a crucial moment in the Civil Rights Movement made an impact on the type of therapist she became. Dr. Comas Diaz's article is a great reflection of how circumstances particular to her country and the period of time during which she trained shaped her as a therapist at least as much as the experience of growing up in Latin America.

I mentioned the importance of the migration story as a factor that individualizes each Latino's experience. As a therapist, one must consider that the time of migration will affect where one is trained; this can have a tremendous influence on the kind of therapist one becomes. The experiences vary from Latino therapists who have done all of their training in the United States to therapists who trained and practiced in Latin America before moving and seeing patients in the United States. The place and culture in which training happens and in which one practices affects the therapist, the patient, and the therapeutic relationship. A study comparing different perceptions on boundary excursion between mental health professionals in the United States and Brazil showed how the culture in which one lives and trains can account for different perceptions regarding boundary excursion (Miller, Commons, and Gutheil, 2006). "While some kinds of behavior may be universally proscribed, others may differ in acceptability, depending on cultural norms" (p. 34). For example, the study found that Brazilian mental health professionals felt that displaying diplomas, professional awards, and/or revealing one's credentials were more harmful to the patient and professionally unacceptable. Mental health professionals from the United States saw shaking hands and kissing on the cheek (a very common way of greeting in Brazil) as more harmful and professionally unacceptable.

Latino therapists who have trained and practiced in Latin America must learn to adapt to a broad range of challenges upon moving to the United States:

- They often come from countries in which health care is provided by the government and are inexperienced in the matters of charging fees. Consequently, they lack the understanding of how money-related matters can enter the psychotherapeutic dialogue in disguised ways.

- They might be viewed as having a special therapeutic interest in seeing only Latino patients, which may or may not be the case. They might also be seen as needing to give back to their particular ethnic community. In reality, Latino therapists might end up in this position because of an expectation of them to cover a growing Latino population in the absence of other Spanish-speaking therapists. The therapist can grow resentful of having to fill such positions that may be administratively imposed and not chosen.
- Like other immigrants, Latino therapists often struggle with their dual ethnic identity (i.e., American and Hispanic). Such struggles can lead them into working with Latino patients as an unconscious means to explore their own ethnic conflicts. Other times, the Latino therapist's identity struggle can translate into a negative opinion of Latino culture.

Generally speaking though, a Latino patient might be best cared for by a Latino therapist, even if only to overcome the language barrier. It is up to the Latino therapist to recognize that language might be the predominant common thread and that there is still a need to learn about the specific cultural background and individual migration story of each patient.

As anybody else, a Latino therapist can make erroneous cultural generalizations and assumptions when treating Latino patients. For example, a Latino therapist can wrongfully underestimate the risk of suicidal behavior and suicide in a Latino youth, based on the thought that Latinos' religious beliefs and use of family as a strong support system would be protective. Some of the literature on suicide (Zayas and Pilat, 2008) states that Latino youth suicide rates are "lower than those of non-Hispanic White", but it also reveals that "Latino youth of both sexes have shown consistently higher rates of suicidal ideation, plans, and behavior than their non-Hispanic counterparts" (p. 334).

To complement the clinical material in this chapter, I have compiled a series of vignettes to help illustrate some of the challenges and rewards that I have experienced as a Latina therapist, altering parts of the narratives and changing names to protect my patients' identity and confidentiality. I do not want to generalize these experiences to all Latino therapists whose own therapy-related stories must be as diverse as their own backgrounds. I have found that my own experience has consistently changed as the years pass since I migrated. These changes have been difficult to predict. For example, I have found, in the past two years, that when treating a Spanish-speaking patient, the countertransference, both positive and negative, seems to be more noticeable to me. I feel this is due, in part, to speaking my native language, which is one that I have begun to relate more to my past than to my present.

TREATING LATINO PATIENTS

What defines a "Latino patient" can be as subjective and inaccurate as a categorization system based on a patient's name or phenotype. This categorization decision might have been made by the person setting up an initial appointment in a clinic and who had the best intentions. Needless to say, this way of characterizing patients is useless. Many people have a "Latino" sounding name because of their ancestry and yet they do not identify themselves as Latinos. On the other hand, many Latinos go undetected with this system because of their fair skin and "non-Latino" sounding names. Many clinics have decided to correct this problem by having the patient check the box that best describes their background. It is interesting that not uncommonly, the patient must choose between options that do not differentiate between race and ethnicity. Therefore a black Latino, will check "Hispanic" but feels that his race was ignored. A Brazilian will likely check the box for "Hispanic" in the absence of an option for "Latino," even though the former term mostly refers to those who speak Spanish and people from Brazil mostly speak Portuguese. Ideally, the patients should be allowed to describe their cultural background.

The primary goal of identifying a Latino patient as such could be that she or he can be paired with a Latino therapist, the assumption being that this would be the former's preference. This makes sense if the goal is to avoid a language barrier. Otherwise, it is an assumption to think that a therapist of a culture similar to the patient could be most helpful. An English-speaking Latino patient might benefit more by seeing a therapist who knows best about a particular disorder rather than a Spanish-speaking therapist. Furthermore, a Latino patient might be more willing to have a preference based on gender than on cultural background.

Cultural Expectations and Erroneous Generalizations

In an article by Suarez-Morales and colleagues (2010), the authors reviewed the literature on "ethnic match" (i.e., matching patients and therapists of similar ethnical background). Most of the studies reviewed showed "that ethnic matching in Hispanic populations' yields positive results in psychotherapy" (199). Critics argue that this position is too all-encompassing and that "even when clients and their therapists are ethnically similar, they may differ in cultural attitudes and levels of acculturation; thus, ethnic match does not ensure cultural match" (p. 199). Like the authors, I have found that the interesting issue to explore is for such a heterogeneous population of Latinos (i.e., "What factors in ethnic matching account for the positive results?") (Suarez-Morales et al, 2010).

There are three factors that I have seen Latino patients might have as cultural expectations of "ethnic matching" and they can be, at least in part, misleading. (i) Latino patients might expect a Latino therapist to be more comfortable with physical expressions of care, to assume a more paternal or maternal role in therapy, and to understand the Latino family dynamics better. The expectation that a Latino therapist will be more accepting of demonstrating or accepting physical manifestations of affection probably comes from the fact that Latinos in general are seen doing so in social events. It is not unusual for Latinos to hug or kiss someone who is just being introduced. Many cultures have similar ways of interacting socially but the perception that as a group, we need much less personal space than other groups seems overly assigned to us. This became clear to me when, along with trainees from other countries, I took a course in the United States on how to perform medical evaluations on patients. The instructor asked Latino trainees to raise their hands and then warned us to keep the patient at an arm's length unless strictly necessary because patients from the United States were bothered by our tendency to get too close. If patients from the United States are bothered by this proximity, do Latino patients long for it? I have wondered if Latino patients, in some conscious or unconscious way, seek a Latino therapist, thinking this will allow for some physical closeness that they fear would be denied by a therapist from another culture. If that is the case, are these patients disappointed to find out that such therapeutic boundaries hold true even for Latino therapists?

The (ii) second cultural expectation is that the Latino therapists will provide a more paternalistic model of treatment, which is still commonly seen in some parts of Latin America. The term "paternalistic medicine" is used more in medicine than in therapy and it commonly refers to a doctor practicing medicine in an authoritarian way and making decisions for patients as opposed to a model that reinforces the importance of patients' autonomy. A Latino patient might hope that a Latino therapist will tell him or her what to do in different areas of their life. A Latino therapist's rejection of such a model, even with an explanation as to why this is not the goal of therapy, can come off as detached and as a clear deviation from the patient's expectation. This explanation would likely be the same that a Latino therapist would give to a patient in Latin America. Still, when the Latino therapist tries to correct such expectations in a Latino patient in the United States, the patient might blame the therapist's stance on a perceived distancing of the latter with his or her ethnic background.

Clinical Vignette 1

Mr. Gutierrez was a sixty-year-old man who had emigrated from Colombia six months ago. He was a retired engineer who relocated to the United States with his wife and daughter. The family moved because of a great job opportunity for his wife. Over a period of three months, Mr. Gutierrez became severely depressed and emaciated because he refused to eat. Mr. Gutierrez's family took him to a therapist who used a translation service to communicate with him. He did not improve, and after a few sessions, declined to continue therapy. He was admitted to a hospital where several tests showed no physical abnormalities impairing his ability to eat, and a psychiatrist determined that he was mentally competent to decline food. Mr. Gutierrez' family decided to bring him to the hospital where I work as they found out that I speak Spanish.

Mr. Gutierrez, a six-foot man weighting 104 pounds, sat in front of me quite indifferent to whatever I had to say even if I spoke in Spanish. My explanations about why it was best for him to accept treatment and food and about the risks involved elicited a "maybe," which after a few days, I found out always turned into a "no, thank you." Mr. Gutierrez would grab my hand, ask me not to take his refusal personally, and would tell me not to worry "*mijita*" (abbreviation for *mi hijita*, "my dear daughter," a term of endearment commonly used by older Latino men to address younger Latino women). I explained to him that if my father was in a similar situation, I would treat him with the same treatment I was proposing to him. I spoke with his family, who were supportive of the plan. Mr. Gutierrez agreed to go along with my recommendations, not without some initial anxiety.

I saw him almost daily for two months. He improved and whenever I approached him with the plan for the next step in treatment, he waived away my explanations and instead focused on talking about the foods he liked and which his family brought every shift. I never discouraged him from calling me "*mijita*" and accepted hugs from him and his family when he was discharged.

Finally, (iii) a third factor of "cultural matching" that Latino patients might hope for is that a Latino therapist will better understand Latino family dynamics. Latino patients have a strong belief in the family unit and integrity and even though this is not exclusive to our culture, many see the Latino family dynamics as a special group of alliances and rivalities that non-Latinos would have difficulties understanding. Unfortunately, as in many other cultures, sometimes there are challenging cultural and/or religious beliefs that the family's integrity must be maintained despite abuse and unhappiness. It is therefore particularly challenging when Latino patients assume that Latino therapists have these same beliefs. Furthermore, the family member who might be the source of discord or abuse might feel threated by the patient seeking help and Latino patients' pathways to help-seeking are "influenced by family perspectives about the appropriateness of disclosing problems to people outside of the family" (Ishikawa, Cardemil, and Falmagne, 2010, p. 1562). Early confrontation in therapy about enmeshed or dysfunctional dynamics can lead to the family pressuring the patient to terminate therapy.

Clinical Vignette 2

Ms. Lopez was a thirty-five-year old Puerto Rican who was raised by an abusive mother. At the age of eleven, she was sexually abused by one of her mother's boyfriends. Ms. Lopez's mother blamed her and punished her by delegating to her all the household chores and the responsibility of raising her younger siblings. When Ms. Lopez was still in her early teens, her mother moved to the United States with a new partner and her younger children, and she left Ms. Lopez with the latter's grandmother. Ms. Lopez's grandmother was nurturing and encouraged her to focus on her studies. About two years later, Ms. Lopez's mother sent for her and she left knowing that her mother's promises of frequent trips back to see her grandmother would not hold true. Ms. Lopez's grandmother died shortly after.

Once in the United States, Ms. Lopez resumed her past obligations of housekeeping and caring for her younger siblings. She met her future husband, got pregnant, and left her mother's house and dropped out of school. She spent most of her time raising her three children and working odd jobs while her husband did little to contribute to the household responsibilities. Ms. Lopez helped her mother by giving her a big portion of her income. Ms. Lopez's children became her only source of happiness. She became anxious when they were not around her and she limited their ability to go out and play with other children. Ms. Lopez's middle child became an "anxious child" and the other two rebelled against her rules.

Ms. Lopez came to therapy despite her husband's and mother's worries that this would be a distraction from her responsibilities. In therapy, she had a difficult time allowing herself to talk about feeling anger towards her mother and her husband. When she talked about her difficult circumstances, she immediately "normalized" them as part of "our culture." She phrased comments and questions using "us" to refer to herself and myself as Latinas. She would say things like "you know how important it is for us Latinas to stay close to our mothers," and "you know how important it is for us Latinas to take care of our man." The therapy included a revision of what her cultural identity meant for her and her use of cultural stereotypes as a way of avoiding conflict.

Ms. Lopez's anxiety symptoms improved but her husband and mother disapproved of some of her changes, including her enrollment in high school. Ms. Lopez's children were pleased that she was less anxious and that she allowed them to go play outside. They motivated her to stay in therapy. Ms. Lopez completed high school and she told me how in the ceremony, she dedicated this accomplishment to her grandmother. Shortly after I terminated therapy (I was leaving for a different job) with Ms. Lopez, her children surprised me with a box of chocolates and a card.

Cultural Sensitivity versus Condescension

One of the possible advantages of being a Latino therapist to a Latino patient is the ability to understand the limitations of textbooks' take on cultural differences and of administratively imposed classes on "cultural sensitivity." Although sometimes these might have genuinely good intentions, they frequently leave me with an aftertaste. The problem might be that the teachings on other cultures tend to focus on traditions or subcultures that are seen as "less Western" and people who read this generalize what they have learned to all Latin America. For example, someone can learn about regions in Latin America where there are beliefs on *mal de ojo* (evil eye) and *brujeria* (witchcraft). Still, for many of the Latinos who have college degrees and who live in a Latin American metropolis, it is offensive that these beliefs are seen as representative of all Latin America.

Clinical Vignette 3

Ms. Arias was a forty-year-old Venezuelan female who had completed her studies in finance in a prestigious university in her country and who now had an important position in a multinational company. She was fluent in English. After she got a promotion, she developed episodes of intense anxiety with associated physical symptoms. She was insightful about how her problem was, at least in part the result of increased anxiety about the added responsibilities. The therapist who had seen her before diagnosed her with *ataque de nervios.*[1] From my impression after reading that therapist's notes, the diagnosis was not entirely a reflection on the symptoms she presented or even on his perception of Ms. Arias. I think he just wanted to show that he knew about culture-bound syndromes. In my opinion, Ms. Arias had panic attacks, which are described in the literature as intense periods of anxiety with somatic symptoms and without that underlying reference of social disadvantage and psychological immaturity that "*ataque de nervios*" has.

The Migration Story of the Latino Patient

A person's migration story is truly unique and tends to have an ill-defined beginning and end. An article in the *American Journal of Public Health* points to the importance of understanding the "premigration circumstances" because they tend to be highly related to the "postmigration psychological and physical health" (Torres and Wallace, 2013, p. 1622). Being a Latino therapist might have given me leverage in understanding Latino patients but it did not prepare me any better in understanding the importance of the migration story. What helped me most was being an immigrant and making friends who were immigrants as well. I found that the migration story is vital in understanding the patient's strengths, challenges, interpersonal dynamics, and support system. A common mistake in the therapy of a Latino patient is undervaluing the impact of migration on that person. There are many factors that define the experience of leaving one's native country, masterfully described by Akhtar (2011b) in his book *Immigration and Acculturation*.

> How traumatic the situation will become depends upon the age at which the move occurs, the depth of attachment to the original abode, the degree of choice in leaving it, the extent of anticipatory planning for such change, the intrapsychic capacity to tolerate separations, and the magnitude of difference between the two places of residence. (3)

I will present some of the common issues that come in therapy with Latino patients by detailing each factor from the above-mentioned citation.

(i) Age In my experience in treating Latinos, the elders face many more challenges. Latino families can make the decision to bring elders to the United States with good intentions, for example, because of the promise of a better financial situation. The decision may sometimes have less noble reasons, such as having grandma or grandpa care for the younger children while other family members go to work. Whatever the reason might be, I feel families sometimes do not fully consider the older person's psychological distress of losing the country they have lived in for most of their lives and the friends and neighbors they have known for years. I frequently see that the older Latinos are less likely to learn the language and this further limits their independence. Latino immigrants who come to the United States later in life, even if fluent in English, are those who will benefit the most from seeing a Latino therapist because many of their stories and emotions were lived in Spanish and too much would be lost in translation.

The cultural identity of Latino immigrants who move to the United States as young children might be defined by their parents' or guardians' own attachment to Latino culture. The young immigrant might decide to follow the parents' or guardians' cultural identity, rebel against it, or develop an identity that blends the different cultures. A common example comes in the use of Spanish. In years past, some parents discouraged their children from speaking Spanish, partly to protect them from being seen as part of a minority group. Currently, it seems as if most parents or guardians encourage their children to speak Spanish, particularly because knowing Spanish has become a great asset in many professions. In my own experience as a Latino therapist, what creates the greatest cognitive dissonance and what I still struggle with is when I provide therapy for young Latinos, who proudly identified themselves as Latino, who have a very traditional Hispanic name, who want to talk in Spanish, but who speak in a heavily accented Spanish.

(ii) Attachment There is therapeutic value in exploring the depth of attachment to the native country. I find that a common mistake a therapist can make is to presume there is a strong positive bond. The references that Latino patients make about their countries might reflect being proud of their background but it may come from an idealized memory of their past. The patients' longing for their homeland might be expressed in comments about Latin food, music, or politics. As a therapist, I frequently perceive these comments may also be due to the patient's desire to start a conversation about these shared memories and to bond over the experience of being Latinos. I have noticed that when I tell my patients about dates during which I will be away, the usual question is "are you going home?" The fact that my answer does not satisfy their curiosity seems to matter little. The idea of my absence for some days is enough for patients to bring their own fantasies of what they would do if they went back to their native countries. Patients tell me what food they would eat, what holiday tradition they would participate in, what important site they would visit, and so on. Sometimes I sense they hope for recognition or acknowledgment of the beauty in their country. In "Immigrants' Continuing Bonds with their Native Culture", the authors (Henry et al, 2009) present the case studies of "Diego," a Mexican immigrant who "explained his internalization of his native culture by using the metaphor of a "giant backpack that has his background in it" (275). He explained that this "backpack" filled with his morals, ethics, education, intimate friendships, and memories, allowed him to cope with the stress of migration. What he considered his "Mexican voice," the backpack, had always guided him in the US, and provided an ever-present connection to Mexico.

In other Latino immigrants, the relationship with their country is complex and the immigrant can feel anger or disapproval toward it, or, what I find most challenging, a love tainted by recent war or persecution. If not for any other reason than to allow these patients the safety to open up about their feelings, one must be careful not to make comments that reflect the assumption of a positive connection between the patient and his or her country, particularly early on in therapy. A patient who had escaped her country in the midst of a civil war and poverty once told me about resentment toward her country, as much of its population had been indifferent to the pain of her minority group. She told me about prior therapists making comments about her country being beautiful and about how much she probably missed it. She said that her reply as to the pain she had endured there created an awkward moment in the session that was not easily repaired and which had, at least in one case, permanently damaged the therapeutic relationship.

(iii) Choice and Planning A Latino immigrant might have had several factors to consider before moving to the United States. A therapist can look at political refugees as an example of those with little choice but to move; there are many other reasons that can make the migration the only reasonable option. An example of the latter is discrimination based on sexual orientation, which was once a reason for someone to be turned down for asylum and which is now an acceptable reason to be granted it in the United States (Dudley, 2013). Common examples of those having little choice are children, elders, and disabled relatives whose families might not consider their opinions.

The stressful impact of migrating to the United States can be lessened if there is a chance to participate in planning for it. In some Latin American families, the plan starts early on when parents with some financial assets invest in providing their children with a private education that provides English classes early on and that tailors programs to prepare students for graduate education in the United States. Many of these children build their life and curriculum as a preparation not only to study in the United States but also to move there. In some families even though this is not originally the plan, the presence of a particularly brilliant student will lead institutions, mentors, friends, and relatives to encourage the above-mentioned path. These case scenarios are commonly known as "*fuga de cerebros*" (brain drain) and it is a worldwide phenomenon.

Many Latinos flee with little time to plan and with very few resources. In many cases in which time permits for some planning, the strategy crumbles during the migration process as the immigrant is confronted with broken promises, unrealistic expectations, and laws that try to contain immigration. A common example is that of Cuban immigrants who use savings in the United States to pay smugglers to bring them in from Cuba. Smugglers have been known to abandon their human "cargo," or force the people in their care to swim to land, when threatened with interdiction (Walser, McNeill, and Zuckerman, 2011).

Clinical Vignette 4

Ms. Sanchez was a thirty-five-year-old Honduran woman who was thirteen years old when her family immigrated to the United States. Ms. Sanchez had not wanted to move but was not given an option. Her family had done well financially and socially in Latin America, but her father's dream was to pursue a career in the United States' hospitality industry; they sold all of their assets to invest in that dream. When they arrived, Ms. Sanchez parents' lied to the school system, stating that she was fluent in English, to facilitate the process of enrolling her in school. She struggled until a teacher figured out the problem some weeks later and gave her private English lessons. Ms. Sanchez excelled, but her father did not. He became increasingly angry and made her work long hours, but she made an effort to keep her good grades.

Ms. Sanchez had adapted to her new life and had made friends so she worried when her father threatened her with returning to Honduras if she did not make more money. She left home but her dad reminded her that her visa was dependent on his and that at any time he could get her deported if she did not continue to financially support her parents. She never questioned whether this was the case and he kept her passport and visa locked. She continued to give most of her income to her parents even though her father invested it in fruitless projects. Ms. Sanchez landed a job with an attorney who helped her get legal immigration documents. She stopped giving money to her father even though he chided her for being ungrateful. Ms. Sanchez and her parents stopped talking and despite her further career achievements, she struggled with feeling unsuccessful because she did not have her parents' recognition or love.

(iv) Separations With whom did the Latino patient come to the United States? Who was already waiting here? Who was left behind? These questions are an extremely important component of the migration story. One common case scenario is that where one parent, usually the male, comes alone first to the United States, gets a job and some financial stability, and then sends for his family. The truth is that in most cases there are multiple stages of who leaves first, who is left behind, who goes back and forth, and who disappears within these transitions. This process leads to traumatic separations and great losses. A question that elicits a flood of emotions in my Latino patients is that of the pending and broken promises of reunification, such as mentioned in the case of Ms. Lopez. Departures usually come with promises of visits or calls or promises to come back. This applies to the Latino who stays in Latin America or the immigrant who sees a family member or friend go back to their native country. In many cases, these promises are broken or were never meant to be carried out.

An interesting variant of these stories of separation is shown in the movie, *Entre Nos* (2009). The movie is inspired by the true story of a woman who leaves Columbia for New York City along with her two small children to reunite with her husband. Shortly after her arrival and without having established any sort of support system, he leaves for a job in Miami and never returns. Thus, he creates a second separation, one that occurs within the foreign country. People left behind can feel betrayed and, if there is no contact, sometimes are left to wonder if their family member died along the way. Don Bartletti (2010), a photojournalist with the *Los Angeles Times*, won the Pulitzer Prize for his feature story and photographs on the dangerous, and sometimes lethal, journey that Latino teens go through in order to cross the border and reunite with their parents in the United States. He described it as the migration route with the most danger he'd ever seen. Other Latino patients struggle because they are the ones that left their family behind. Sometimes they cannot afford to bring their loved ones to stay in the United States or they may have formed a new family here and feel guilty about those they left behind.

An article by Mitrani and associates (2004) focuses on the impact of the separation of children and their mothers and the challenging process of reunification. The children have to first deal with the separation from their mother and once the mother is settled and gets the child back, the child has to separate from whoever were the caretakers while the mother was absent. The study showed that the average age at separation was seven years old and the average length of separation was a little over three years. The article focuses on a group of youngsters who developed behavioral problems because the separation from their mothers not only led to a disruption in "key parenting practices" but also resulted in overwhelming intrapsychic pain and anger. One positive thing was that in some cases where siblings were left behind together and then migrated together, "sibling bonds were helpful in providing at least one point of attachment that was not disrupted by immigration" (p. 222).

(v) Different Residences Latin American countries comprise all sorts of surface features: desolate areas, aboriginals' clusters, small towns, big towns, even huge metropolises. People tend to assume that the situation of the Latino immigrant is that of someone from a small town in Latin America who moves to a big city in the United States. This assumption may originate from the Latino immigrant being perceived not just as coming from a different culture, but also as coming from an underdeveloped country. In the age of globalization, the differences between the family's wealth and resources between birth country and the now host country might be less than expected. However, people residing in the United States might still believe that *all* Latino immigrants come from a background of financial hardship with limited access to education. This reminds me of the controversy created by comedian Barry Humphries while impersonating a character named Dame Edna. "Dame Edna" answered readers' questions in a satirical advice column in the magazine, *Vanity Fair*. A reader shared with Dame Edna that she wanted to learn a different language and was told by many to learn Spanish but wondered upon this decision. Dame Edna replied: "Forget Spanish. There's nothing in that language worth reading except *Don Quixote*, and a quick listen to the CD *Man of La Mancha* will take care of that. There was a poet named Garcia Lorca, but I'd leave him on the intellectual back burner if I were you. As for everyone's speaking it, what twaddle! Who speaks it that you are really desperate to talk to? The help? Your leaf blower? Study French or German, where there are at least a few books worth reading, or, if you're American, try English." (*Vanity Fair*, February 2003, p. 116) Sure, *Vanity Fair* apologized for this but it still reflects a perceived stereotype that isn't verbalized.

The perceptual differences between native and host countries and comments denigrating the country of origin can further alienate the immigrant. These differences can be attenuated if the immigrant feels that his or her cultural traditions are respected and even welcomed in the host country. For many immigrants, the differences among the native and host country can propagate if there is an idealization of the native country or a devaluation of the host country. Both situations can breed negativity and should be explored in therapy.

TREATING NON-LATINO PATIENTS

When treating non-Latino patients, a Latino therapist must confront the stereotypes they feel about people from the United States. I have found that those stereotypes can become more specific and stigmatizing over time after being repeatedly exposed to them in the media and in social situations. Like many other stereotypes, these can dissipate as one meets and makes friends with United States citizens from different areas of the country.

The Unavoidable Question of Background

During the first therapy session, if not during an initial phone call, patients notice that I have an accent and what comes next is for me to see how much time it will take for them to ask about it. As a therapist, I was trained not to disclose personal information and to try to work with the patient on understanding why they feel it is important for them to know a particular aspect of one's own personal life. Still, when it comes to patients asking about my accent, I feel compelled to tell them that I am Latina. I think in part I do it as a way of apologizing for having an accent, even though they are not usually asking about it in the context of not having understood something I said. I am aware that having a Latino therapist might make the patient question whether I can fully understand his or her past experiences, values, their way of living, and so on. I had a residency supervisor who told me once that if you do not do your elementary and high school education in the United States, you would never fully understand United States citizens. Another thought that comes to my mind when patients ask me about my accent is whether they are truly asking about my competency in terms of where I did my training. I remember seeing an episode of a popular television sitcom where one of the main characters seeks medical help and upon recognizing the treating person as a quack, the latter reassures the patient by saying he went to some of the best medical schools in Central America. Finally, of course, there comes the point of confronting ethnic discrimination and realizing that someone might not want to have a Latino therapist based on such feelings.

Carlotta Miles, a psychoanalyst based in Washington, DC, mentioned that along the years, she noticed that sometimes new patients would seem somewhat surprised when meeting her for the first session (personal communication, February 4, 2010). She pointed out, in a candid and humorous way, that she had gotten as far as confronting the patient with the question "you didn't expect me to be black, did you?" In my case, the fact that I'm Latina might also come as a surprise for patients who have set up an appointment with me and who might have been misled by my name. I am aware that some patients might not be pleased by such a surprise and might not be able to freely talk about it in the first session. The question is then: should one interpret an obvious discomfort? And if so, how does one do it in a way that the patient truly feels that she or he can open up about this without being judged? I was recently surprised by my own negative perceptions on questions about my background in a therapy session where a patient, whom I had treated for a few months, asked me about my nationality. I thought of all the above-mentioned concerns she might have had. I asked about her interest in this and she explained that she really appreciated the work we were doing and was worried that my stay in the United States might be only temporary. As I mentioned above, people might not recognize me as Latina and this can lead to patients opening up about their feelings toward Latinos without recognizing my ethnic background. In cases in which patients open up to having negative feelings toward Latinos or make offensive remarks about them, should I bring up that I am Latina? How should I introduce this to the clinical dyad? At what point in the treatment?

Clinical Vignette 5

Mr. Phillips was a fifty-nine-year-old man from Philadelphia. He had worked thirty years for the same company and was forced to retire when the company was downsized. He stayed at home and helped his chronically ill and debilitated wife with the household chores. Mr. Phillips's sixteen-year-old granddaughter had lived with them for the past three years. The girls' parents, Phillips Jr. and wife, had asked for the girl to stay with the grandparents after school because they lived closer to her school. The agreement quickly changed to her staying with them through the weekdays and gradually the parents stopped picking her up for weekends. The girl was verbally abusive to her grandparents and blamed them for her parents' neglect. Mr. Phillips came to therapy seeking help for his depression. He stated that the source of it was the state of the economy, which he blamed on Latinos. In fact,this came frequently in therapy: if he was late was it was because a Latino had cut him off on the highway? If his house had problems, was it because the construction had been done by Latinos? If a loved one had been robbed, hadn't it probably been by a Latino? He would not be stirred into confronting his problems at home which he persistently downplayed.

Transference toward the Latino Therapist Projected on Latino Culture

Sometimes the transference a patient might have toward the therapist might come up in therapy as an expression of emotion towards the therapist's ethnic group. I have collected two vignettes that exemplify this. In the first case, a man's escalating negative transference disguised itself as an increasing disdain toward Latinos. In the second case a woman's positive transference might have led her to a newfound passion for Latino culture.

Clinical Vignette 6

Mr. Smith was a nineteen-year-old man from New Jersey who was enthusiastic about his decision of becoming a Spanish major in college. In preparation, he had spent the summer traveling through South America. He talked with excitement about the places he had visited, foods he had tried, and locals he had befriended. Upon his arrival home, his parents became concerned about his increased drinking. Mr. Smith openly talked about the amount of alcohol he had; he felt that he did not have an alcohol problem because he did not need to drink every day. Nonetheless, his binges resulted in his being arrested for driving under the influence, in his grades dropping, and in his experiencing black-outs, scaring his friends away.

Mr. Smith came to therapy to deal with symptoms of depression. He found through the hospital's website that I am Latina and he brought this up in our first session as he talked about his dreams of doing part of his career studies in South America. As the therapy progressed, it became apparent to me that his drinking was a bigger problem than he was willing to admit. Mr. Smith was upset when I confronted him about it. He became angry, but instead of addressing this directly, he started making comments reflecting his change of mind towards Latin America. He no longer saw this culture as interesting; it certainly was not worth further studies on it or further travels to it. The only way in which he was able to direct his anger towards me was by correcting my pronunciation of certain words, which he had never done prior to me confronting him on his alcohol abuse. And yes, he even corrected my Spanish when I referred to proper names of cities in Latin America. Mr. Smith's alcohol problem worsened, he eschewed my suggestion to enter substance abuse treatment, and stopped therapy.

Clinical Vignette 7

Ms. Jules was a twenty-three-year-old woman from Colorado who came to therapy after years of problems in dealing with interpersonal relationships. She was raised by a mother who had made several suicide attempts in front of her children. The father was mostly absent because of business trips and expected Ms. Jules to monitor her mother and report to him on any crisis. Ms. Jules developed patterns of self-destructive behavior that included self-mutilation and drug use.

She came to therapy and had two initial questions for me. First, she wondered whether I could tolerate her suicidality without recurring to frequent involuntary admissions and she seemed pleased with my answer. Second, Ms. Jules asked about my ethnic background and after discussing why this was important for her, I told that I am Latina. She came to sessions consistently, consciously fought the idea of blaming others for her situation, and internalized what we worked on. Ms. Jules's self-destructive behavior decreased and she slowly established healthy relationships. I gradually noticed that she developed a taste for Latino food, music and movies, even though the neighborhood where she lived had little Latino presence. As she continued to do better, she tolerated intimacy in romantic relationships better. She dated a Latino man, further embraced the culture, and became an advocate on laws that favor Latino immigrants.

TREATING NON-LATINO IMMIGRANTS

My immigration experience allows me to connect with other immigrants, whether they are Latino or not. I do not mean to imply that I can reduce their experiences to just being immigrants. Still, I had to immigrate and that personal experience has allowed me to understand some of the challenges, rewards, and impact of immigration. Immigrants to the United States have to deal with experiences ranging from subtle to life-changing. They may or may not talk about these experiences openly. A person native to the United States may simply not be aware of the impact of immigration, and won't bring up the subject with the immigrant. In the ensuing paragraphs, I will delineate some of the changes that have created a greater impact on my own development as a therapist.

Health Care

Shortly after I moved to the United States, I had a severe headache. I had an imaging study done, I took medication, and I was reassured that I was going to be fine. Weeks later, I got a letter stating the cost of the study—it was thousands of dollars. I was overwhelmed and frightened because I did not have that amount of money. I then realized that the letter was a statement about the cost but not a bill. I emigrated from a country whose healthcare is run by the government and in which private healthcare is paid and charged as the care is given, therefore nothing had prepared me for this fright. The experience helped me understand the need to explain such things and other healthcare nuances to immigrants who are dealing with this for the first time. There are other chapters in this book that deal with the factors that prevent immigrants from accessing care, but the one that I want to highlight is that of the fear that seeking help will affect immigration status.

Clinical Vignette 8

Ms. Salenko was a fifty-year-old Ukrainian woman who was brought to therapy by her daughter. Ms. Salenko had become increasingly preoccupied with the thought that she had a terrible body odor. She had become so self-conscious about it that she had missed days at work despite her daughter's reassurances that she did not smell unpleasant. There was an unclear history of associated symptoms, as Ms. Salenko was guarded in talking about them. She and her daughter were accepting of Ms. Salenko coming and seeing me, but they would not accept hospital admission or tests as they feared records of these could be used to deny Ms. Salenko United States citizenship.

I looked for options and I presented the case to my supervisor. My supervisor felt that such fear was irrational and reflective of their paranoia. I explained how I could see their perspective, as in my own process of getting a green card, I had been asked about whether I had received mental healthcare along with questions about whether I had been a prostitute or committed criminal offenses. My supervisor did not agree with me and chastised me for projecting my own fears regarding the immigration process on the patient.

Feelings about the United States

Some immigrants come from countries that have been or are in conflict with the United States. In my experience, these immigrants are particularly sensitive when it comes to talking about their culture. They are even more cautious when it comes to talking about their experience of living in United States. They are afraid to be judged as ungrateful or as traitors if they disagree with policies or actions taken by the US government. In many of these cases, patients have commented they are grateful to be talking to an immigrant therapist as opposed to someone born in the United States, even though they are aware that some people born in the United States share their thoughts.

Clinical Vignette 9

Ms. Ahmadi was a forty-five-year-old woman who was born in the Iran. She had been a child when she and her family moved to the United States. She grew up in a household where academic excellence was encouraged and she was accepted in a program in Humanities at an Ivy League University in New York. She worried about the struggles of people in her native country and in the early eighties, while Iran was at war, she moved there. She worked as a social worker and dealt with horrific situations that developed when there were clashes with the United States or among internal groups in Iran. Ms. Ahmadi came back to New York when her father died, shortly after the events of September 11, 2001. She faced some people who belittled her and even threatened her because of her clothes and her religion.

Ms. Ahmadi came to therapy to work on the anxiety she had developed while working in Iran and on the sadness and confusion that the bullying had caused upon her return. Ms. Ahmadi opened up about her disappointment on some of the policies the United States had implemented while she lived in Iran. She said that upon coming back, she had briefly seen a therapist whom she assumed was from the United States and that she had been afraid of being less than complimentary about the United States' foreign policy and about admitting she was considering going back to Iran. We talked about her plans and about the issues she perceived as cons and pros of going back. As I knew little about her culture and about the political, financial, and other challenges she would face if she decided to go back, I asked her to describe these for me. I also asked about the things she liked and missed about

Iran. Ms. Ahmadi decided to move back to Iran and in our last session she brought me a gift that had artisanal work typical to Iran.

Although I could expand on the topic of receiving gifts, I will simply quote from an article by Savin and Martinez (2006): "If the professional has made an effort to help him and to understand his culture, he may want to give a gift that will remind the professional of him and his culture. Such gifts often consist of traditional foods, clothing or artwork. Acceptance of such gifts indicates to the client that the relationship is valued. In contrast, refusal may be detrimental" (249).

Feelings about Their Own Countries or Communities

Some immigrants very much depend on the small communities that people from their country have built in the United States. Anything that jeopardizes their place within that small community can lead to complete isolation and to being shunned by their own family. As part of being culturally sensitive, many health care providers and institutions try to pair patients with providers that have a similar ethnic background. Although this is mostly a good idea, I have written and lectured about the pitfalls of generalizing this approach (Margery Bertoglia, S., 2011, 2012, 2013).

Clinical Vignette 10

Ariana was a seventeen-year-old girl from Pakistan. She and her family had moved to the United States when she was just an infant. Ariana was raised in a traditional household and her parents had begun talking about an arranged marriage. Ariana suffered from a chronic illness which resulted in frequent visits to her doctor and she had fallen in love with him. She wrote him a passionate love letter; upon reading it, he transferred her care to another physician. Ariana overdosed on pills and called her doctor, who asked her to go to the emergency room. The resident there was happy to tell her that the psychiatry resident covering that day was a Pakistani too. I happened to be the one who got the call; I was covering for the latter. I felt sad that as a replacement, I would not be able to provide the same level of cultural understanding. Ariana appeared strained but she seemed to relax when she saw me. She explained that had been told that a Pakistani doctor would see her but she felt that despite any training he would still judge her by their cultural mores. She explained that an admission to a psychiatric unit would bring shame to her parents and her community. We identified a mental health counseling resource through her school and I did not admit her.

CONCLUSION

Being a Latino therapist in the United States is a unique experience that I do not pretend to generalize to other Latino colleagues. Many of the things that define a Latino patient, such as their individual migration story, the age at which they migrated, and their attachment to different aspects of Latino culture, also define the Latino therapist. Misconceptions and generalizations made about Latino culture abound within our community and among people born in the United States.

Latino patients are often happy about having Latino therapists in their community as it ameliorates some of the challenges in help-seeking, the most obvious being the language barrier. Latino therapists can find it rewarding, too, to provide therapy to the Latino community. On the other hand, Latino therapists can become overwhelmed by the challenge of treating a growing Latino population when they are part of only a small number of providers who are fluent in Spanish. Latino therapists also have the challenge of being therapists to a majority group and/or to another immigrant group who might have a negative transference toward Latino culture or who might be skeptical of a Latino therapist understanding their own culture. Despite this, the experiences tend to be positive and rewarding and to be a further opportunity to learn about other cultures and even about our own. Not all Latino patients will be referred to a Latino therapist, although the latter have an important role in educating administrators and other health trainees and professionals about this population. Through case presentations, interactive discussions, and even conjoined interventions, a Latino therapist can push these efforts forward. Although there is still much to do in terms of providing empathic mental health care for Latinos as well as other immigrant groups, there is a growing awareness of the gaps in present service, and the importance of taking responsible steps to address the needs of the Latino community by closing those gaps in the near future.

NOTES

1. "'*Ataque de nervios*' is characterized by sudden onset of uncontrollable shouting, trembling, heart palpitations, a sensation of heat in the chest rising to the head, fainting, and seizure-like activities in response to acute stressful experiences, such as grief during funerals, threats, the scene of an accident, or a family conflict. Often a person may temporarily lose consciousness. Amnesia of the episode may occur upon regaining consciousness. Considered a culturally sanctioned response to acute stresses among Puerto Ricans and Latinos, *ataque* usually afflicts socially disadvantaged women older than forty-five years with less than a high school education" (Gaw, 2008, p. 1537).

Selected References

Acevedo-Midgette, V. (2008). *The Relationship of Acculturative Stress, Machismo and Self-esteem as Predictors to Aggression for Latino Males.* Dissertation, University of Wisconsin-Madison, June 2008.

Ainslie, R. (1995). *No Dancin' in Anson: An American Story of Race and Social Change.* Northvale, NJ: Jason Aronson.

——— (1997). *The Psychology of Twinship.* Northvale, NJ: Jason Aronson.

——— (1998). "Cultural Mourning, Immigration, and Engagement: Vignettes from the Mexican Experience." In *Crossings: Immigration and the Socio-Cultural Remaking of the North American Space,* ed. Marcelo Suarez-Orozco, pp. 283–300. Cambridge, MA: Harvard University Press.

Akhtar, S. (1995). "A Third Individuation: Immigration, Identity, and the Psychoanalytic Process." *Journal of the American Psychoanalytic Association* 43: 1051–1084.

——— (1999) *Immigration and Identity: Turmoil Treatment and Transformation.* Northvale, NJ: Rowman and Littlefield.

——— (2003). "Things: Developmental, Clinical, and Technical Aspects of Inanimate Objects." *Canadian Journal of Psychoanalysis* 11: 1–44.

——— (2006). "Technical Challenges Faced by the Immigrant Psychoanalyst." *Psychoanalytic Quarterly* 75: 21–43.

——— (2011a). *Immigration and Acculturation: Mourning, Adaptation, and the Next Generation.* Lanham, MD: Jason Aronson.

——— (2011b). "The Trauma of Geographic Dislocation." In: *Immigration and Acculturation: Mourning, Adaptation and the Next Generation,* pp. 3–29. Lanham, MD: Jason Aronson.

——— (2015). "Patience: Developmental, Cultural, and Clinical Aspects." *Psychoanalytic Review* (in press).

Alfonso, C. A, Schwartz, S. (1999) *La Virgen en el Nuevo Mundo, Madre Dolorosa y Cariñosa.* Panel presentation at the Universidad de Guanajuato Faculty of Music, November 15, 1999, unpublished manuscript.

Altman, N. (2006). "Whiteness." *Psychoanalytic Quarterly* 75: 45-72.

Alvarez, J., Jason, L. A., Olson, B. D., Ferrari, J. R., Davis, M. I. (2007). "Substance Abuse Prevalence and Treatment among Latinos and Latinas." *Journal of Ethnicity in Substance Abuse* 6: 115-141.

American Psychiatric Association (2003). *Practice Guideline for the Assessment and Treatment of Patients with Suicidal Behaviors.* Arlington, VA: American Psychiatric Association.

——— (2008). *Mental Health: A Guide for Latinos and their Families.* Available at: http://www.psychiatry.org.

Aneshensel, C. S., Becerra, R. M., Fielder, E. P., and Schuler, R. H. (1990). "Onset of Fertility-related Events during Adolescence: A Prospective Comparison of Mexican

American and Non-Hispanic White Females." *American Journal of Public Health* 80: 959-963.

Arciniega, G. M., Anderson, T. C., Tovar-Blank, Z. G., and Tracey, T. J. (2008). "Toward a Fuller Conception of Machismo: Development of a Traditional Machismo and Caballerismo Scale." *Journal of Counseling Psychology* 55: 19-33.

Augustine J, and Bridges E. (2008). "Young People and HIV." *Advocates for Youth*; 2008. http://www.advocatesforyouth.org/publications/publications-a-z/430-young-people-and-hiv. Accessed February 22, 2013.

Bartletti, D. (2010). "Enrique's Journey," from the *Los Angeles Times*, August 24 and September 11, 2002. In *The Pulitzer Prize Photographs: Capture the Moment*, ed. by C. Rubin, E. Newton, pp. 204–205. New York, NY: Newseum Inc.

Baumrind, D. (1966). "Effects of Authoritative Parental Control on Child Behavior." *Child Development* 37: 887–907.

Bem, S. L. (1981). "Gender Schema Theory: A Cognitive Account of Sex Typing Source." *Psychological Review* 88: 354.

Berry, J. (1997) "Immigration, Acculturation and Adaptation." *Applied Psychology: An International Review* 46: 5–68.

Blum, R., Beuhring, T., Shew, M., Bearinger, L., Steving, R., and Resnick, M. (2000). "The Effects of Race/Ethnicity, Income, and Family Atructure on Adolescent Risk Behaviors." *American Journal of Public Health* 90: 1879–1884.

Bourdieu, P. (2005). *Language and Symbolic Power*. Cambridge, MA: Polity Press.

Brewer, J. D. (2000). *Ethnography*. Philadelphia, PA: Open University Press.

Bruce, J. 2007. *Nos habiamos choleado tanto. Psicoanalisis y racismo.* Lima, Peru: Fondo Editorial Universidad de San Martin de Porres.

Bui, K., and Takeuchi, D. (1992). "Ethnic Minority Adolescents and the Use of Community Mental Health Care Services." *American Journal of Community Psychology* 20: 403–417.

Bureau of Labor Statistics (2014). *Economic News Release: Employment Situation Summary*. Retrieved 4-12-2014.

Burke, K. (1968). *Language as Symbolic Action: Essays on Life, Literature, and Method.* Berkeley, CA: University of California Press.

Burke, P. (2009). *Cultural Hybridity*. Cambridge, UK: Polity Press.

Bullón, A. (2000). *The Acculturation Process of the Latino Psychiatrist in the USA.* Presentation at the Annual Meeting of the Latin American Psychiatric Association and the Peruvian Psychiatric Association. Lima, Peru. August 2000, unpublished manuscript.

Cabaniss, D. L., Cherry, S., Douglas, C. J., Schwartz, A. (2011) *Psychodynamic Psychotherapy—A Clinical Manual*. Oxford, UK: Wiley-Blackwell.

Canino, G., and Roberts, R. (2001). "Suicidal Behavior among Latino Youth." *Suicide and Life Threatening Behavior* 31S: 122–130.

Cardemil, E., Reivich, K., Beevers, C., Seligman, M., James, J. (2007) "The Prevention of Depressive Symptoms in Low-income Minority Children: Two Year Follow-up." *Behavioral Research and Therapy* 45: 313–327.

Carrigan, W., and Webb, C., (2003). "The Lynching of Persons of Mexican Origin or Descent in the United States, 1848 to 1928." *Journal of Social History* 37: 411–413.

Centers for Disease Control and Prevention Injury Center: Violence Prevention. *National Suicide Statistics at a Glance.* Atlanta, GA: National Center for Injury Prevention and Control. http://www.cdc.gov/ViolencePrevention/suicide/statistics/-index.html. Accessed July11, 2012.

Centers for Disease Control and Prevention. *Web-based Injury Statistics Query and Reporting System (WISQARS). Leading Causes of Death Reports.* Atlanta, GA: National Center for Injury Prevention and Control. http://www.cdc.gov/injury/wisqars/index.html. Accessed July 11, 2012.

Centers for Disease Control and Prevention (2011). *Youth Risk Behavior Surveillance System.* Atlanta, GA: National Center for HIV/AIDS, Viral Hepatitis, STD, and TB Prevention. Division of Adolescent and School Health. http://www.cdc.gov/healthyyouth/yrbs. Accessed July 11, 2012.

Centers for Disease Control and Prevention (2011). "Youth Risk Behavior Surveillance—United States, 2011." *Morbidity and Mortality Weekly Report, 8 June 2012.* http://www.cdc.gov/mmwr/pdf/ss/ss6104.pdf.

Cervantes, M. (1605). *Don Quixote de la Mancha.* New York, NY: Penguin Classics, 1982.

Cespedes, Y. and Huey, S. (2008) "Depression in Latino Adolescents: A Cultural Discrepancy Perspective." *Cultural Diversity and Ethnic Minority Psychology* 14: 168–172.

Chang, N., and Liou, T. (2009). "A Study of Latino Parenting Culture and Practices: Listening to the Voices of Latino Parents." *Hsiuping Journal of Humanities and Social Sciences* 12: 1–36.

Chodorow, N. J. (2005). "Gender on the Modern-postmodern and Classical-relational Divide: Untangling History and Epistemology." *Journal of the American Psychoanalytic Association* 53: 1097–1118.

Chung, G., Flook, L., and Fuligni, A. (2009). "Daily Family Conflict and Emotional Distress among Adolescents from Latin American, Asian, and European Backgrounds." *Developmental Psychology* 45: 1406–1415.

Comas-Diaz L. (2005). "Becoming a Multicultural Psychotherapist: The Confluence of Culture, Ethnicity, and Gender." *Journal of Clinical Psychology* 61: 973–981.

Comas-Diaz, L., Jacobsen, F. (1991) "Ethnocultural Transference and Countertransference in the Therapeutic Dyad." *American Journal of Orthopsychiatry* 61: 392–402.

Constantino, G., Malgady, R., and Rogler, L. (1994). "Storytelling through Pictures: Culturally Sensitive Psychotherapy for Hispanic Children and Adolescents." *Journal of Clinical Child Psychology* 23: 13–20.

Cross, T., Bazron, B., Dennis, K., and Isaacs, M. (1989). *Towards a Culturally Competent System of Care.* Washington, DC: Georgetown University, Child Development Center.

Cunneen, S. (1996) *In Search of Mary—The Woman and the Symbol.* New York, NY: Ballantine Books.

Cyrulnik, B. (2008). "Children in War and Their Resiliences." In *The Unbroken Soul: Tragedy, Trauma, and Resilience,* eds. H. Parens, H. Blum, and S. Akhtar, pp. 21–36. Lanham, MD: Jason Aronson.

Darling, N., and Steinberg, L. (1993). "Parenting Style as Context: An Integrative Model." *Psychological Bulletin* 113: 487–496.

De la Garza, R., DeSipio, L., Garcia, E. C., Garcia, F. C., Garcia, J., and Falcon, A. (1992). *Latino Voices: Mexican, Puerto Rican, and Cuban Perspectives on American Politics.* Boulder, CO: Westview Press.

Dean, R. S. (2009). *Countries and Their Cultures: Panamanian American.* http://www.everyculture.com/multi/Pa-Sp/Panamanian-Americans.html. Retrieved February 11, 2014.

Delgado, R. (2009). "The Law of the Noose: A History of Latino Lynching." Harvard Civil Rights-Civil Liberties Law Review 44: 297–312.

Díaz de Chumaceiro, C. L. (1996). "The Macho Don Juan: A Reply to Javier and Yussef." *Journal of the American Academy of Psychoanalysis* 24: 555–562.

Dihn, K., Roosa, M., Tein, J., and Lopez, V. (2002) "The Relationship between Acculturation and Problem Behavior Proneness in a Hispanic Youth Sample: A Longitudinal Mediation Model." *Journal of Abnormal Child Psychology* 30: 295–309.

Doddakashi, V., Wilcox, R., and Hauser, L. (2003). "Female Suicides in Major Texas Cities, 1994 through 1998." *Texas Medicine* 99: 50–58.

Duarte, C., Bird, H., Shrout, P., Wu, P., Lewis-Fernandez, R., Shen, S., and Canino, G. (2008) "Culture and Psychiatric Symptoms in Puerto Rican Children: Longitudinal Results from One Ethnic Group in Two Contexts." *Journal of Child Psychology and Psychiatry* 49: 563–572.

Dudley, R. (2009). *Asylum in the United States Based on Sexual Orientation: The Intersection of Mental Health and the Law*. Abstract presented at XXXIst International Congress on Law and Mental Health, Amsterdam. https://www.ialmh.org/NewYork2009/final.

Eaton, D., Kann, L., Kinchen, S., Shanklin, S., Flint, K., Hawkins, J., Harris, W., Lowry, R., McManus, T., Chyen, D., Whittle, L., Lim, C., and Wechsler, H. (2012) "Youth Risk Behavior Surveillance—United States, 2011." *Mortality and Morbidity Weekly Reports* 61: 1–162.

Ebin, V. J., Sneed, C. D., Morisky, D. E., Rotheram-Borus, M. J., Magnusson, A. M., Malotte, C. K. (2001). "Acculturation and Interrelationships between Problem and Health-promoting Behaviors among Latino Adolescents." *Journal of Adolescent Health* 28: 62–72.

Eckert, P. and McConnel-Ginet, S. (1992). "Communities of Practice Where Language, Gender and Power All Live." In *Locating Power*, eds. K. Hall, M. Bucholtz, and B. Moonwomon, pp. 89–99. Berkeley, CA: Berkeley Women and Language Group.

Eigo, T. (2014). *Bolivian Americans: Overview*. Countries and their Cultures. http://www.everyculture.com/multi/A-Br/Bolivian-Americans.html. Accessed February 25, 2015.

Ember, C., Ember, M. (2006) *Cultural Anthropology*. Upper Saddle River, NJ: Prentice Hall.

Engel, G. L. (1977). "The Need for a New Medical Model: A Challenge for Biomedicine." *Science* 196: 129–136.

Entre Nos. (2009). Directed by G. La Morte and P. Mendoza, produced by IndiePix Studios.

Erikson, E. (1950). *Childhood and Society*. New York, NY: W.W. Norton.

Escobar, J. I., Burnam, M. A., Karno, M., Forsythe, A, and Golding J. M. (1987). "Somatization in the Community: Relationship to Disability and Use of Services." *Archives of General Psychiatry* 44: 713–718.

Escobar J., and Vega W. (2000). "Mental Health and Immigration's Three AAA's: Where Are We and Where Do We Go from Here?" *Journal of Nervous and Mental Disorders* 188: 736–740.

Falicov, C. J. (1996). "Mexican families." In *Ethnicity and Family Therapy* (2nd ed), eds. M. McGoldrick, J. Giordano, and J. D. Pearce, pp. 169–181. New York, NY: Guilford Press.

Flores, E., Eyre, S. L., and Millstein, S. G. (1998). "Sociocultural Beliefs Related to Sex Among Mexican American Adolescents." *Hispanic Journal of Behavioral Sciences* 20: 60-82.

Fonagy, P., Gergely, G., Jurist, E. L., Target, M. (2002). *Affect Regulation, Mentalization and the Development of the Self.* New York, NY: Other Press.

Fontes, L. A. (2005). *Child Abuse and Culture.* New York, NY: Guildford Press.

Fuller, B., and García Coll, C. (2010). "Learning from Latinos: Contexts, Families, and Child Development in Motion." *Developmental Psychology* 43: 559–565.

Gaw, A. C. (2008). Cultural issues. In *The American Psychiatry Publishing Textbook of Psychiatry*, 5th Edition, eds. R. Hales, S. Yudofsky, G. Gabbard, pp. 1529–1547. Washington, DC: American Psychiatric Publishing.

Goldwert, M. (1985). "Mexican Machismo: The Flight from Femininity." *Psychoanalytic Review* 72: 161–169.

González, N. L. (1969). *The Spanish-Americans of New Mexico: A Heritage of Pride*. Albuquerque, NM: University of New Mexico Press.

Good, M. J., Willen, S., Hannah, S., Vickery, K., and Park, L. (2011) *Shattering Culture. American Medicine Responds to Cultural Diversity*. New York, NY: Russell Sage Foundation.

Grames, H. (2006) "Depression, Anxiety, and *Ataque de Nervios*: The Primary Mental Health Care Model in a Latino Population." *Journal of Systemic Therapies* 25: 58–72.

Green, A. (1980). "The Dead Mother." In *Life Narcissism, Death Narcissism*, transl. A. Weller, pp. 185–221. London, UK: Free Association Books.

Grinberg, L., and Grinberg, R. (1989). *Psychoanalytic Perspectives on Migration and Exile.* transl. N. Festinger. New Haven, CT: Yale University Press.

Guarnaccia, P. J., Rodriguez, O. (1996) "Concepts of Culture and Their Role in the Development of Culturally Competent Mental Health Services." *Hispanic Journal of Behavioral Sciences* 18: 419–443.

Guilamo-Ramos, V., Dittus, P., Jaccard, J., Goldberg, V., Casillas, E., and Bouris, A. (2006). "The Content and Process of Mother-adolescent Communication about Sex in Latino Families." *Social Work Research* 30: 169–181.

Guilamo-Ramos, V., Dittus, P., Jaccard, J., Johansson, M., Bouris, A., and Acosta, N. (2007). "Parenting Practices among Dominican and Puerto Rican Mothers." *Social Work* 52: 17–30.

Guilamo-Ramos, V., Jaccard, J., Pena, J., and Goldberg, V. (2005). "Acculturation-related Variables, Sexual Initiation and Subsequent Sexual Behavior among Puerto Rican, Mexican, and Cuban Youth." *Health Psychology* 24: 88–95.

Hamilton, B. E., Martin, J. A., Ventura, S. J. (2007). "Births: Preliminary Data for 2006." *National Vital Statistics Reports 2007.* http://www.cdc.gov/nchs/data/-nvsr/nvsr56.pdf. Accessed December 17, 2007.

Hanratty, D. (1991). *Ecuador: A Country Study.* Washington, DC: Library of Congress Research Division.

Harding, S. (1986). *The Science Question in Feminism.* New York, NY: Cornell University Press.

Harkness, S. and Super, C. (2015). "Themes and Variations: Parental Ethnotheories in Western Culture." In: *Parental Beliefs, Parenting and Child Development in a Cross Cultural Perspective*, ed. K. Rubin. New York, NY: Psychology Press (in press).

Harrison, A. O., Wilson, M. N., Pine, C. J., Chan, S. Q., and Buriel, R. (1990). "Family Ecologies of Ethnic Minority Children." *Child Development* 61: 347–362.

Hayakawa, S. (1972). *Language in Thought and Action.* New York, NY: Harcourt Brace.

Henry, H. M., Stiles, W. B., Biran, M. W., Mosher, J. K., Brinegar, M. G., Banerjee, P. (2009). "Immigrants' Continuing Bonds with Their Native Culture: Assimilation Analysis of Three Interviews." *Transcultural Psychiatry* 46: 257–284.

Hoare, C. H. (2002) *Erikson on Development in Adulthood: New Insights from the Unpublished Papers*. New York, NY: Oxford University Press.

Hollinger, D. A. (1995) *Postethnic America: Beyond Multiculturalism*. New York, NY: Basic Books.

Humes, K. R., Jones, N. A., Ramírez, R. R. (March 2011) "Overview of Race and Hispanic Origin 2010." 2010 Census Briefs, *U.S. Department of Commerce Economics and Statistics Administration*, US Census Bureau, 1–23.

Humphries, B. (2003). "Ask Dame Edna." *Vanity Fair*, February 2003 issue, p. 116. New York, NY: Condé Nast Publications.

Hwang, W. (2006) "Acculturative Family Distancing: Theory, Research, and Clinical Practice." *Psychotherapy: Theory, Research, Practice, and Training* 43: 397–409.

Hwang, W., and Wood, J. (2009). "Acculturative Family Distancing: Links with Self-reported Symptomatology among Asian Americans and Latinos." *Child Psychiatry and Human Development* 40: 123–138.

Inclan, J. (2015). *Family Therapy with Latin American Immigrants: A Systemic Ecological Model*. (in press).

Institute of Medicine. (2003). *Unequal Treatment: Confronting Racial and Ethnic Disparities in Healthcare*. Washington, DC: National Academies Press.

Ishikawa, R. Z., Cardemil, E. V., Falmagne, R. J. (2010). "Help Seeking and Help Receiving for Emotional Distress among Latino Men and Women." *Qualitative Health Research* 20: 1558–1572.

Jimenez, J., Potts, M. K., Jimenez, D. R. (2002). "Reproductive Attitudes and Behavior among Latina Adolescents." *Journal of Ethnic and Cultural Diversity in Social Work* 11: 221–249.

Juni, S., Rahmim, E. and Brannon, R. (2001). "Sex Role Development as a Function of Parent Models and Oedipal Fixation." *Journal of Genetic Psychology* 146: 89–99.

Juszczak, L., Melinkovich, P., and Kaplan, D. (2003) "Use of Health and Mental Health Services by Adolescents across Multiple Delivery Sites." *Journal of Adolescent Health* 32S: 108–118.

Kagitcibasi, C. (1996). "The Autonomous-relational Self: A New Synthesis." *European Psychologist* 1: 180–186.

Kaplan, C., Turner, S., Piotrkowski, C., and Silber, E. (2009) "Club Amigas: A Promising Response to the Needs of Adolescent Latinas." *Child and Family Social Work* 14: 213–221.

Kataoka, S., Stein, B., Jaycox, L., Wong, M., Escudero, P., Tu, We, Zaragoza, C., and Fink, A. (2003). "A School-based Mental Health Program for Traumatized Latino Immigrant Children." *Journal of the American Academy of Child and Adolescent Psychiatry* 42: 311–318.

Kataoka, S., Langley, A., Stein, B., Jaycox, L., Zhang, L., Sanchez, N., and Wong, M. (2009) "Violence Exposure and PTSD: The Role of English Language Fluency in Latino Youth." *Journal of Child and Family Studies* 18: 334-341.

Kernberg, O. F. (1995). *Love Relations: Normality and Pathology*. Binghamton, NY: Vail-Ballou Press.

Khan, M. (1963). "The Concept of Cumulative Trauma." In *The Privacy of the Self*, pp. 42–58. New York, NY: International Universities Press.

Kieffer, C. (2013). "Betrayal, Shifting Loyalties, Identity, and Love in Adolescence." In *Betrayal: Developmental, Literary, and Clinical Realms*. ed. S. Akhtar, pp. 37–60. London, UK: Karnac Books.

Kirmayer, L. (2012) "Rethinking Cultural Competence." *Transcultural Psychiatry* 49: 149–164.

Kirmayer, L. J., Robbins, J. M. (1991). *Current Concepts of Somatization: Research and Clinical Perspectives*. Washington, DC: American Psychiatric Press.

Klein, M. (1935). "A Contribution to the Psychogenesis of Manic Depressive States." In *Love, Guilt and Reparation and Other Works—1921–1945*, pp. 267–289. New York, NY: Free Press, 1975.

Konczal, L. (2001). "Nicaraguan Immigrants." In *Multicultural America: An Encyclopedia of the Newest Americans*, ed. R. Baylor. Westport, CT: Greenwood Press.

Lahey, B., Flagg, E., Bird, H., Schwab-Stone, M., Canino, G., Dulcan, M., et al. (1996) "The NIMH Methods for the Epidemiology of Child and Adolescent Mental Disorders (MECA) Study: Background and Methodology." *Journal of the American Academy of Child and Adolescent Psychiatry* 35: 855–864.

Landale, N. S., Hauan, S.M. (1996). "Migration and Premarital Childbearing among Puerto Rican Women." *Demography* 33: 429–442.

Lapp, M. (1990). *Managing Migration: The Migration Division of Puerto Rico and Puerto Ricans in New York City, 1948–1968*. Doctoral dissertation: Johns Hopkins University.

Lara, M., Gamboa, C., Kahramanian, M. I., Morales, L. S., and Bautista, D. E. (2005). Acculturation and Latino Health in the United States: A Review of the Literature and its Sociopolitical Context. *Annual Review of Public Health* 26: 367–397.

Laria, A. J., Lewis-Fernandez, R. (2006). "Latino Patients." In *Clinical Manual of Cultural Psychiatry*, ed. R. F. Lim, pp. 119–173. Washington, DC: American Psychiatric Publishing.

Layton, L. (2006). "Racial Identities, Racial Enactments, and Normative Unconscious Processes." *Psychoanalytic Quarterly* 75: 237–269.

Leslie, L., Weckerly, J., Landsverk, J., Hough, R., Hurlburt, M., and Wood, P. (2003) "Racial/Ethnic Differences in the Use of Psychotropic Medication in High-risk Children and Adolescents." *Journal of the American Academy of Child and Adolescent Psychiatry* 42: 1433–1442.

Levi-Strauss, C. (1958) *Structural Anthropology*. New York, NY: Basic Books.

——— (1969). *The Elementary Structures of Kinship*. Boston, MA: Beacon Press.

Lipowski, Z. J. (1988). "Somatization: The Concept and Its Clinical Application." *American Journal of Psychiatry* 145: 1358–1368.

Lissardy, G. (2013). "Feminicidio, el principal problema para las mujeres latinoamericanas." *BBC Mundo America Latina*. http://www.bbc.co.uk/mundo/noticias/2013/03/-121231_femicidio_feminicidio_experta_america_latina.shtml. Retrieved December 15, 2013.

Love, J. A., and Buriel, R. (2007). "Language Brokering, Autonomy, Parent-child Bonding, Biculturalism, and Depression: A Study of Mexican American Adolescents from Immigrant Families." *Hispanic Journal of Behavioral Sciences* 29: 472–491.

Mambo Kings, The. (1992). Directed by A. Glimcher, produced by Alcor Films.

Margery Bertoglia, S. (2010) "Immigrants: A Vulnerable Population." In *Ethical Issues in Forensic Psychiatry: Minimizing Harm*, ed. RL. Sadoff, pp. 155–166. Chichester, UK: John Wiley and Sons, Ltd.

——— (2012). *Race, Culture and Socio-Economic Status: Three Heads of Bias in Forensic Psychiatry*. Cross-Cultural Issues in Forensic Psychiatry Panel, presented at the Annual Meeting of the American Academy of Psychiatry and the Law. Montreal, Canada, October, 2012.

——— (2013). *Immigrants: A Vulnerable Population*. Panel presented at the XXXIIIrd International Congress on Law and Mental Health Migration, Asylum, and Families, Amsterdam, July, 2013.

Martinez, C., McClure, H. and Eddy, J. (2009) "Language Brokering Contexts and Behavioral and Emotional Adjustment among Latino Parents and Adolescents." *Journal of Early Adolescence* 29: 71–98.

Marzuck, P., Tardiff, K., Leon, A., Stajic, M., Morgan, E., and Mann, J. (1992). "Prevalence of Cocaine Use among Residents of New York City who Committed Suicide during a One-year Period." *American Journal of Psychiatry* 149: 371–375.

McDonald, J., Manlove, J., Ikramullah, E. (2009). "Immigration Measures and Reproductive Health among Hispanic Youth: Findings from the National Longitudinal Survey of Youth, 1997–2003." *Journal of Adolescent Health* 44: 14–24.

Mena, M., Mitrani, V., Muir, and Santiestaban, D. (2008) "Extended Parent-child Separations: Impact on Hispanic Substance-abusing Adolescents." *Journal of Specialists in Pediatric Nursing* 13: 50–52.

Miller, P. M., Commons, M. L., Gutheil, T. G. (2006). "Clinicians' Perceptions of Boundaries in Brazil and the United States." *Journal of the American Academy of Psychiatry and the Law* 34: 33–42.

Mirande, A. (1997). *Hombres Y Machos: Masculinity and Latino Culture*. Boulder, CO: Westview Press.

Mitrani, V. B., Santisteban, D. A., Muir, J. A. (2004). "Addressing Immigration-related Separations in Hispanic Families with a Behavior-problem Adolescent." *American Journal of Orthopsychiatry* 74: 219–229.

Miville, M. L. (2013). *Multicultural Gender Roles: Applications for Mental Health and Education*. Hoboken, NJ: John Wiley and Sons, Inc.

Modood, T. (2007). *Multiculturalism*. Cambridge, UK: Polity Press.

Montejano, D. (1987). *Anglos and Mexicans in the Making of Texas 1836–1986*. Austin, TX: University of Texas Press.

National Alliance on Mental Illness Website. Available at: http://www.nami.org.

National Campaign to Prevent Teen and Unplanned Pregnancy (2010). *National Educational Longitudinal Study of 2002/2004*. Washington, DC: The National Center for Educational Statistics. Retrieved March 2013 from http://nces.ed.gov/edat/

O'Donnell, L., and O'Donnell, C., Wardlaw, D., Stueve, A. (2004). "Risk and Resiliency Factors Influencing Suicidality among Urban African American and Latino Youth." *American Journal of Community Psychology* 33: 37–49.

Olvera, R. (2001). "Suicidal Ideation in Hispanic and Mixed Ancestry Adolescents." *Suicide and Life Threatening Behavior* 31: 416–427.

Oquendo, M., Ellis, S. Greenwald, S., Malone, K., Weissman, M., and Mann, J. (2001) "Ethnic and Sex Differences in Suicide Rates Relative to Major Depression in the United States." *American Journal of Psychiatry* 158: 1652–1658.

Oquendo, M., Dragatsi, D., Harkavy-Friedman, J., Dervic, K., Currier, D., Burke, A., Grunebaum, M., and Mann, J. (2005). "Protective Factors against Suicidal Behavior in Latinos." *Journal of Nervous and Mental Disease* 193: 438–443.

Orlov, A., Reed, V. (1980). "Central and South Americans." In *Harvard Encyclopedia of American Ethnic Groups*, pp. 210–217. Cambridge, MA: Harvard University Press.

Ortner, S. (2006) *Anthropology and Social Theory*. Durham, NC: Duke University Press.

Papps, E., Ramsden, I. (1996). "Cultural Safety in Nursing: The New Zealand Experience." *International Journal of Quality in Health Care* 8: 491–497.

Parens, H. (1998). "The Impact of Cultural Holding Environment on Psychic Development." In *The Colors of Childhood: Separation-Individuation Across Cultural, Racial, and Ethnic Differences*, eds. S. Akhtar and S. Kramer, pp. 199-230. Northvale, NJ: Jason Aronson.

Passel, J., Cohn, D. (2008) *U.S. Population Projections: 2005-2050*. Washington, DC: Pew Hispanic Center.

Pérez y González, M. (2000). *Puerto Ricans in the United States*. Westport, CT: Greenwood Press.

Perez Botello, M.T. (2008). "El refrán como texto oral y escrito." *Estudios Sociales* 2: 183–197.

Perper, K., Peterson, K., and Manlove, J. (2010). "Diploma Attachment among Teen Mothers." *Child Trends*. Washington, DC. http://www.childtrends.org /Files// Child_Trends-010_01_22_FS_DiplomaAttainment.pdf. Retrieved March, 3, 2013.

Pina, A., Silverman W. (2004) "Clinical Phenomenology, Somatic Symptoms, and Distress in Hispanic/Latino and European American Youths with Anxiety Disorders." *Journal of Clinical Child and Adolescent* Psychology 33: 227–236.

Portes, A., and Rumbaut, R. (1996). *Immigrant America: A Portrait* (2nd ed.). Berkeley, CA: University of California Press.

Pumariega, A., Swanson, J., Holzer, C., Linskey, A., and Quintero-Salinas, R. (1992). "Cultural Context and Substance Abuse in Hispanic Adolescents." *Journal of Child Family Studies* 1: 75–92.

Pumariega, A., Glover, S., Holzer, C., and Nguyen, N. (1998). "Utilization of Mental Health Services in a Tri-ethnic Sample of Adolescents." *Community Mental Health Journal* 34: 145–156.

Pumariega, A. J., Rothe, E., and Rogers, K. (2009). "Cultural Competence in Child Psychiatric Practice." *Journal of the American Academy of Child and Adolescent Psychiatry* 48: 362–366.

Pumariega, A., Rothe, E., Swanson, J., Holzer, C., Linskey, A., and Quintero-Salinas, R. (2012) "Suicidality and Acculturation in Hispanic Adolescents." In *Immigration and Mental Health: Stress, Psychiatric Disorders and Suicidal Behavior among Immigrants and Refugees*, eds. L. Sher and A. Vilens, pp. 57–70. Hauppauge, NY: Nova Science Publishers.

Queralt, M. (1993). "Risk Factors Associated with Completed Suicide in Latino Adolescents." *Adolescence* 28: 831–850.

Quinceñeara (2006). Directed by R. Glatzer and W. Westmoreland, produced by Cinetic Media.

Quinones-Mayo, Y., and Dempsey, P. (2005). "Finding the Bicultural Balance: Immigrant Latino Mothers Raising 'American' Adolescents." *Child Welfare* 84: 649–667.

Quintana, C. (2014). *Perceptions and Experiences of Physical Punishment in Childhood and Their Subsequent Impact on Social and Psychological Functioning in American and Mexican Populations*. Dissertation, 2014, Fielding Graduate University.

Quintana, S. (1998). "Children's Developmental Understanding of Ethnicity and Race." *Applied and Preventive Psychology* 7: 27–45.

Qureshi, A., Collazos, F., Ramos, M., Casas, M. (2008). "Cultural Competency Training in Psychiatry." *European Psychiatry* 23S: 49–58.

Raffaelli, M., Zamboanga, B.L., Carlo, G. (2005). "Acculturation Status and Sexuality among Female Cuban American College Students." *Journal of American College Health* 54: 7–13.

Ramirez, S., Jain, S., Flores-Torres, L. L., Perez, R., and Carlson, R. (2009) "The Effect of Cuento Therapy on Reading Achievement and Psychological Outcomes in Mexican-American Students." *Professional School Counseling* 12: 252–262.

Rew, L., Thomas, N., Horner, S., Resnick, M., Beuhring, T. (2001). "Correlates of Recent Suicide Attempts in a Tri-ethnic Group of Adolescents." *Journal of Nursing Scholarship* 33: 361–367.

Ridgway, C. L. and Smith-Lovin, L. (1999). The Gender System and Interaction. *Annual Review of Sociology* 25: 191–216.

Risman, B. J. (2001). "Calling the Bluff of Value-free Science." *American Sociological Review* 66: 605–611.

Rodriguez-Del Toro, V. (2011) "La lucha por la perspectiva de genero." *Kalathos: Revista Transdisciplinaria Metro-Inter.* http://kalathos.metro.inter.edu/kalathos_mag/publi-cations/archivo1_vol5_no1.pdf.

Romero, A., Carvajal, S., Valle, F., and Orduña, M. (2007) "Adolescent Bicultural Stress and Its Impact on Mental Well-being among Latinos, Asian Americans, and European Americans." *Journal of Community Psychology* 35: 519–534.

Rosello, J., Bernal, G. (1999) "The Efficacy of Cognitive-behavioral and Interpersonal Treatments for Depression in Puerto Rican Adolescents." *Journal of Consulting and Clinical Psychology* 67: 734–745.

Rotheram-Borus, M., Piacentini, J., Van Rossem, R., Graae, F., Cantwell, C., Cstro-Blanco, D., and Feldman, J. (1999) "Treatment Adherence among Latina Suicide Attempters." *Suicide and Life Threatening Behavior* 29: 319–336.

Russell, D. E. H. (2011). *The Origin and Importance of the Term Femicide.* http://www.dianarussell.com/origin_of_femicide.html.

Santisteban, D., Coatsworth, J., Perez-Vidal, A., Mitrani, V., Jean-Gilles, M., and Szapocznik, J. (1997). "Brief Structural/Strategic Family Therapy with African American and Hispanic High-risk Youth." *Journal of Community Psychology* 25: 453–471.

Santisteban, D. and Mena, M. (2009) "Culturally Informed and Flexible Family-based Treatment for Adolescents: A Tailored and Integrative Treatment for Hispanic Youth." *Family Process* 48: 253–268.

Sartre, J. P. (1943) *Being and Nothingness*. New York, NY: Editions Gallimard.

Satow, R. (1983). "A Severe Case of Penis Envy: The Convergence of Cultural and Individual Intra-psychic Factors." *Journal of the American Academy of Psychoanalysis* 11: 547–556.

Saulny, S. (2011) "Multiracial Nation, Multiple Ways to Tally." *New York Times*, February 10, 2011.

Savin, D., Martinez, R. (2006). "Cross-cultural Boundary Dilemmas: A Graded-risk Assessment Approach." *Transcultural Psychiatry* 43: 243–258.

Serrat, J. M. (1981) "Esos locos bajitos," from the album *Serrat en Tránsito, La Compañia Ariola.*

Snowden, L., Evans-Cuellar, A., and Libby, A. (2003) "Minority Youth in Foster Care: Managed Care and Access to Mental Health Treatment." *Medical Care* 41: 264–274.

Suarez-Morales, L. and Lopez, B. (2009) "The Impact of Acculturative Stress and Daily Hassles on Preadolescent Psychological Adjustment: Examining Anxiety Symptoms." *Journal of Primary Prevention* 30: 335–349.

Suarez-Morales, L., Martino, S., Bedregal, L., McCabe, B. E., Cuzmar, I. Y., Paris, M., Feaster, D. J., Carroll, K. M., and Szapocznik, J. (2010). "Do Therapist Cultural

Characteristics Influence the Outcome of Substance Abuse Treatment for Spanish-speaking Adults?" *Cultural Diversity and Ethnic Minority Psychology* 16: 199–205.

Substance Abuse and Mental Health Services Administration (2011). *Results from the 2010 National Survey on Drug Use and Health: Summary of National Findings*. Rockville, MD: Substance Abuse and Mental Health Services Administration. Available at: http://www.samhsa.gov/data.

Substance Abuse and Mental Health Services Administration (2012). *Results from the 2010 National Survey on Drug Use and Health: Mental Health Findings*. Rockville, MD: Substance Abuse and Mental Health Services Administration. Available at: http://www.samhsa.gov/data.

Super, C. and Harkness, S. (1997). "The Cultural Structuring of Child Development." In *Handbook of Cross Cultural Psychology, Volume 2: Basic Processes and Human Development*. eds. J. W. Berry, P. Dasen, and T. S. Saraswathi, pp. 1–39. Boston, MA: Allyn and Bacon.

Swanson, J., Linskey, A., Quintero-Salinas, R., Pumariega, A., and Holzer, C. (1992). "Depressive Symptoms, Drug Use and Suicidal Ideation among Youth in the Rio Grande Valley: A Binational School Survey." *Journal of the American Academy Child and Adolescent Psychiatry* 31: 669–678.

Szapocnik, J., Kurtines, W., and Fernandez, T. (1980). "Bicultural Involvement and Adjustment in Hispanic-American Youth." *International Journal of Intercultural Relations* 4: 353–365.

Tajfel, H. (1981). "Cognitive Aspects of Prejudice." In *Human Groups and Social Categories: Studies in Social Psychology*, pp. 127–141. Cambridge, UK: Cambridge University Press.

Tajfel, H., Turner, J. C. (1986). "The Social Identity Theory of Intergroup Behavior." In *Psychology of Intergroup Relations*, eds. S. Worchel and W G Austin, pp. 7–24. Chicago, IL: Nelson-Hall.

Taylor, P. Lopez, M. H. Martinez, J. H., Velasco, G. *When Labels Don't Fit: Hispanics and their Views of Identity*. Washington, DC: Pew Hispanic Center Survey.

Tervalon, M, Murray-Garcia, J. (1998) "Cultural Humility Versus Cultural Competence: A Critical Distinction in Defining Physician-training Outcomes in Multicultural Education." *Journal of Health Care for the Poor and Underserved* 9: 117–125.

Toro-Alfonso, J. (2012). "Como el diablo a la cruz: los hombres y la terapia psicológica." *Revista Psicólogo* 2: 7–11.

Torres, J. B. (1998) "Masculinity and Gender Roles among Puerto Rican Men: Machismo on the US Mainland." *American Journal of Orthopsychiatry* 68: 16–26.

Torres, J. M., Wallace, S. P. (2013). "Migration Circumstances, Psychological Distress, and Self-rated Physical Health for Latino Immigrants in the United States." *American Journal of Public Health* 103: 1619–1627.

US Census Bureau (2011) "The Hispanic Population 2010." *Census Briefs*. http://www.census.gov/prod/cen2010/briefs/c2010br-04.pdf. Accessed February 12, 2013.

US Census Bureau (2012) "The Foreign Born Population in the United States: 2010." *American Community Survey Reports*. http://www.census.gov/prod/2012pubs/acs-19.pdf. Accessed February, 12, 2013.

US Department of Health and Human Services (2003). *Developing Cultural Competence in Disaster Mental Health Programs: Guiding Principles and Recommendations*. Rockville, MD: Center for Mental Health Services, Substance Abuse and Mental Health Services.

US Department of Health and Human Services (2001). *Mental Health: Culture, Race, and Ethnicity – A Supplement to Mental Health: A Report of the Surgeon General*. Rockville, MD: U.S. Department of Health and Human Services, Substance Abuse and Mental Health Services Administration, Center for Mental Health Services.

US Department of Health and Human Services (2000). *Cultural Competence Standards in Managed Mental Health Care Services: Four Underserved/Underrepresented Racial/Ethnic Groups*. Rockville, MD: U.S. Department of Health and Human Services. Substance Abuse and Mental Health Services Administration, Center for Mental Health Services.

US Department of Health and Human Services (1999). *Mental Health: A Report of the Surgeon General*. Rockville, MD: U.S. Department of Health and Human Services, Substance Abuse and Mental Health Services.

US Department of Health and Human Services, Centers for Disease Centers for Disease Control and Prevention (2006). *HIV/AIDS surveillance report*. http://www.cdc.gov/hiv/topics/surveillance/resources/reports/2006report/. Accessed February 18, 2013.

US Department of Health and Human Services. Centers for Disease Control and Prevention (2007). "Sexually Transmitted Disease Surveillance, 2006." http://www.cdc.gov/std/stats/toc2006.htm. Accessed February 18, 2013.

Vander Stoep, A., Evens, C., and Taub, J. (1997) "Risk of Juvenile Justice Systems Referral among Children in a Public Mental Health System." *Journal of Mental Health Administration* 24: 428–442.

Van Oss Marín, B. (2003). "HIV Prevention in the Hispanic Community: Sex, Culture, and Empowerment." *Journal of Transcultural Nursing* 14: 186–192.

Varela, R. E., Vernberg, E. M., Sanchez-Sosa, J. J., Riveros, A., Mitchell, M., and Mashunkashey, J. (2004). "Parenting Style of Mexican, Mexican American, and Caucasian-Non-Hispanic Families: Social Context and Cultural Influences." *Journal of Family Psychology* 18: 651–657.

Vega, W., Gil, A., Warheit, G., Apospori, E., and Zimmerman, R. (1993). "The Relationship of Drug Use to Suicide Ideation and Attempts among African American, Hispanic, and White Non-Hispanic Male Adolescents." *Suicide and Life-Threatening Behavior* 23: 110–119.

Vélez-Pastrana, M. C., González-Rodríguez, R. A., and Borges-Hernández, A. (2005). "Family Functioning and Early Onset of Sexual Intercourse in Latino Adolescents." *Adolescence* 40: 777–791.

Vexler, E. and Suellentrop, K. (2006). *Bridging Two Worlds: How Teen Pregnancy Prevention Programs Can Better Serve Latino Youth*. Washington, DC: National Campaign to Prevent Teen Pregnancy.

Volkan, V. (1997). *Bloodlines: From Ethnic Pride to Ethnic Terrorism*. Boulder, CO: Westview Press.

Waelder, R. (1936). "The Principle of Multiple Function: Observations on Multiple Determination." *Psychoanalytic Quarterly* 41: 283–290.

Weininger, E. (2009). "Bourdieuian Class Analysis." In *Alternative Foundations of Class Analysis*, ed. E.O. Wright, pp. 119–166. http://www.ssc.wisc.edu/~wright/Found-all.pdf. Retrieved April 14, 2014.

Wharton, A. (2012) *The Sociology of Gender: An Introduction to Theory and Research (2nd Ed.)*. Oxford, UK: Wiley-Blackwell.

Willen, S. S., Bullón, A., and Good, M. D. (2010) "Opening up a Huge Can of Worms: Reflections on a 'Cultural Sensitivity' Course for Psychiatry Residents." *Harvard Review of Psychiatry* 18: 247–253.

Winnicott, D. (1967). "The Location of Cultural Experience." In *Playing and Reality*, pp. 95–103. New York, NY: Basic Books.

——— (1969). "The Use of an Object." *International Journal of Psychoanalysis* 50: 711–716.

Yamamoto, J., and Acosta, F. X. (1982). "Treatment of Asian Americans and Hispanic Americans: Similarities and Ddifferences." *Journal of the American Academy of Psychoanalysis* 10: 585–607.

Yeh, C. (2003). "Age, Acculturation, Cultural Adjustment, and Mental Health Symptoms of Chinese, Korean, and Japanese Immigrant Youths." *Cultural Diversity and Ethnic Minority Psychology* 9: 34–48.

Yeh, M., McCabe, K., Hough, R., Dupuis, D., and Hazen, A. (2003) "Racial/Ethnic Differences in Parental Endorsement of Barriers to Mental Health Services for Youth." *Mental Health Services Research* 5: 65–77.

Zamboanga, B., Schwartz, S., Jarvis, L., and Van Tyne, K. (2009) "Acculturation and Substance Use among Hispanic Early Adolescents: Investigating the Mediating Roles of Acculturative Stress and Self-esteem." *Journal of Primary Prevention* 30: 315–333.

Zambrana, R. E., Logie, L. A. (2000). "Latino Child Health: Need for Inclusion in the US National Discourse." *American Journal of Public Health* 90: 18–27.

Zayas, L. H., Gulbas, L. E., Fedoravicius, N. and Cabassa, L. J. (2010). "Patterns of Distress, Precipitating Events, and Reflections on Suicide Attempts by Young Latinas." *Social Science and Medicine* 70: 1773–1779.

Zayas, L. H., Pilat, A. M. (2008). "Suicidal Behavior in Latinas: Explanatory Cultural Factors and Implications for Intervention." *Suicide and Life Threatening Behavior* 38: 334–342.

Zayas, L. H., and Solari, F. (1994). "Early Childhood Socialization in Hispanic Families: Context, Culture, and Practice Implications." *Professional Psychology: Research and Practice* 25: 200–206.

Index

About the Contributors

Maria Elena Aguilo-Seara, MD, Resident, Department of Psychiatry, Drexel University School of Medicine, Philadelphia, PA.

Ricardo Ainsle, PhD, Professor of Educational Psychology, University of Texas at Austin, Austin, TX.

Salman Akhtar, MD, Professor of Psychiatry, Jefferson Medical College, Training and Supervising Analyst, Psychoanalytic Center of Philadelphia, Philadelphia, PA.

César A. Alfonso, MD, Past President of the American Academy of Psychoanalysis and Dynamic Psychiatry; Clinical Associate Professor of Psychiatry, Columbia University School of Medicine, New York, NY.

Pedro Bauza, MD, Clinical Faculty, Department of Psychiatry, Michigan State University; Inpatient and Consultation-Liaison Psychiatrist, St. John Hospital and Eastwood Clinic, St. Clair Shores, MI.

Solange Margery Bertoglia, MD, Clinical Assistant Professor of Psychiatry, Jefferson Medical College, Philadelphia, PA.

Antonio Bullón, MD, Clinical Assistant Professor of Psychiatry, Harvard Medical School, Cambridge, MA.

Consuelo Cagande, MD, Assistant Professor and Director, Psychiatry Residency Program, Cooper Health System and Cooper Medical School of Rowan University, Camden, NJ.

April Fallon, PhD, Professor, Fielding Graduate University School of Psychology; Clinical Associate Professor of Psychiatry, Drexel University School of Medicine, Philadelphia, PA.

Amaro J. Laria, PhD, Clinical Instructor, Department of Psychiatry, Harvard Medical School, Cambridge, MA.

Kelly Lopez, MD, Resident, Department of Family Medicine, Jefferson Medical College, Philadelphia, PA.

Andres J. Pumariega, MD, Professor and Chair, Department of Psychiatry, Cooper Health System and Cooper Medical School of Rowan University, Camden, NJ.

Carol Quintana, PhD, Bilingual Mental Health Clinician, Youth Protection Services at the Helen May Strauss Clinic, Union City, NJ.

Eugenio Rothe, MD, Professor of Psychiatry and Public Health, Florida International University, Miami, FL.

Félix Torres, MD, Founder and President, New York Forensic Psychiatry Consulting, PC; Clinical Assistant Professor of Psychiatry and Behavioral Sciences, New York Medical College, New York, NY.

www.ingramcontent.com/pod-product-compliance
Ingram Content Group UK Ltd.
Pitfield, Milton Keynes, MK11 3LW, UK
UKHW012038150926
475560UK00001B/73

9 781442 248564